UNIVERSITY OF NORTH CAROLINA
STUDIES IN THE ROMANCE LANGUAGES AND LITERATURES
Number 58

A DANTE SYMPOSIUM

A DANTE SYMPOSIUM

IN COMMEMORATION OF THE 700th ANNIVERSARY OF THE POET'S BIRTH (1265-1965)

EDITED BY

WILLIAM DE SUA AND GINO RIZZO

SPONSORED BY

THE 1965 DANTE CENTENARY COMMITTEE
DANTE SOCIETY OF AMERICA
SOUTH ATLANTIC REGION

CHAPEL HILL

THE UNIVERSITY OF NORTH CAROLINA PRESS

DEPÓSITO LEGAL: V. 2.513 - 1965

ARTES GRÁFICAS SOLER, S. A. — VALENCIA, 1965

TABLE OF CONTENTS

	Page
PREFACE	9
DANTE'S STYLE AND GOTHIC AESTHETIC By Rocco Montano	11
UEBER DIE *VITA NUOVA* By Ulrich Leo	35
DANTE'S DIVINE COMEDY: THE VIEW FROM GOD'S EYE By Aldo Bernardo	45
FEATURES OF THE POETIC LANGUAGE OF THE *DIVINA COMMEDIA* By Helmut Hatzfeld	59
METRICAL PATTERNS IN THE *DIVINE COMEDY* By George H. Gifford	75
DANTE'S NOBLE SINNERS: ABSTRACT EXAMPLES OR LIVING CHARACTERS? By Glauco Cambon	87
BEATRICE IN DANTE'S PLOT By Allan H. Gilbert	99
DANTE AND THE VIRTUOUS PAGANS By Gino Rizzo	115
THE *ALTRA VIA* AND GUIDO AS *ATTENDANT LORD* By John Mahoney	141
"THERE IS A PLACE DOWN THERE..." (*INFERNO* XXXIV) By Mark Musa	151
IL *PEREGRIN* E I *NAVICANTI* DI *PURGATORIO* VIII, 1-6 By Giovanni Cecchetti	159

DANTE AND ISLAM: HISTORY AND ANALYSIS OF A CONTROVERSY
 BY VICENTE CANTARINO 175

DANTE AND ITALIAN NATIONALISM
 BY CHARLES T. DAVIS 199

PREFACE

The editing of this symposium was undertaken at the invitation of the 1965 Centenary Committee of the Dante Society of America, South Atlantic Region. We are greatly indebted to its Chairman, Urban Tigner Holmes, Kenan Professor of Romance Languages in the University of North Carolina, who was the moving force behind this venture, for his advice and encouragement. Our gratitude is also extended to our contributors for their generosity and patience during the making of this volume, and to Mrs. Helen Leo for allowing us to reprint her late husband's essay.

The essays in this volume are not meant to represent anything like a comprehensive set of *letture dantesche*, although it is our hope that they will provide some indication of the range of Dante scholarship and criticism as it is being practiced currently in America. If they have any collective value in addition to their intrinsic merit, it is as an expression of homage to the great poet, born seven hundred years ago this year, whose work inspired our efforts.

WILLIAM DE SUA and GINO RIZZO

DANTE'S STYLE AND GOTHIC AESTHETIC

Rocco Montano
University of Maryland

According to views which, despite some marginal corrections, are still held true by the great majority of scholars and students of art and literature, humanism in the 15th and 16th centuries meant reaction to medieval transcendentalism and instauration of the world of man. The Renaissance is presented as the result of a general reversion from the contemplation of the supernatural to physical and human reality. Burckhardt's chapter title, "The Discovery of the World and of Man", may not be so frequently used now as it was some decades ago, but the idea that with Petrarch and Boccaccio and the revival of the classics a new trend toward secularism and naturalism started laying the basis of the great achievements of the new civilization, is substantially undisputed. If we look more specifically to the world of art, it seems even clearer that the starting point of the great realizations of the Renaissance was the new interest in nature and the things of the world. Sir Anthony Hunt, an authority in this field whose book *Artistic Theories in Italy* has been recently published in a paperback edition, states:

> As the last remains of Gothic disappear, a style emerges which expresses men's new approach to the world, their Humanist confidence, and their reliance on the methods of reason. In painting and sculpture naturalism flourished, but a naturalism based on the scientific study of the outside world by means of the new weapons of perspective and anatomy. In architecture the revival of Roman forms was used to create a style which answered

to the demands of human reason rather than to the more mystical needs of medieval Catholicism.[1]

There seems to be no surer way to explain the passage from the architecture of the great cathedrals of the Middle Ages to the style of the Renaissance than to refer to the departure from the mysticism and symbolism of the Gothic art and to the instauration of the Greco-Roman naturalism. I do not think that there is the need of quoting other authors who agree on this view. My idea is that these theories are as sharply in contrast with the most important trends of the culture of the 15th and 16th century as with the essence of the medieval art. If we take the pain of going closer to the texts we can easily see first of all, that what brought about the revival of the ancient authors was the belief that through them the spiritual values of the Christian world could be defended and re-established. To Petrarch and to all those who followed him and exalted with him the studies that they called *studia humanitatis* or *humanae litterae,* these same studies were by no means a way of breaking away from the world of religion. They were searched and passionately pursued as a mean of perfecting the soul and guiding it with more certain steps toward the goal of the Christian life. Petrarch leaves no doubt on this point. In the introduction to his *De remediis utriusque fortunae* he says:

> How grateful should we be to those writers who lived so many centuries before us and who were endowed with divine minds and saintly customs and now live, dwell, talk with us! Among the perpetual storms of our souls, like propitious and caressing zephyrs, like expert and industrious pilots, not only do they point out for us the harbour of peace, but toward it they stimulate the weak strings of our will and hold the helm of our wavering soul so that it may be steady and moderate among so many windstorms. This is the true philosophy; not the one which with fallacious wings and arrogance swollen with sterile arguments whirls into the void, but the one which with firm and modest steps lends help to our salvation.

---

[1] A. Hunt, *Artistic Theories in Italy. 1450-1600,* Oxford, Oxford Univ. Press, 1940; paperback ed. 1962, p. 1.

De sui ipsius ignorantia, one of the most resolute enterprises of his late years, Petrarch asserted or rather re-asserted in this way what had been the main constant theme of his spiritual career:

> The Latin poets — shake those who are lazy, raise the fallen ones, awake those who are sleeping, sustain those who are uncertain and lift them to pure desires and elevated thoughts —. To those who are directed to these sacred things the authors whom I mentioned are of great help and assistance ... Although our goal is not virtue as the ancient philosophers thought, nevertheless the straight road which leads to our true goal passes through Virtue; through virtue, I mean, not because we know it, but because we love it. [2]

When friends or adversaries, or his own religious scruples seemed to recall him from this love and his familiarity with the Ancients his answer was most firm:

> But why should I separate myself from those authors to whom I see Augustine himself so deeply attached? How Cicero and Plato could be of any hindrance to the knowledge of the truth while the latter's school not only does not contrast with our faith but even teaches and exalts it, and the Books of the former show the way which more directly leads to it? [3]

To Petrarch as well as to those who followed him, the study of *humanae litterae* was the most appropriate means to defend the principles of faith and to give them deeper acceptance in the world. Marsilio Ficino, who in the second part of the 15th century became the most authoritative exponent of the philosophy of humanism, said precisely this in the *Introduction* of his vast work *Theologia platonica:*

> I think — and it is not a vain belief — that by the Divine Providence things have been ordained so that

---

[2] F. Petrarca, *Prose* ed. by C. Martellotti et al. (Milano-Napoli, 1955), p. 747.
[3] *F. Petrarchae Familiarum Rerum Libri* ed. by V. Rossi, Firenze, 1933, II, 9.

the wicked minds of many persons who would not yield to the authority of the divine word alone, will be won by the philosophical arguments of Plato's work which uphold our faith. [4]

It is clear that the opposition to the Middle Ages did not stem from an attitude of revolt against Christian transcendentalism. It was as a reaction against the failures of Medieval Christianity that the movement originated. It grew out of the deep dissatisfaction with the sterility of late scholasticism, the prevailing dialectics, the arid subtleties and the spread of Greek naturalism which had invaded Christian education. Following the great synthesis of St. Thomas and St. Bonaventure, universities had become palestrae of subtle arguments, schools of logic and physics devoid of every religious inspiration. During the same time war, superstition, violence, anarchy had become the sad characteristics of the Christian civilization. The papacy in the captivity of Avignon was at the lowest spiritual level of its history. It was to all this that Petrarch opposed the *studia humanitatis*. They appeared to him as the means for fighting ignorance and superstition, and for substituting the sterile dialecticism and the atheistic naturalism of the "schools" with a learning provided with deep moral values, capable of perfecting the mind and the soul and of spreading *humanitas*, temperance, virtue, and understanding in the world. Through them, Petrarch felt, Christianity could be brought back to its purity and regain its influence among man.

The main target of the revolt was what humanists after Petrarch used to call *scholasticum vulgus*: namely, theologians who, according to the same Petrarch, from theologians have turned to be dialecticians and perhaps sophists. [5] They were those whom Coluccio Salutati, Petrarch's faithful heir, called "Barbari Britanni"; a direct reference to the followers of Duns Scotus, or Scotists who had become the symbols of sillogistic subtleties. They were also called *modern*, and very often were associated or confused with Occamists and Averroists, all responsible for the corruption of religion and the spread of incredulity. As Benvenuto da Imola says:

---

[4] M. Ficino, *Opera*, Basilea, 1961, p. 78.
[5] *F. Petrarchae Familiarum Rerum Libri*, ed. cit., I, 12.

Modern theologians have transformed sacred theology into a vain sophistication. [6]

To Luigi Marsili, an Augustinian monk, who was to become the promoter of fervid and learned religious meetings in the Monastery of Santo Spirito, Petrarch had already written:

> Write a treatise against that rapid dog who is Averroes, who, stirred with infernal furor outrages and mangles the holy name of Christ and the Catholic faith. [7]

The same reaction —I would like to state— took place in the world of art and poetry: it was not a turn toward secularism, but a revolt against intellectualism. Those Scotists and Goths were responsible not only for the corruption of religion but also of literary taste. As Roger Ascham, the late 16th-century English heir of this Petrarchean movement, was to say in his *Schoolmaster*:

> When apte and good wordes began to be neglected, and properties of those two tonges (Latin and Greek) to be confounded, then also began ill deeds to spring, strange manners to oppress good orders, newe and fond opinions to strive with old and truwe doctrines, first in Philosophie and after in Religion. [8]

Lorenzo Valla, one of the exponents of the humanism of the 15th century, attacked with much greater violence those "Goths and Vandals," philosophers, as he said, "whose basic source of error consisted in their lack of expression," and grammarians

> Who at high price taught people how to ignore everything and who were only able to render more silly those who attended their schools. [9]

There is great quantity of texts which could be quoted with regard to this point. They all show very clearly from which source the

---

[6] Cfr. E. Garin, "La cultura fiorentina nella seconda metà del '300 e i 'barbari britanni'", *La Rassegna della Lett. It.*, 1962, 2, p. 189.

[7] F. Petrarca, *Lettere senili*, XV, 6.

[8] R. Ascham, *The Schoolmaster*, in O. B. Hardison, Jr., *English Literary Criticism. The Renaissance*, New York, Appleton-Century-Crofts, 1963, p. 59.

[9] L. Valla, *Elegantiarum Libri VI* selection in: Prosatori latini *del '400* a cura di E. Garin, Milano-Napoli, 1952. Prefaces to books II and III.

distaste for the literature, art, and thought of the past centuries originated. The word *gothic* is used by L. B. Alberti, the great architect and humanist of the first part of the 15th century, as a synonym of *ugly;* he says "a gothic woman" for an "ugly old woman." In no case do these texts point to the new trends in thought and aesthetic ideals as the result of a more secularized vision of the world. It is the Middle Ages, mainly the late Middle Ages, the era of the Gothic and Scholasticism which according to the representatives of the new culture had brought about corruption of religion as well as barbarism of taste. We may recall that L. B. Alberti was himself a devout attendant of the mentioned religious meetings of Santo Spirito. Giotto, the universally praised initiator of the new art, the man who determined the most firm departure from the taste of the Middle Ages and inaugurated the realism of the Renaissance, was the painter who found the most inspired pictorial expression for St. Francis' miraculous life. A friend of Dante, probably a genius and a man of a deeply religious nature as great and sincere as the poet of the *Divine Comedy*. Giotto also painted in the Cappella degli Scrovegni in Padua perhaps the most moving and intense representation of Christ's passion that has ever been made.

Evidently the opinion held by Petrarch, L. B. Alberti, L. Valla or Pierre de La Ramée in France about the religious failures and the artistic ugliness of the age that preceded them, does not need to be taken at face value. There is always injustice in the attitude of a new generation toward the older one. We also recognize now the great artistic values of the literature of the Gothic Age, namely of the poetry of the troubadours and of the *dolce stil nuovo,* as well as of the great cathedrals of the time. But the reasons for the humanist revolt against the age that had come before them tell us better than any other fact about the characteristics of the Gothic world. In some ways we have to see from their stand-point in order to understand the process. We will be able to perceive then that the essence of the Gothic aesthetic is the same strong intellectualism which characterized the theological speculation of the age.

We are accustomed to think of the Middle Ages and of the Gothic cathedrals in terms of deep mysticism and tension toward the supernatural. This is what the books on the aesthetic and the architecture of the 13th century tell us. But the facts and the texts do not agree with such a perspective.

The basic point we may discern, if we go closer to the texts than is usually done, is the clear-cut separation that all the theologians of the Middle Ages established between the content, religious or prophane, of the work of art and the task of the artist. St. Thomas Aquinas, to mention only one, states most definitely:

> The perfection of art does not consist in the artist but in the work which is accomplished... Art concerns things that are made... Therefore it is not requested that the artist operates according to the good, but that his work is well made. [10]

Elsewhere he says:

> The excellence of the works of art does not depend on the fact that human will is directed in a certain way but in the works themselves if they are well formed. [11]

Dante also makes clear that "the goodness and the beauty of a speech are separate and different things." [12] The definition of beauty that the poet also gives does not concern problems of content, but only of the organization of elements. In the *Convivio* he says:

> We say that a speech is beautiful when its parts correspond to each other — we call a poem beautiful when the voices correspond to each other according to the rules of art. [13]

This definition does not differ from the one that St. Augustine had given and all the Middle Ages had repeated: "beauty is congruity of elements with some suavity of colors." But the characteristic trait of the late Middle Ages is the great emphasis on skill and technique as the basic element for the formation of the work of

---

[10] St. Thomas A., *Summa Theologiae* I, II, Q. 57, ar. 3-5.
[11] St. Thomas A., *Summa Theologiae*, loc. cit.
[12] Dante, *Convivio* II, 11.
[13] Dante, *Convivio* I, 5.

art. The renewed knowledge of the books on logic by Aristotle in the 12th century stirred the deepest enthusiasm for the achievements of mind and intellectual ability. Logic literally invaded the schools of Western Europe. At the same time we observe the propagation of *artes,* treatises on writing, poetry, speaking, building. The *artes poeticae* or *poetriae* by John of Garland, or Matthew of Vendrôme, had the largest diffusion. And they were all based on the assumption that artistic activity is a matter of skill and is completely independent of the content. Dante speaks with great contempt of those who:

> lacking skill and science, trusting only their talent, pretend to speak of high matters and use the high style.[14]

To him only the poets who follow the rules, *regulati poetae* can be properly called poets; the others are only *versificatores,* makers of verses. The qualities which are necessary to the poet are "strength of mind," "assiduity with art" and the "habit of science." This statement is from the poet's *De vulgari eloquentia.* At no point in these treatises do we find any reference to content, or to moral or religious aims.

Of course, one could recall at least the title of St. Bonaventure's work, *Reductio artium ad theologiam,* in the way of directing all arts to theology. But the advice of this small treatise to make the best use of each art in the service of the truth does not mean that the function of the artist consists in the pursuit of happiness and the discovery of the truth. In this matter, St. Bonaventure would not differ from St. Thomas, for whom the proper task of the artist is not "to operate according to the good, but to form something valid in itself."[15] The artist is a man and as such his acts fall under the moral decision, but the good of the work of arts is in itself. We have to ask that the bridge be strongly built; the good or evil moral intentions of the artist do not have anything to do with it. We only need to go beyond the titles to see that the position of St. Bonaventure or St. Thomas is absolutely clear. Unfortunately the great majority of those who speak of this matter

---

[14] Dante, *De Vulgari Eloquentia* II, 4.
[15] St. Thomas A., *Ethica* I, 4.

do not look farther than titles and isolated quotations. Often the weight of views which have been universally accepted seems to be too great. But the conceptions as well as the art and literature of the Middle Ages do not allow any doubt on this point. In his work *De eruditione didascalica,* one of the most important documents of the culture of the Middle Ages, Hugh of St. Victor speaks of the various degrees of wisdom through which the soul rises to the vision of God. They include also practical arts. We can and we must utilize them. But the task of the artist as artist remains, to use Hugh's own words:

> *disgregata coniungere vel coniuncta segregare* (to connect things which are separate and to divide things which are connected). [16]

The idea that art may have in itself the power of discovering the truth or approaching the good is most alien to the mentality of the Middle Ages. Art and *poetria* have to do with the ability of making *(recta ratio factibilium)*. They are called *sciences, instruments*. The beauty which results from the activity and the skill of the poet does not have anything to do with good or evil. Dante makes the clearest distinction on this point. The beauty and the goodness of each expression, he says:

> are separate and diverse the one from the other; for the goodness lies in its meaning, and its beauty in the adornment of the words.

He addresses the reader who may be unable to understand the meaning of his ode and invites him to give heed to its beauty, which, he says:

> is great, both in virtue of syntax, which pertains to grammarians; and in virtue of the ordering of the discourse, which pertains to rhetoricians; and by virtue of numbers in its parts, which pertains to musicians. [17]

---

[16] See for all these texts my: *L'estetica nel pensiero cristiano* in: *La Grande Antologia Filosofica* ed. by C. Marzorati (Milan, 1955), vol. V. See also my book in 2 volumes: *Storia della Poesia di Dante,* Naples, Quaderni di Delta-Ferraro, 1962-63.

[17] Dante, *Convivio* II, 11.

These remain the basic elements of a poem for Dante, as for all the Middle Ages. The work of art, in this conception, results from a process which we may call pure art, exclusive of attention to problems of form, harmony, sounds and colors. This, of course, does not imply disregard for the contents of the poem; it only requests the most complete awareness, on the part of the poet, of those qualities of correspondences of sounds and elements of which a work of art properly consists. The definition that Dante gives of poetry —a very important one for the knowledge of the aesthetic of the whole age— is this: *"fictio retorica musicaque poita"* [18] which may be translated: "a work of inventiveness made by mean of music and rhetoric". The *De vulgari eloquentia*, the work from which the previous quotation is taken, was written for the purpose of giving *"those who write poetry by chance"* the necessary rules. Then we should probably recall that the title itself of the *Divine Comedy* does not refer to the contents of the work but only to problems of style. Our modern mentality would expect that the title of a poem dealing with the supreme experiences of the soul and the highest reality should point to matters such as: the Itinerary to God, the Ascent of the Soul, the Journey to the Light, and such. But Dante has only taken into account that the poem was written in a humble, "comic", low style.

This is very indicative of the aesthetic conceptions of the Middle Ages. To us, style is the direct manifestation of our mind; it must be personal, inspired. "The style is the man himself", it has been said. For the Middle Ages there are different styles which have to be used according to the subject matter. There is a tragic, a pastoral and a comic style, plus some minor ones. Each has its own meter, words, sounds, and imagery. They are objective. Once a poet has chosen the style that he wants to adopt, he must be faithful to the definite nature of it. In the *De vulgari eloquentia* Dante intended to show the characteristics of each style. The work was not completed. He wrote only one and a half books. But we can nonetheless see how he selected the words, the sounds, the meter of each style. There is a wide exemplification of "comic" sounds and words. Most interesting of all is the study of meter, especially of the hendecasyllable, and of the canzone

---

[18] Dante, *De Vulgari Eloquentia* II, 4.

which Dante considered alone appropriate for the illustrious style. The poet shows the sounds, namely the combination of double letters, of labials, of z, x that are not suitable for the tragic style. He shows that the hendecasyllable can only be accompanied by the septenary and points out that monosyllables and words of more than three syllables have to be avoided by the poet who uses this style.

The *De vulgari eloquentia* is very often mistaken for a treatise on the Italian language. The common opinion is that Dante expressed the conviction that Italian has to be formed by taking the best of each dialect of the peninsula. In this respect, the treatise was at the center of the centuries—long controversy, the Italian *Questione della lingua*. But actually Dante's work does not concern the language that the Italians should speak. The poet deals with problems of styles, and he aims at establishing the rules and the elements proper for the tragic style. The treatise shows the extreme refinement of Dante's literary taste and, although incomplete, is the most important theoretical document of the aesthetic and the taste of the Middle Ages. Probably only the ancient treatise *On the Sublime*, by Longinus can offer a term of comparison. And we must add that it shows most faithfully the literary perspective and the aesthetic conceptions on which the *Divine Comedy* was also based. Dante has given both the most important theorization and the greatest concrete manifestation of the aesthetic of the Middle Ages.

The *Divine Comedy* too, we wish to point out, is faithful to the partition of styles, not only in the title but in the form in which it is written. Of course we cannot here attempt any treatment of Dante's style in detail. I have given a large number of indications in my book, *Storia della poesia di Dante*. Here we may say at least that such descriptions of Dante's style as powerful, realistic, biblical, classical, dramatic, sincere, as we find in many studies, remain purely generic. They can be applied to Shakespeare and to Milton as well, and they do not take into account the fact that there are different, very distinct styles in Dante's poem. According to the matter which the poet deals with, we find extremely beautiful and most definite examples of comic, tragic or pastoral styles. The opinion expressed by Erich Auerbach, already held by the Romantic critics, that Dante's is a mixed style textured with tragic and comic elements absolutely does not give a correct picture of the *Divine Comedy*. There are different, but completely separate manners in Dante's poem. In the 21st canto of *The Inferno* we find the most evident example of Dante's comic style. In the 28th of the *Purgatorio* one may have a clear picture of a pastoral style; in many parts of *The Paradiso* Dante has realized those compositions of tragic style of which he had spoken in *De Vulgari eloquentia*. The poem, as we have said, is entirely faithful to the principles of medieval poetics.

Certainly no one can ignore the famous *terzina* of canto 24 of the *Purgatorio* which reads, or seems to read:

> I am one who, when Love inspires me take note,
> and go setting it forth after the fashion which
> he dictates within me.

This is the translation given by the Temple Classics, generally the most accurate among Dante translations. Binyon's translation, probably the most consistent from the point of view of poetry, has:

> I am one who hearkens when
> Love prompteth, and I put thought into word
> After the mode which he dictates within.

Ciardi has:

> When Love inspires me with delight,
> or pain, or longing, I take careful note,
> and as he dictates in my soul, I write.

The Italian text reads, or seems to read:

> I' mi son un che quando
> Amor mi spira noto e a quel modo
> Che ditta dentro vo' significando.

The words in the second line seem to refer very clearly to love, or Love with the capital letter, *Amore*, which inspires (*mi spira*, inspires me). But there are many elements that we should take into account before accepting such a reading. The first is this: in his answer to Bonagiunta Orbicciani, the poet of the former Tuscan school, who has asked Dante whether he is the poet who first started the "sweet new style", Dante makes a statement about his own way of poetizing which he intends should apply also to Guido Guinizelli and Guido Cavalcanti, his predecessors and teachers in the school of the "sweet style". We learn this from the very clear reply of the same Bonagiunta. The above terzina, therefore, should be considered as a description not only of Dante's own poetry but of that of the two Guidos as well. But there is absolutely no way of considering Guido Cavalcanti's poetry as inspired by love, let alone by Divine Love, capitalized. Guido was unmistakably a follower of the atheistic doctrines of Latin Averroism. He was known, as Boccaccio tells us, as one who was endeavoring to demonstrate that God does not exist. His most famous poem, the philosophical manifesto of the school, expounds the doctrine that love, being a passion of the sensible appetite which hinders or prevents the activity of the intellect, is really death to man. Only the intellectual activity was the mark of human life for Cavalcanti and for the followers of Averroistic Aristotelianism. Love was looked at with contempt by those stern, proud philosophers. Guido's poetry not only expresses this contempt but represents the most characteristic example of poetry free from every sentimental effusion, and firmly organized as a rigorous reasoning. Obviously, if the "sweet new style" is a school of poetry to which words such as sentiment, inspiration, Love, sincerity should be applied, then Guido, the poet who according to Dante had taken the lead away from Guido Guinizelli in poetry, cannot be assigned to the *dolce stil nuovo*. As a matter of fact this school of the "sweet new style" had very little to do, in its basic trends, with inspiration by love or with inspiration at all. Not only is Cavalcanti's most representative poem a rigorous, stern composition excluding any personal reference, but Guinizelli's poem "Al cor gentil ripara sempre Amore", universally recognized as the starting point of the "new style", is purely a philosophical statement on the nature of love and its ennobling effects. What was new in it was the limpid, almost scientific straightforwardness of its language and the smoothness that the poet was able to attain. Dante praises these poems and his own for the subtlety and the sweetness of the style; he mentions Cavalcanti's skill in using rhyme also in the middle of the verse, the excellence of his tragic style. The refinement and the consistency of the style together with their philosophical insights were the things that nourished the pride of the new poets. The former Tuscan poets —Bonagiunta among them— charged the new school with being too difficult and of substituting philosophy for the pleasant words of love. There is no reference in all this to the expression of sentiment and sincerity of feeling, or to love as the inspiring motive of poetry. All references are to style, "sweet style". When Dante, in the *Divine Comedy*, meets Guinizelli and is asked by him which is the reason for his attraction to the poetry of the same Guinizelli, again he speaks only of "sweet words".

As for the problem of the terzina we have quoted above, there is really no problem. It is rather a matter of misreading. The word *spira*, that we have seen interpreted and translated as "inspires", does not have anything to do with inspiration. Truly, the word *spira* can be the shortened form of *ispira*, inspires. But it is properly a regular form of the verb *spirare*, which means, *to breathe, to blow*, as we find in sentences like *spira un forte vento*, a strong wind blows. In the episode of Francesca da Rimini we find the verse:

> Come l'arena quando turbo spira.
> (like sand when the storm blows)

The poets of the *dolce stil nuovo* used the verb *spirare* to speak of the movements of the passion, the breathing or the flowing of love. We find it in the verse:

> Amor che drittamente spira

Spira is said of anguish: "angoscia spira". The poets of the school used to speak of *spiriti d'amore*, spirits of love. A sonnet by Cavalcanti contains in each of its 14 lines the word *spirito*. It was the technical word of the school. It is clear that the words "*Amor mi spira*" should be substituted with "*Amore spira*", as many good manuscripts have. The idea that *love inspires* is a romantic one, completely alien to the mentality of the Middle Ages and certainly cannot apply to the poetry of the *Dolce stil nuovo*. As a matter of fact, Dante's words are simply the answer to the charge made in his real life by Bonagiunta that the poetry of the *sweet new style* was too doctrinal and obscure. They say that the new poetry and its smoothness had originated from a closer attention to the process of the passions. The tercet should be translated approximately in this way:

> I am one who
> when love develops, take note and I try to
> describe it according as it teaches within.

The verb *ditta* which Dante uses has reference to the teachers of rhetoric who were called *dettatori*. In his answer Dante wants to stress that the achievements of the new poets depend on the fact that they are able to follow the movements of love more closely, and that therefore love itself becomes the teacher of a better style. This, Bonagiunta understands, is the knot that prevented the other poets from reaching the "sweet new style".

I have found it necessary to elaborate at some length on this analysis, for the terzina is quoted in all the books that have some reference to the aesthetic of Dante and the Middle Ages, always with the implication that it represents a kind of romantic aesthetics based on sincerity of expression and adherence to inner inspiration. In numerous essays recently collected in two volumes, Professor J. A. Mazzeo, who is one of the leading scholars in this field, has made use of his vast erudition and remarkable scholarship to demonstrate, also on the basis of this *terzina*, that Dante's poetry is inspired by God and love and beauty, which are in Dante's world an avenue to the supreme light. Beatrice, according to the critic, leads "through her ever increasing beauty to the threshold of absolute reality".[19]

Such assumptions have always been dear to romantic readers and I am sorry that I am not able to share the belief in this beautiful myth. But Dante, I think, does not have anything to do with this kind of romantic Platonism. In his first youth he had accepted Guinizelli's theory that love is a ladder to perfection. But a long, long time had passed for the poet since then. In the *Divine Comedy* Beatrice leads her beloved to the Empyrean not because she is a beautiful lady, but because she is dead, a saint of

---

[19] J. A. Mazzeo, *Structure and Thought in the Paradiso*, Ithaca, Cornell Univ. Press, 1958. Cfr. my book-review in: *Comparative Lit.*, 1962, 3.

the Christian Paradise, and as such can show the way. There is no possibility of error. Dante, the author of the *Divine Comedy*, would be the last author to believe that beautiful women lead to the divine Light. More likely, for Dante and for us, I think, they take us to Hell. Francesca da Rimini, who believed in the Platonic theories of Guinizelli, is in Hell, among the lustful souls. Guinizelli himself is among the lustful of Purgatory. On the other hand, the assumption that poetry is, as Mazzeo says, the rival of Metaphysics, and that the poet "is a prophet expressing what he receives by divine inspiration," could not be farther from Dante's views. What the poet says, in fact, is that the matter has been impressed by God on his mind, and that there is a "vision" granted to him as could have been granted to other prophets, to St. Paul or to Joachim of Floris. This does not have any connection with poetry. As a poet, Dante has only to render faithfully what he has seen or, as he says, to show "the image visibly of the holy realm imprinted in my brain." [20] They are two separate things. Praying to Apollo to give him the force to carry on his task, Dante explicitly says that he shall earn the crown of the poets "both through the theme and thee."

This distinction is always absolutely clear in the *Divine Comedy* as well as in Dante's theoretical writings and in the whole literature of the Middle Ages. The concept of inspiration in poetry, the idea that the poet is a seer and that the artist detects or reveals divine reality, these romantic myths are far from the mentality of the epoch.

The theories which describe the aesthetic of the Middle Ages as a mystic aesthetic, subordinating art and poetry to metaphysics, and which are so confidently and universally accepted, are based on the false assumption that, since the Middle Ages is an epoch of mysticism and subordination of human activities to the supernatural goal, art and poetry too are the means of a mystic ascent. The depiction of Gothic art as an expression of these same mystic trends has the same origin, a very weak one. It could or should be remembered that starting with the beginning of the 12th century until the first half of the 14th century the Western world knew one of the most rich and intense developments of

---

[20] *Paradiso*, I.

studies on logic in its whole history. We know now that even the most extremely rigorous representatives of modern logical positivism can hardly rival in subtlety, intellectual force and audacity of conclusions, the movement which goes from Berangarius and Roscellin to Occam. We could also wonder why, if Gothic architecture stemmed from deep currents of mysticism, it developed so late, after ten centuries of Christian asceticism. The fact is that Gothic architecture literally exploded throughout Europe when first the Aristotelian books on logic, and then the *Physics* and *Metaphysics*, invaded the universities of the Christian world. John of Salisbury's *Metalogicus* bears an unmistakable, almost frightened, testimony of the irrepressible enthusiasm for logic in Chartres at about the time of the foundation of the Cathedral. The school of Chartres was also at the same time the center of the pantheistic doctrines of Amaury of Bène and David de Dinant. In 1210, we know, the first condemnation of Aristotle's book on "natural philosophy" was enacted by the Church, but this and other bans that followed did not halt the rapid, overwhelming expansion of Greco-Arab naturalism. Through the unmistakable testimonies of Roger Bacon, St. Albertus Magnus and St. Thomas we know that Aristotelian culture, in its extreme Averroistic interpretations, was dominating in Paris, Bologna and elsewhere about the middle part of the 13th century. At this same time a movement led by Guglielmo di Sant'Amore went close to excluding religious orders from teaching in Paris and to establishing a lay system in the *studium* itself of Christianity. It was hardly a time of mysticism. The statutes of the universities, as E. Gilson [21] among other historians has clearly shown, present a widespread substitution of courses on science for the study of letters which had characterized the culture of the 12th century before the advent of Aristotle. Even grammar had become a science: *grammatica speculativa*. Theology was now a rigorous intellectual construction. It was no longer the time of the warmth, the affection, the personal approach of a St. Bernard or of R. of St. Victor. If we listen to St. Albertus Magnus, one of the representatives of this new extremely intense interest in science, "man is nothing but intellect."

---

[21] E. Gilson, *History of Christian Philosophy in the Middle Ages*, New York, 1955.

To Dante too, "mind is deity." [22] The treatises on *De intellectu, De intelligentia* with their subtle distinctions among the various forms of intellects (*passibilis, passivus, agens, activus* and so on) represent the most remarkable aspects of the speculation of these decades.

This is the time when the expansion of Gothic art takes place. It is the time of the impetuous growth of economic life, of the extraordinary development of the communes, of the origin of *l'esprit laique* (as Lagarde has shown) and of *l'esprit bourgeois*. The works by St. Bernard, Richard of St. Victor and all the great mystics were composed in a prose rich in effusiveness, devoid of logical arguments and scientific divisions. On the other hand, we have the extremely complex organization of thought of the medieval *Summae*. Gothic art is the result of this latter attitude. It shows the same rigorous structure, the intellectual force, the complexity of organization, the multiplicity of elements which we find in the great constructions of St. Thomas and St. Albertus Magnus. We are at the antipodes of mysticism. Everybody is accustomed to think of the Gothic arch as the manifestation of the medieval ascent of the soul. There are so many descriptions of this kind in our books. Actually the pointed arch has nothing more mystic than the Romanesque arch which, in fact, was the arch of the intensely suggestive churches of the epoch of deeper asceticism. Persuaded that the Middle Ages in their entirety were an epoch of ascetic flights to God, historians of art did not have difficulty in interpreting the Gothic arch in that perspective. The truth is that this art is fully consistent with the aesthetic ideals which supported the literary production of the age. The search, also here, is for the extreme articulation of elements, the subtlety and intricacy of forms, the great number of correspondences, the strenuousness and ingenuity of the construction. The work was always the result of an extreme intellectual tension and of a characteristic, profound ambition to create something difficult, subtle, high.

Speaking of the highest forms of style, Dante uses the word *fastigiosus,* which means "high", sublime, with no reference, however, to profundity or saintliness of thought. *Fastigiosus* refers only to style and extreme refinement of forms. Other words that Dante

---

[22] Dante, *Convivio* III, 2.

uses to describe the most complex stylistic compositions are *"pexus," "irsutus," "excelsus,"* which all refer to consummate elaboration, search for difficult tasks, height and technique. Not once are we referred to the depth or the spiritual quality of the work. As artist, we read in the *Commedia*, Dante "upholds" his matter. He is the scribe: *quella materia ond'io son fatto scriba*. His concern is artistry. What is important is the quest for difficulty, the complexity and the subtlety of the task performed. Dante praises his own and his friends' poetry for being sweet and subtle. He also exalts Arnault Daniel above all other troubadours because of his ingenuity. Arnault, he says, was the best craftsman. And we have only to look at the complexity of the *sestina*, the meter in which Arnault excelled, to understand the extremely high degree of virtuosity reached by the poetry of the time. We may recall that Dante himself vied successfully with Arnault in the composition of the *sestina*, a canzone in which six strophes of 12 lines each have the same rhyme-words repeated in a prefixed order that varies in each stanza; obviously here it is not a question of mysticism. Provençal poetry is the expression of a completely secular outlook. But we can see here the same complexity, intellectual strength, love for subtlety, artistry, technical ingenuity, and tension which we find in Gothic architecture. Symbolism, I would firmly state, cannot explain the characteristics of this art. The idea that the artistic design of the Gothic cathedral "was inspired by a definite metaphysical system" I regard as very vague and dubious. This last quotation is from *The Gothic Cathedral* by Otto von Simson, who is an authority in this field. He tries to establish a direct relationship between the foundation of St. Denis in Paris, the first great example of Gothic art, and the mystic theology of the pseudo-Dionisius Areopagite. The critic also insists that the Cathedral of Chartres is the result of the mystic neoplatonism that developed in the famous school of that town. The basic fact for him is "the symbolic interconnection between cosmos, Celestial City, and sanctuary..." [23]

---

[23] Otto von Simson, *The Gothic Cathedral. Origins of Gothic Architecture and the Medieval Concept of Order*, First ed. New York, 1956, paperback ed. Harper Torchbooks, New York, 1964, p. 37.

Erwin Panofsky has also pointed to *manifestatio*, the transcription of supernatural truth into visible forms, as the first element of Gothic art. Ernst Gall has often repeated that the Gothic cathedral with its verticalism is

> a symbol of transcendental forces which are to fill the soul of worshipers with deep longing for the celestial Kingdom of God. [24]

I do not have the authority of the scholars whom I have just mentioned. Yet I am persuaded that mystic neoplatonism, symbolism, and the Dionysian metaphysics of light and number do not give any real explanation for the characteristics of Gothic art and literature Christian symbolism did not change from the 11th to the 13th, and even to the 16th, centuries. The doors of St. Denis and of the Catedral of Chartres were supposed to be the *porta coeli* for the same reason for which the doors of the *Battistero* of Florence were called "the doors of Paradise." The numbers of Christian symbolism can be found in the Cathedral of Chartres as well as in the *Colonnato* of St. Peter in Rome. The problem is *how* this symbolism is expressed. Christian liturgy can suggest that the artist follows a pattern based on the number three or nine or seven, and we may find three or seven windows in Gothic as well as in Romanesque or Renaissance architecture. But this, obviously, does not tell us in which way those windows were arranged and it is exactly the arrangement, the particular shape, the way in which they are adorned or not that make a style.

We can even recognize that Suger, the architect of St. Denis, might be influenced in his thought by the metaphysics of Dionysius the Areopagite. Actually, we only know that he was a very dear friend of St. Bernard and as a person concerned with action, practical and political matters, the Crusade, the buildings of his Abbey, the response of people to his projects. His approach to religion was probably much closer to St. Bernard's deeply personal experience than to the abstractions of the neoplatonic philosophy. Like all other religious artists and architects of the Middle Ages or of the Renaissance he certainly had the ambition of creating a fa-

---

[24] E. Gall, book-review of S. M. Crosby, *L'Abbaye royal de Saint-Denis* (Paris, 1953) in *The Art Bulletin*, XXXVII, 1955.

çade that, in Von Simson's words, could "evoke the idea that the sanctuary is, in the words of the liturgy, the gate of heaven." But this has very little to do with his introducing a rose window over the main entrance of his cathedral, and the new way in which he turned the vaults and formed its columns. All this depends only on what looked beautiful and impressive to him. Even if his Christian theology were based on the works of Dionysius —and this is far from being proved— in order to understand the extraordinary expansion of Gothic style in the 12th and 13th centuries we have to consider what in his work possibly appealed to the other builders of cathedrals and to the people of the Middle Ages. Neoplatonism was no longer the philosophy of the 13th century. Yet the new style proliferated in a really astonishing way. Evidently it was a system of architectural forms which was admired and imitated. We are not speaking of the work of a single artist who may be inspired by one philosophy or another. We have to see what the populations of Italy, England and France appreciated and wanted to be reproduced in their Churches in a time when Aristotle's *Physics* and *libri naturales* and a deeply secular culture had taken the place of mystic conceptions.

Above all other elements, it was the pointed arch that was universally adopted: not because of its mystic character; but because it offered the only way to push the height of the new structures. The arch itself was known long before; but now it responded in a unique, almost miraculous way to the need of raising the height of the naves, of multiplying the number of the vaults and the columns, according to the new taste, without expanding in an impossible way the extent of the Church. We have to recall that space in the medieval town was extremely limited. Houses were clustered very closely within the city walls. The pointed arch represented an incomparable technical solution to the basic urbanistic and aesthetic problems of the age. By itself alone it can explain what we have called the explosion of Gothic architecture throughout Europe. The ambition of the time was toward height, arduousness, culmination together with multiplicity and concatenation of elements. One can hardly conceive now of what amount of skill, audacity, ambition, what mobilization of means were necessary to build those great cathedrals for towns which in most cases had only twenty or thirty thousands of inhabitants. It was infinitely more complex for them, from every point of view, than building the Empire State or higher, more formidable buildings. There were no exact measures, no tools, no materials but stones. What was achieved was really astonishing, miraculous from the point of view of technique and ambition as well. It was a feat of incredible ingenuity and intellectual tension, the opposite of mystic absorption and mere playing with symbols. The cathedral of Beauvais crumbled down in 1284 when the piers of the choir proved to be too lofty. The same thing happened elsewhere; but the fever and the ambition of building higher and higher remained. Those people were truly "builders," in the highest sense of the word. And then there was the quest for subtlety, plurality and complexity of elements. One may recall the multitude of spears, statues, arches, decorations. There was no moment of dullness; space was filled; everything was carried to the extreme point of cleverness and ingenuity. The most appropriate words for all this are those we have found in Dante's *De vulgari eloquentia: fastigiosus, subtilis, pexus, grandiosus, superbus.*

There is, I wish to make clear, a very definite link between Gothic art and the literature of the 12th and 13th centuries, between the architecture of the cathedrals and the poetry of the troubadours and Dante. We cannot speak of the symbolism of the medieval aesthetic ignoring the fact that the literature of the time, from the Troubadours to the "sweet new style," is characterized by a thoroughly secular mentality and an extreme, almost exclusive concern with artistry and formal inventiveness. In my opinion a closer consideration of the works of art and literature in the light of the theoretical texts of the Middle Ages provides very clear evidences of the true aesthetic sensibility from which both literature and art stem. As a matter of fact the humanistic reaction to the art and literature of the Middle Ages of which I have spoken earlier can be understood only as a revolt against the excess of ingenuity, the technicalities, the intellectual complexity and subtlety of the Gothic world. At a certain moment there was the need of something more plain, of a purer elegance, of measure, simplicity, space. The classics helped to form a new taste entirely opposed to the rules, the figures, the strictures of medieval art. What mattered was the example of the great classical authors. *Imitatio* took the place of *ars*. The definition that Petrarch was to give of the poetical activity could not be more suggestive. Poetry, he said, "is remembrance of things experienced and proved." [25] The distance from Dante could not be greater. And clearly it is not a matter of a developing secularism. It is clearly a reaction against the irrepressible intellectualism of the preceding age. The *Ospedale degli Innocenti* by Brunelleschi, the first great architect of the new age, shows the same attitude, the same substitution of plainness, simple harmony, spaciousness and chaste elegance for the strenuous complexity of the Gothic world. The change is astonishing. It can explain the profound aversion of the humanists to the art and literature of the preceding centuries. It tells us, first of all, better than any other fact, which were the characteristics of the medieval system. We have only to contrast any Gothic building with the spaciousness, the plain elegance, the naked simplicity, the purity of the church of San Lorenzo by Brunelleschi. It will also be very clear, I think, that the passage from the aesthetic system of the Middle Ages to that of the Renaissance does not imply any shift toward secularism and naturalism. The return to nature, for Brunelleschi, L. B. Alberti, and Donatello, was only the means for eliminating the intellectualism and the complicacy of Gothic art. The same was the case of Petrarch.

There are, I think, many current views that need to be corrected in this field. My hope is that in this year of Dante's centenary, through the same process which is leading to a completely new interpretation of Dante's work, also the knowledge of the basic trends of medieval art and literature will be renewed. It is of great importance for all our studies.

---

[25] F. Petrarca, *Lettere senili* II, 3.

UEBER DIE "VITA NUOVA" [1]

ULRICH LEO
University of Toronto

Dante Alighieris "kleinere" Werke zeigen uns den außerordentlichen Mann, jedes von einer anderen Seite; alle diese Aspekte zusammen haben dann dem Dichter der "Commedia" sein unverkennbares Gesicht gegeben. — Im "Convivio" ("Gastmahl") ist er der mehr als Autodidakt denn als Professioneller sich äußernde, aber selbständig und persönlich denkende, leidenschaftliche und dichterisch beschwingte Lehrer christlicher Scholastik für Laien; in "De vulgari eloquentia" ("Uber die italienische Dichtersprache") der Begründer moderner Grammatik, Sprachgeographie und Dichtungs-Ästhetik; in der "Monarchia" ("Das Weltkaisertum") ein Wortführer in den ethisch-politischen Grundfragen seiner Epoche. In den "Rime" ("Gedichte") zeigt sich der bedeutendste Reformator mittelalterlicher Liebesdichtung, wie die Provenzalen sie geschaffen und die Italiener —mit anderen europäischen Völkern— sie seit etwa hundert Jahren von den Troubadours übernommen hatten; und im übrigen ein Lyriker nicht nur der sublimsten Spiritualisierung irdischer Dinge, sondern fähig vulgärer Invektive und auch des Ausdrucks einer alle Dämme überflutenden Erotik. [Die Sonettensammlung "Il Fiore" ("Die Blume") ist in ihrer Zuteilung bestritten.] In den zwei lateinischen "Egloghe" finden wir den eleganten, klassizistisch gebildeten Korrespondenten in einem freundschaftlichen Dichterstreit; in der

---

[1] This article appeared first as "Nachwort" to *Dante: Vita Nuova: Das Neue Leben*. Fischer Bücherei, 1964.

"Questio de aqua et terra" ("Problem betreffend Wasser und Land") den Kosmographen, der aus der naturwissenschaftlichen Bildung seiner Zeit heraus spricht. In den lateinischen "Epistole" ("Briefe") —leider sind nur dreizehn erhalten— spricht der immer lebendig wache, rhetorisch strömende, oft aggressive Mann; und seine Themen gehen vom Persönlichsten —seiner lebenslänglichen Verbannung und dem Stolz, mit dem er sie trug —über das Politische— die ihn ganz verzehrende, dann ganz enttäuschte Hoffnung auf den deutschen Kaiser als den Retter Italiens und dieses Verbannten —bis zum Literarisch-Ästhetischen— jenem großen, kostbaren Schreiben an Cangrande della Scala, in dem wir den ersten Kommentar zur "Commedia" haben und das die heute wieder verbreiteten Zweifel an seiner Echtheit überleben möge, so wie es frühere Zweifel dieser Art überlebt hat.

Alle diese Werke und Schriften stehen, wie gesagt, in irgendeiner Beziehung zu dem einen großen Werk, das ihnen allen nachgefolgt ist: sachliche, thematische, weltanschauliche, formale Beziehungen verbinden sie mit der "Commedia". Nur die "Vita Nuova" ("Das Neue Leben") aber —die zärtlich-tragische, höchst vergeistigte Liebesnovelle in Versen und Prosa aus Dantes Jugend (wohl 1292 geschrieben; doch sprechen gute Gründe auch für 1295)— könnte als ein direkter Vorläufer der "Commedia" angesehen werden. (Der Titel ist in erster Linie zu verstehen im Sinne von "innerer Erneuerung"). —In der Mitte der "Vita Nuova" steht die irdische Beatrice, wie in der Mitte der "Commedia" die himmlische; in der "Vita Nuova" herrscht Amore, der heidnische Liebesgott, wie in der "Commedia" der christliche Gott der Liebe. Florenz ist die Stätte, an welcher die unter der Form des Erzählten mehr verborgene als offen hingestellte Wirklichkeit der "Vita Nuova" sich abspielt; in der "Commedia" ist Florenz nur noch der Ort, auf den das Heimweh, der Haß, die Kritik des Dichters sich richten — er selber lebt nun in Italien und darüber hinaus im Universum. Aber Zentrum ist Florenz hier wie dort. Ferner: in der "Vita Nuova" wird Florenz nicht ein einziges Mal genannt (wie auch sonst kein Ort und keine Person); stattdessen sagt der Dichter etwa: "die Stadt, in welcher meine Herrin nach dem Willen des höchsten Gottes das Licht erblickt hatte" (VI); "die Stadt, in der die holdseligste Herrin geboren ward, lebte und starb"— (XL); "die trauervolle Stadt" (XL, Son. V. 6). Aber "trauervolle Stadt" ("città dolente") ist der erste Name für die Hölle in der "Commedia" (*Inf.* III, 1).

Namen also sind ausgeschlossen vom Stil der "Vita Nuova"; der distanzierte Eindruck des gleichsam in verdünnter Luft oberhalb der Wirklichkeit sich abspielenden lyrischen Berichtes beruht sehr wesentlich auch auf dieser streng durchgeführten Anonymität. Die Herrin selber heißt in der "Vita Nuova" nicht etwa "Bice", wie ihr Urbild von ihren Angehörigen und Freunden genannt wurde (nur ein einziges Mal findet sich "Bice", und zwar im Reim, in einem Sonett [XXIV, Son. V. 9], das —wie wohl fast alle Gedichte in der Novelle— früher entstanden war als die erzählende und kommentierende Prosa, die es umgibt). Die Herrin wird vielmehr eingeführt als "die verklärte Herrin meines Geistes..., die von vielen, die nicht wußten, wie sie sie nennen sollten, Beatrice genannt wurde" (II); und zwar bedeutet ja "Beatrice" "die Segenspendende" — ein Doppelsinn, der den Namen durch das ganze Büchlein hindurch in einem Zwielicht zwischen Wirklichkeit und höherer Bedeutung hält. Ferner: wenn Beatrices Freundinnen unter sich von ihr als "questa donna" sprechen (XXII), so kann auch dies nur als Folge des Stilgesetzes der Anonymität verstanden werden: in Wirklichkeit sagten sie natürlich "Bice". —Und warum wollte Dante eine "epistola in forma di sirventese" nicht in die "Vita Nuova" aufnehmen (VI)? Einer der Gründe hierfür war offenbar der Umstand, daß sie zusammem mit sechzig florentinischen "donne" dort bei Namen genannt wurde. (Infolgedessen ist jenes "sirventese" uns verloren gegangen.)

Den Namen der Geliebten zu verhüllen ist nun Vorschrift aller Liebeslehren des Altertums und Mittelalters, und diese Vorschrift wird aufs strengste eingehalten bei Dantes lyrischen Vorbildern, den Troubadours, mit ihrem *senhal* ("Zeichen" für die Dame). Ja, ein moderner Nachfahre der vergeistigten Liebesdichtung wie Giacomo Leopardi nennt keine der von ihm ohne Gegenliebe angebeteten Damen bei ihrem wirklichen Namen. Aber die Anonymität der "Vita Nuova" umfaßt jedes Lebensgebiet, nicht nur das der Liebe. Den Dichter Guido Cavalcanti nennt Dante hier nur den "ersten meiner Freunde" (III, und öfter); während jener in einer berühmten Szene del "Commedia" (*Inf.* X, 63) als "Guido" erscheint. Denn die "Commedia" beruht in ihrem Stil geradezu auf dem Grundsatz der Namennennung, so wie die "Vita Nuova" auf deren Verschweigung. Florenz, der Arno erscheinen hier nur in der Umschreibung; durch die Gesänge der "Commedia" hallt der Name "Firenze" hundertfältig.

Im Bemühen, das künstlerische Verhältnis der "Vita Nuova" zur "Commedia" auszudrücken, könnte man sagen: die "Vita Nuova" erzählt verhüllte irdische Wirklichkeit; die "Commedia" erzählt enthüllte transzendente Wirklichkeit. Das lyrische Werk der Jugendzeit entschleiert seine geheimnisvolle Diesseitigkeit gleichsam in der veröffentlichten Jenseitigkeit des didaktisch-epischen Werkes der Reife. Die Lyrik der "Vita Nuova" zittert in der didaktischen Epik der "Commedia", durch und durch. Von der "città dolente" (*Inf.* III, 1) an bis zum letzten fernen Lächeln der Beatrice hin zu ihrem einstigen Freunde und jetzigen Zögling (*Par.* XXXI, 91 f.) ist latent gegenwärtig jene zarte Stimme des jugendlich liebenden Lyrikers, leise mitschwingend in der männlich gewaltigen Rede des dichterischen Propheten. Die unaussprechlich süße, zu Tränen rührende Erschütterungskraft der eben erwähnten Verse aus dem obersten Paradiese geht aus folgender Inspiration des Dichters hervor: unter dem Lichte Gottes gibt die himmlische Führerin ihrem Schüler im allerletzten Augenblick für Erdenzeiten jenes Lächeln und jenen Gruß zurück, welche die "engelhafte Dame" ("donna angelicata") einst, vor Jahrzehnten, unter dem Lichte Amors ihrem Liebhaber entzogen hatte ("Vita Nuova" X). Das heißt aber: die "Vita Nuova" ist fast vom ersten bis fast zum letzten Verse der "Commedia" im Dichter gegenwärtig und wirksam gewesen. (Eine Einsicht, durch die ein "rifacimento" ["Überarbeitung"] der "Vita Nuova" in Dantes späteren Jahren noch wahrscheinlicher wird —wir kommen darauf zurück.) Die zitierte Szene aus dem Ende des Paradiso könnte überschrieben werden: Das letzte Kapitel der "Vita Nuova".— Und schon gegen Ende der zweiten "Cantica" der "Commedia", des Purgatorio, vom Wieder-Erscheinen der Beatrice ab, wie sie unter Blumenwolken, von Engeln gegrüßt, auf dem "Wagen" steht —in rotem Gewande, so wie sie einst, als neunjähriges Kind, dem Dichter der "Vita Nuova" zuerst erschienen war ("Vita Nuova" II: *Purg.* XXX, 33)—, bis zur Absolution des Pilgrims Dante (*Purg.* XXXI, Ende) ist die Erinnerung an die letzten Abschnitte der "Vita Nuova" in einem Maße gegenwärtig —des Dichters vergeblicher Kampf gegen die Verlockung irdischer Anmut und

Teilnahme nach Beatrices Tode ("Vita Nuova" XXXVI ff.)—: daß man fast wieder von einer Fortsetzung der Jugend-Erzählung sprechen möchte, wieder *sub specie aeternitatis*.— In der "Vita Nuova" war Beatrice dem gegen seine Sinne kämpfenden Dichter im irdischen Traum erschienen, um ihn zu mahnen (XXXIX): nun (*Purg*. XXX u. XXXI) erscheint sie in der überirdischen Wirklichkeit; und aus der Mahnung einer gekränkten Geliebten ist nun eine vollständige kirchliche Bußhandlung geworden. —Auch sei in diesem Zusammenhang nicht vergessen: von allen Werken Dantes weist nur die "Vita Nuova" direkt auf das künftige große Gedicht hin— mit der das Büchlein abschließenden Andeutung einer "wunderbaren Vision", die dem Dichter zuteil wurde und unter deren Eindruck er hofft, einst von Beatrice "in einer Weise zu sprechen, wie noch von keiner je gesprochen worden" (XLII).

Aus all diesem ist zu ersehen: alle "kleineren" Werke Dantes könnten verloren sein, ohne daß uns das Verständnis der "Commedia" *als einer Dichtung* —und das ist die "Commedia" mehr als irgend etwas anderes— durch solchen Verlust unmöglich gemacht würde. Die "Vita Nuova" dagegen —das andere im echtesten Sinne dichterische Werk Dantes— bestimmt durch ihre latente Gegenwart einige Hauptstellen und sogar ganze Strecken des späteren Hauptwerkes; und wir würden viel verlieren, wäre es uns nicht vergönnt, das große Gedicht durch die Perspektive der kleinen Novelle su sehen. —Ja, die "Vita Nuova" ist in ausschließlicherem Sinne dichterisch als die "Commedia". Nie wieder hat Dante so ganz und nur als Lyriker gesprochen wie in seinem Jugendwerk. Die erhabensten dichterischen Flüge der "Commedia" sind in ihrer Ausdrucksqualität vorgedeutet in der "Vita Nuova".

Ist die "Vita Nuova" eine Allegorie? Die Antwort muß —übrigens ebenso für die "Commedia"— lauten: "nein".

Eben jene lyrische Bewegtheit, jener bei aller Distanz unmittelbare Ausdruck von Melancholie, Entzücken, Selbstbetrachtung, persönlichster Erinnerung, sowie die Schilderung der eigenen inneren Entwicklung vom jungen Liebenden zum lyrischen Dichter —dies ist die "innere Handlung" der "Vita Nuova"— weisen jedes nur zweitsinnige Verständnis des Büchleins zurück. Es ist einfach nicht glaubwürdig, daß ein junger Dichter solche Töne gefunden haben sollte, nur um ein zuvor ausgedachtes religiöses, philosophisches, literarästhetisches oder politisches Begriffsgebäude in vorsichtiger Verhüllung vorzulegen. Eine vielbesprochene Theorie, wonach die ganze "Vita Nuova" unter dem Deckmantel einer Liebesgeschichte ein politisch-häretisches Denksystem in einer nur den Eingeweihten vertrauten Geheimsprache zum Ausdruck bringe, verurteilt sich selbst in diesem Sinne; zu schweigen von weniger bedeutenden Versuchen, ihr den Boden der Wirklichkeit zu entziehen, über dem sie schwebt. — Beatrice "ist" vor allem einmal Bice Portinari aus Florenz, Tochter des Folco Portinari, geboren 1265, gestorben am 8. Juni 1290 als junge Ehefrau; freilich nun erscheinend in zartester Veredelung im Sinne der Troubadour-Dichtung, und schließlich verklärt bis zur Ver-Engelung, im Sinne des "Süßen neuen Stils", Dantes poetischer Schöpfung; vielleicht sogar verabsolutiert als schließliche Verkörperung christlicher *caritas*. — Wieso hätte Dante fremde Kalendersysteme herangezogen, um Beatrices Todestag mit der heiligen Zahl Neun — dem Symbol der Herrin als eines "Wunders" — mühselig genug auf einen Nenner zu bringen (XXIX): hätte er die Freiheit gehabt, ihren Todestag zu erfinden, anstatt den wirklichen Todestag umdeuten zu müssen! Und selbst wenn dies eine pseudogelehrte Mystifikation sozusagen zweiten Grades wäre: wozu könnten innerhalb eines allegorischen Schemas Szenen mit dem Charakter der Erlebtheit dienen wie die Abendgesellschaft (XIV), wo Dante die ihm nicht mehr gewogene Beatrice unerwartet sieht und fast ohnmächtig wird, während sie sich mit ihren Freundinnen über ihn lustig macht? oder Beatrices Traurigkeit beim Tode ihres Vaters (XXII)? oder die Schilderung, wie Dante im Andenken ihres eigenen Todestages in tiefer Versunkenheit sitzt und Engel zeichnet (XXXIV)? oder seine unheimliche Krankheit mit Fieberträumen und Todesahnungen (XXIII)? oder die ergreifende Szene mit den Rompilgern (XL)? — Solche Szenen, beruhend geradezu auf individuellem Erlebnis trotz aller Sublimierung ins Anonyme, wären in einem allegorisch gemeinten Ganzen einfach fehl am Platze gewesen. Die Kapitel XIV bis XVII sind eine der tiefsten und lebendigsten Stellen der Weltliteratur über das Thema "Liebe, Dichtung und Tod": dergleichen wäre einfach verloren gewesen innerhalb einer beabsichtigten "Allegorie". Man weiß aus einer Fülle mittelalterlicher Beispiele zu genau, wie echte allegorische Dichtung klingt, um die "Vita Nuova" "allegorisch" nennen zu können: es sei denn man wollte in den — freilich in unseren Tagen wieder wie einst im frühen Mittelalter unter unkritischem Beifall gepflegten — Grundfehler verfallen, einem Text die allegorische Auslegung aufzuzwingen, anstatt vor allem den Text selber sein Ja oder Nein dazu sprechen zu lassen.

Der Stil der "Vita Nuova" steht also unter dem Zeichen einer einst geschehenen Wirklichkeit, die sie aber umformt, indem sie sich von ihr distanziert. Anstelle des einst Erlebten, Gesehenen und Benannten stehen abstrahierte und unbenannte Gefühle und Aspekte. Eine Diatribe über die Zahl Neun steht an Stelle einer Beschreibung von Beatrices Tod (XXXVIII: XXIX). (Freilich war die Beschreibung schon vorweggenommen worden innerhalb jenes Fiebertraumes [XXIII].) — Wir wohnen nur wenigen natürlichen Ausbrüchen bei, wenig unmittelbarem Echo durchgemachter Erschütterungen; vielmehr ist dies zumeist aufgesogen in eine überaus kunstvolle Literatursprache — noch mehr der Wirklichkeit entfremdet durch Andeutungen scholastischer und klassizistischer Gelehrsamkeit eines jugendlichen Einzelgängers; ferner durch astrologische Symbolisierungen, durch Digressionen über Dichtungs-Ästhetik, Liebestheorie, asketische Moral. Inhaltlich liegt diesem ganzen Vorgang der Distanzierung von der geschehenen Wirklichkeit Dantes Bestreben zugrunde, eine mehr oder weniger lange Reihe einst gehabter und gewiß nicht immer nur geistiger Liebes-Erlebnisse nachträglich zu vereinheitlichen, als habe es in des jungen Dichters Leben nur ein einziges, und zwar aufs äußerste spiritualisiertes Erlebnis dieser Art gegeben: dasjenige mit der "Beseligenden", die — zuerst als irdische Frau, dann als engelgleiche Entrückte — den jungen Liebenden zum Dichter gemacht habe. (Die übrigen erotischen Begegnungen zu Beatrices Lebenszeit haben hier ihren Nachklang in den "donne di schermo", die das eigentliche Erlebnis angeblich nur haben verdecken sollen.) — Die "donna pietosa" (XXXV-XXXIX) steht dann für sich.

Hier ist ein Wort am Platze über das Verhältnis der lyrischen Gedichte der "Vita Nuova" zu ihrer Prosa. Nicht sind sie parallel und jeweils glechzeitig entstanden wie etwa die — wenig dichterischen — Verskapitel und Prosakapitel in Boethius' "Consolatio Philosophiae", einem formalen Vorbilde Dantes. Vielmehr waren die meisten — nicht alle — Gedichte der "Vita Nuova" schon fertig und im Umlauf (seit etwa 1283); ja sie hatten aus ihrem Verfasser schon einen bekannten jungen Lyriker gemacht, bevor er, etwa zehn Jahre später, eine Auswahl aus ihnen mit kommentierenden Nachträgen ("divisioni") versah und durch dichterisch erzählende Prosa verband. Die Gedichte sind das vergleichsweise unmittelbarere Echo des einst Erlebten — ob nun mit Beatrice oder einer ihrer Vorgängerinnen —; die Prosa — ganz auf Beatrice bezogen — ist das entferntere. Andererseits ist aber die Prosa der vollere, oft sogar blutvollere Widerklang einer schon entfernten Wirklichkeit: sie verhält sich oft zum jeweiligen Gedicht wie ein Gemälde in brennenden Farben zu einer vorhergegangenen sorgfältigen Bleistift-Skizze. (Als Beispiel vergleiche man etwa die Prosa in Kap. III mit dem nachfolgenden Sonett.) Speziell die Sonette in ihrer knapp vorgezeichneten metrischen Form sind im Ausdruck sozusagen zwangsläufig zurückhaltender als die äußerlich durch nichts gehemmte Prosa. Bei den weit längeren und formal weniger begrenzten Canzonen ("canzoni") — der vornehmsten lyrischen Dichtungsart nach Dantes Lehre — und auch bei den "Balladen" ("ballate"; Bsp.: Kap. XII) — ist der Ausdruck nicht von vornherein so eingeschränkt; aber hier geht etwa die Erzählung im Gedicht genau den umgekehrten Weg wie in der entsprechenden Prosa (Bsp.: Kap. XXIII): und man fragt sich, wieso? Die Antwort für das Kap. XXIII kann nur sein: das Gedicht — die geschehene Wirklichkeit unmittelbar wiedergebend — läßt den Dichter aus einem schlimmen Traum erwachen und den Traum den umhersitzenden, teilnehmenden "donne" erzählen; diese bleiben im Mittelpunkt. Die Prosa — Jahre später das einst Geschehene künstlerisch gestaltend — läßt den Traum selber (erst hier einen Fiebertraum) als direkte grausige Wirklichkeit erlebt werden; das Erwachen und die Teilnahme wurden nur als versöhnendes Ende aufbewahrt.

Wir handeln mit solchen Fragen von der "Struktur" unseres Dichtwerkes, seiner künstlerischen Gestalt, und von der Art, wie sie zustande gekommen ist. Hierher gehört auch das zuvor schon gestreifte Problem vom "rifacimento" der "Vita Nuova": d. h. die Frage, ob das Büchlein von Anfang an so war, wie wir es vor uns haben, oder ob der Dichter es später überarbeitet hat. Dies ist eines von jenen "Dante-Problemen", die mit nur inneren Gründen schwerlich je definitiv beantwortet werden können; andererseits ist die Hoffnung gering, daß jemals noch Original-Manuskripte sich finden, die eine von außen gestützte Entscheidung gestatten. Es ist ja von Dantes Hand bisher nicht eine Zeile aufgetaucht, — nicht einmal eine Unterschrift. Man muß also auf Grund von Erwägungen Stellung nehmen; und der Verfasser dieses Nachwortes ist für sein Teil überzeugt, daß ein "rifacimento" in der Tat stattgefunden hat; und zwar auf Grund innerer und textlicher Erwägungen — nicht um der angeblichen Notwendigkeit willen, die "Vita Nuova" mit dem späteren "Convivio" restlos in Einklang zu bringen. Als später hinzugefügt oder zum wenigsten erweitert würden in Frage kommen hauptsächlich die Kap. XXV und XL und ein Stück in XLI. Mit den Begründungen sollen die Leser dieser Zeilen nicht belästigt werden; um so mehr als das eigentliche Ethos eines solchen "rifacimento" aus der früher gezeigten innigen Verbundenheit der "Vita Nuova" mit der etwa fünfzehn Jahre später begonnenen "Commedia" erwächst. Der Gedanke, daß Dante im Exil die "Vita Nuova" wiedergelesen und sogar auf Grund seiner inzwischen getriebenen philosophischen und ästhetischen Studien ergänzt habe, kurz bevor er (etwa 1308) die Arbeit an der "Commedia" endgültig aufnahm, hat etwas ungemein Überzeugendes, ja etwas Ergreifendes. Aber in Gewißheit verwandelt werden kann die so überzeugende Vermutung schwerlich.

Die Betrachtung über die "Struktur" der "Vita Nuova" gipfelt in der Frage, ob man geradezu von einer bewußten "Architektur" des Büchleins sprechen dürfe. Wieder möchte der Unterzeichnete "Ja" antworten. Unverkennbar hat das kleine Werk drei nahezu gleich lange Teile: die Erlebnisse mit Beatrice und ihre seelische Wirkung auf den Liebenden, vom ersten Treffen bis zur Entzweiung (I-XVI); die Periode der "neuen Materie", nämlich des "Preisens" der Herrin, deren Dichter der vergeblich Liebende nun sein möchte (XVII-XXVII); die Trauer nach ihrem Tode, der Abfall zur "donna pietosa" und die Vision von Beatrices Berklärung (XXVIII-XLII). Die einunddreißig Gedichte verteilen sich zu je zehn auf die drei Teile; doch kommt im dritten Teile — dem höchstfliegenden — noch eine Canzone hinzu. Andererseits: fast im Zentrum des Werkes (XXIII) steht die zweite Canzone, der fünfzehn Gedichte vorausgehen und 15 folgen. Die drei großen Canzonen (Kap. XIX, XXIII, XXXI) sind durch je vier Gedichte voneinander getrennt. (Die zweistrophige Canzone [Kap. XXXIII] ist nur ein Ansatz, und die angeblich abgebrochene einstrophige [Kap. XXVII] war schwerlich der Anfang einer Canzone, sondern ist vielmehr ein mit Absicht leicht umgeformtes Sonett.) — Diese nahezu exakten schematischen Einteilungen, dazu noch auf Grund der "heiligen Drei", entsprechen zu solchem Grade Dantes geistiger Anlage und formaler Neigung, daß man an ihrer Absichtlichkeit kaum zweifeln kann.

Soviel sei hier gesagt zum seelischen und künstlerischen Verständnis dieser süß-traurigen, altertümlich-fremdartigen, tief besinnlichen, höchst lyrischen Dichtung in Vers und Prosa, die ihresgleichen in der europäischen Literatur des Mittelalters und vielleicht darüber hinaus schwerlich haben dürfte.

DANTE'S *DIVINE COMEDY*: THE VIEW FROM GOD'S EYE

ALDO BERNARDO

State University of New York at Binghamton, Harpur College

I would like to justify the adjective "Divine" which was prefixed to the simple title of *Comedy* some 200 years after the death of the poet. And I would like to justify this adjective in terms that I believe Dante would perhaps modestly have agreed with, for in this adjective is contained the essential perspective that Dante, the poet, deliberately chose when he set out to depict what he calls "the state of souls after death." Most readers have some idea as to why the adjective, "divine," was prefixed to the *Comedy*. But I would like to show as clearly as I can why and how it does indeed apply to the entire poem; and I would like to do so by means of an exposition of the poem's meaning on a level which Dante himself tells us he meant to convey. All too often Dante criticism has concentrated so much on the minutiae of the *Comedy* that it has lost sight of the forest because of the trees, if I may use an expression that seems singularly appropriate in talking about the *Comedy*

Everyone will readily agree that the *Comedy* is great both in its whole and in its parts. But since it is difficult to speak of the whole, most of what is said about the poem concentrates on the parts. This would have made Dante very sad, for, after all, his ultimate purpose in writing his poem was, in his own words, "to remove those who live in this life from the state of misery and direct them to the state of happiness." These words would certainly seem to imply the importance of grasping the whole. But somehow the modern aesthetic discourages treatment of this important dimension as a result of its worship of form as pure linguistic technique. And yet, I believe that there is a way to treat the whole in a manner that would at least not clash with modern methodologies. It is simply to focus upon the setting or backdrop that Dante deliberately chose for the unfurling of his poetic journey, i.e. the world of the hereafter, or, if you will, the world of the spirit, and see how it relates and contributes to the artistic structure of the whole.

If there is general agreement that in the *Comedy* we have one of the relatively few instances in the history of mankind when human creativity approached its zenith, then it appears logically incorrect to maintain that the framework of the poem, because of its religious and spiritual nature, contributes minimally to those qualities that make Dante's poem great. It might indeed be said that it is precisely the framework that constitutes the basic originality of the *Comedy*, for unlike Homer and Virgil who depicted man's journey on the frontiers of life, and a Chaucer or a Boccaccio who were later to set their journeys squarely in this life, Dante elected to depict his in the hereafter. Why? Was it simply because he was a religious man? Judging from the finished product, this remains doubtful. Was it not rather because as a great poet and artist he felt that such a setting would provide him with a desired perspective? What was this perspective? I would say that it was the perspective of both ultimate universality and ultimate infallibility, a view of Man at his worst and at his best, not as seen by Man himself, but as seen through the eyes of the Christian God. For what do we have in Dante's setting if not a depiction of the baseness and grandeur of Man when viewed as a potential citizen of the City of God?

How Dante arrived at this choice of perspective and some of its major implications in viewing the poem as a whole constitute the main purpose of this study. I hope as a result to contribute a distinct dimension to the meaning of the adjective "divine" and perhaps leave the reader with a deeper conviction that the *Comedy* does indeed deserve to be so-called. But let us start from the beginning.

As anyone familiar with Dante's thought knows, he felt that everything, from angels to plants, proceeds from God; and everything aspires to return to God with a distinct and visible rhythm. It is this aspiration and rhythm that gives the universe its life; this is the cause of its circular form and accounts for all its intricate motion. Everything is in a constant state of flux because of its unceasing efforts to pattern itself on the spiritual world of God. In other words, the city of Man instinctively strives to become the city of God. Consequently, all social and political problems gain the proper perspective for solution through a revelation of the heavenly order of things, or through a depiction of the infinite and mysterious ways and means offered by God to men for their ultimate happiness and salvation. This brings us to the basic problem facing Dante as a poet: i.e. how to depict most effectively, in all its beauty, this cosmic rhythm in which mankind is unconsciously trying to participate.

What Dante wanted to express was not new. It had to do with the problem of human destiny or man's place in the universe. But his became a much more comprehensive and ambitious attempt than previous ones, for he felt moved to portray through the art of poetry not only the entire spiritual evolution of Man from the lowly worm to the angelic butterfly (to use his own phrase), but to do so on what he considered infallible grounds revealed by God Himself in the Scriptures. At the same time, he wanted to preserve the inherent dignity and freedom instinctively felt by Man while a creature in this life. His ultimate goal thus became to depict as vividly as possible how man can be saved and become eternal through the use of his free will. This is why the *Comedy* is a tremendous hymn both to human dignity and potentiality and to divine mercy and creation, and why it is considered the supreme example of the fusion of poetry, theology and philosophy. And this is why it is essential for the reader who wishes fully to understand and appreciate the poem to suspend disbelief and constantly bear in mind that at the heart of the poem is the full acceptance of the meaning and mystery of the advent of Christ in all its wonder and beauty.

To achieve his goal Dante had to undertake a reproduction of the entire universe, of the senses and of the spirit. What's more, he had to create an impression of infallibility which in his day meant simply abiding by the teachings of the Church and of the Church Fathers. By taking these teachings and using them as foundations for a portrayal of the universe as presumably seen through the eyes of the Christian God, Dante sincerely hoped to help lead Mankind from the miseries of this world to salvation and true happiness.

Dante's main problem, then, was to make us see as God sees. How does God see? Only God's own book, Scripture, can give the answer. There we learn that God certainly sees in a different manner than Man. In Scripture we find that God speaks with events rather than with words. In fact, things and events seem to be, for God, what words are for men. In short God sees consequences and finalities, not as through a glass, darkly, but face to face, timelessly. So Dante decided to model his style on that of the Bible. That is, people, things, events indicated by words had to reveal an ultimate human and divine meaning.

There still remained the problem of what God sees. Here too Scriptures give the answer. There we are taught that God sees essentially the world and life of the supernatural where there is no intrusion of time or space. This is the true life in God's sight. This is what God sees. So Dante's poem concentrates on that other life and reproduces it so convincingly within the Christian frame work that a reader of his day must certainly have come away with the conviction that Man must be blind to believe that the life he sees around him, on this earth, is the true life.

Such considerations made Dante conceive of a poem whose subject matter on the literal level is the life of the hereafter, the life after death, the life of the spirit. Now God Himself teaches in Scripture that there is a connection between this other life and life on earth. So any complete picture of the hereafter had also to teach Man a great deal about this life. How to achieve this was another problem faced by Dante.

To resolve this problem Dante had recourse to three ingenious devices. First, he takes a live man, not yet dead but about to give up, and makes him of his own will take a mysterious journey in that life. This device enabled him really to portray the entire universe, i.e. the natural and the supernatural, the now and the then, the imperfect and the perfect; in short, evil as well as good.

The second device was to project the earthly personalities of the souls encountered in the after-world against a background that reflects God's infallible judgment with respect to ultimate perfection or imperfection. We thus are made to feel that in such cases as Paolo and Francesca, Farinata or Ulysses earthly fulfilment is certainly a far cry from ultimate fulfilment.

A third device employed by Dante to achieve the desired bridge or connection between that life and this was his use of Beatrice as an example of how thin a line divides human from divine love. As everyone knows, the *Comedy* is essentially a hymn to love in all its manifestations. Consequently, Beatrice is but a sign of how divine love penetrates the entire universe, even down to particular individuals.

We have, then, in the *Divine Comedy* the curious situation in which the afterlife is the true life or literal level of meaning while this, our life, is but a reflection of that life. As a result, each sinner of Hell, repented soul of Purgatory, or blessed soul of Paradise, in order to acquire its fullest meaning, must also be viewed within the framework of this life.

But God's world meshes with our world in very mysterious ways. These ways are usually revealed to men through signs or symbols found anywhere and everywhere in Creation. Since the *Comedy* is basically an imitation of God's Creation, it too must contain such hidden signs. Dante himself, the hero of the poem, is but a sign or symbol just as are all the people, things and events found everywhere in the poem. In other words, they all have more than one level of meaning. Furthermore, in order to give the impression of God's Creation since the beginning of time, there had to be a great number of people, things and events, just as in the Bible which is God's account of Creation. But just as in the Bible, there also had to be certain leading leading actors or signposts along the way being pursued by the willing pilgrim. All too often we forget that the real "protagonist" of the *Comedy* is God Himself, the Light toward which the pilgrim moves at the very beginning of the poem. As for the supporting cast, it is very large indeed; but the chief roles are certainly played by Dante himself, Virgil, Beatrice and St. Bernard. These last three, as is well known, are Dante's principal guides on his journey. Therefore, they represent three means offered by God to Man to help him achieve the Light. It is now generally conceded that Reason, Revelation and Intuition are the most appropriate terms for defining these three means.

There are many, many other such signs or symbols scattered throughout the poem that indicate either God's presence or his handiwork. The very structure of the poem reflecting everywhere the numbers 3, 7 or 10 provides eloquent testimony of this, as does the setting of Eastertide and even the year 1300.

But it is about time that we turn to the poem itself and see how it does reflect a perspective that could be defined as "divine" rather than "human", or, to put it another way, as the view from God's eye.

Let us first examine briefly the introductory canto or prologue. What the human eye sees is a relatively simple scene: the figure of a man lost in a dark wood, his arrival at the foot of a mountain topped by the weak rays of the sun; his attempt to climb the mountain; the sudden appearance of three beasts that impede his way; his unsuccessful attempt to bypass all three; and finally the appearance of the shade of Virgil who agrees to lead him to the light via another route. What we basically see is a tableau that seems to reflect mysterious overtones that puzzle us. This sense of mystery is doubtless rooted in the suspicion that the entire tableau must have a deeper meaning. And indeed it does acquire this deeper meaning as we follow Dante in his subsequent journey and ultimately realize with him that this first canto contains in capsule form the essential meaning of the entire journey. Space prevents going into too many details, but let us examine just two.

First of all, let us re-read the first 7 verses so familiar to all.

> Nel mezzo del cammin di nostra vita
> mi ritrovai per una selva oscura,
> che la diritta via era smarrita.
> Ah quanto a dir qual era è cosa dura
> esta selva selvaggia e aspra e forte
> che nel pensier rinnova la paura!
> Tant'è amara che poco è più morte;

Even if we catch the wealth of meaning in the images of the dark wood, the lost way and the speaker's age, very few general readers can be expected to be sensitive enough to something else found in these verses which gives evidence of the incredible extent to which Dante compressed meaning into every nook and cranny of his poem. To put it simply and briefly, we note that the very first verse of the poem ends with the word *vita*, "life;" the seventh verse ends with the word *morte*, "death;" the number seven also plays an important role in the *Comedy* as indicative of the seven days of creation. Now the opening verses of *Genesis* teach us that in creating the universe God started with chaos and ended with life, but as a result of Man's pride Man chose death. Rather than elaborate further, suffice it to point out that the opening of the *Comedy* clearly echoes the opening of Scripture and that the subsequent movement of the poem clearly implies a return to Eden — in fact, a movement from death back to life. But we, like the lost Dante, cannot realize all this until we have completed our reading of the poem, which is the same as saying until we have understood God's ways.

Another example of the same thing can be seen in the vivid tableau depicting Dante partially emerging from the wood, and looking up at the three beasts, the mountain and the sun. In an article published a few years ago I tried to show the strong analogy that exists between this particular position in which Dante finds himself and the position of Satan.[1] If the three beasts symbolically represent the three main divisions of Dante's Hell, and there is strong evidence to support this, then it is possible to equate Dante's stance as he looks up to the three beasts, the mountain and the sun, to the position of Satan stuck fast in the depths of the universe and looking up at the three divisions of his kingdom. The one important distinction between Dante's position and Satan's is that Dante is not stuck fast in the dark forest and that he can also see the mount and the sun. But the positions are analogous and the meaning does emerge that Dante has "hit bottom," as it were. But who can see all this at first glance except the imaginary eye of God whose omnipresence is underscored by the poet in the opening scene of his poem when he clearly defines the main action of his drama as the movement of a Christian pilgrim toward the Light of the Sun? I should perhaps add here that this is an extreme simplification of a complex theological problem which I deal with in detail in the article I have cited.

---

[1] Aldo S. Bernardo, "The Three Beasts and Perspective in the *Divine Comedy*," PMLA, LXXVIII, 1 (March 1963), 15-24.

But let us now enter the Inferno, standing back as far as possible to see what it is all about over and above a strange and horrendous place. As I have indicated, Scripture had taught Dante that God's world is spiritual rather than physical. Hell must, therefore, imply a spiritual state or meaning. If viewed from above, Dante's Hell is actually an extended symbol of sin or evil which Man must thoroughly understand and freely shun in order to deserve God's rewards. Human nature is essentially good, but according to Scripture it created sin by turning away from God. So sin is the absence of God, who is the source of all good and of all spiritual light. Dante's Inferno is therefore a vast void under the surface of the earth created when the best of God's creatures, Satan, was ejected from heaven and became almost synonymous with dirt or matter, in which he is now eternally stuck. It is a realm of darkness, horror and grief into which God's creatures tumble when they turn their backs to Him and begin indulging in self-love. In his self-love Man buries himself deeper and deeper in the egotistic life of the passions — like a body subject to the laws of matter. As such, he is beaten around by the elements and sinks more and more into the clutches of the material world, a process clearly visible throughout the Inferno. It is precisely because such an environment is foreign to Man's true nature that Dante's Hell can be viewed as an extended metaphor of disharmony and discord.

Man without reason and virtue with which he is endowed by God, is like the wild, uncultivated country of Dante's Hell. Here the actions of men appear senseless, but they are actually actions symbolic of the specific sin of which each is guilty, a sin which each willingly chose to pursue and never regretted to the very last moment of his life. Interestingly, these senseless actions now comprise their very punishments and remind them eternally of what it means to have turned their backs to God. This is what they wanted back on earth and this is what they will get eternally.

So in the Inferno, what we really have is Dante, presumably still a live man like any of us, willingly turning to clear human reason (Virgil) and examining sin in all its gory details and learning to know wickedness and evil as it really is, stripped of all false resemblance to the good. Having once learned the nature of sin, it is like being pulled by a new and truer center of gravity. Dante the poet symbolizes this by having Virgil help him turn around at Satan's waist — the dead center of gravity of Dante's universe of matter. Together they climb UP to Satan's feet, and when Dante the pilgrim looks BACK and sees the tremendous monster (Sin) stuck upside down, he realizes what a stupid and silly and perverted thing Sin really is. So does Sin appear to the man who understands all its implications.

So much for the spiritual or "divine" meaning of the Inferno, a meaning which for Dante, as I have previously indicated, was an essential dimension of any great work of art. Let us now try to view the Purgatorio in like manner.

At first glance, Purgatory also, like Dante's Hell, seems to be another series of strange places visited by Dante the wayfarer. But once again, if we step back and view the picture from above, a different image emerges, for Dante's Purgatory also represents a spiritual state as well as a place. What we really have here is the picture of a sinner who, having learned under the guidance of human reason the nature of evil, and having rejected evil, now begins to learn the nature of the good. We are actually back at the foot of the mountain seen in the first canto of the Inferno. This time, however, there are no beasts to cope with and the pilgrim's posture is one of humility rather than self-confidence. We soon realize that Purgatory is essentially a process, a spiritual process, that cleanses and purifies those souls who have shaken off the yoke of sin. Such souls have crossed the threshold of salvation because sometime in their life they sincerely repented for their life of sin and turned to God. They must now rid themselves of their inclination for sin, "the fog of the world," as Dante calls it. Consequently, they suffer torments rather than punishments; torments that are painful yet pleasing. They are pleasing first of all because they are really enforced virtues (and therefore constitute good training for the will) and secondly because they will some day cease. Unlike the case in Hell, there is progress in Purgatory, symbolized by the act of climbing up the mountain side. Whereas Hell had a funnel-like shape, the mount of Purgatory becomes progressively narrower toward the top, representing the focussing of Man's spiritual experience on a single point of reference which is up rather than down.

By exercising their wills on the seven circular shelves of Purgatory, the souls eventually reach a state akin to Adam and Eve's. Upon reaching this state, they are permitted to enter the Garden of Eden or the Earthly Paradise. The entire structure is a symbol of God's mercy and love, pulling us ever upward notwithstanding our natural inclination to go down.

Dante's Purgatory is thus more complicated than his Hell, encompassing as it does certain elements of Hell and some of Heaven. The main thread of meaning, however, is much more clear and positive than in Hell. This thread is to be found in Dante the wayfarer. Whereas in Hell he had undergone a process of negative learning, here it is all positive. He learns things to be remembered rather than forgotten. It is basically a kind of moral growth resulting from the answers that Virgil primarily gives to his questions. As he learns, we learn along with him; and soon we grasp, together with him, the most important single lesson that emerges from the very marrow of the *Comedy*. And this is that what makes the world go round, what causes good and evil and practically every other problem in any way connected with human or divine relations is love in all of its thousands of aspects. In fact, the whole of Dante's Purgatory has been called the drama of the right ordering of love, starting with the mind's release from false objects and ending with its turning to ever wider and truer realities. In short, Dante's journey through Purgatory teaches the wayfarer and us how human love may be transformed into divine love or Charity.

In the dead center of Purgatory and, incidentally, of the poem, Dante the wayfarer gets a truly liberal education from Virgil and a few other souls by forcing his intellect to grasp the rather subtle doctrines of Free Will and of Love. (I might here say parenthetically that this is the best example I know, of what the term "liberal education" was meant to convey in its original meaning of "liberating" man from something.) By the time the episode is over, Dante is truly convinced that love is indeed the seed not only of every virtue but of all evil, and that Man is truly free to use his will as he chooses. He learns further that the entire structure of Purgatory with its ledges and specific location of souls, depends on the way in which each soul directed his love back on earth. He also learns that to direct one's love correctly, i.e. in proper quantities and toward proper objects, all that is needed is the willingness and ability to follow the dictates of one's higher reason. If Man did this, and Dante learns that it is really not as difficult as it appears, Man could enjoy a sort of relative blessedness here on earth, roughly similar to that enjoyed by Adam and Eve before the Fall. Throughout Purgatory one can hear echoes of St. Paul's exhortation, "owe no man anything except to love one another; for he who loves his neighbor has fulfilled the law." (*Rom.* 13, 8.)

Dante's insight and understanding increases as he climbs higher and higher up the mountain. We note, among other things, that his climb is constantly facilitated by the sudden appearance of angels, dreams, visions and the like; and we are puzzled. But once again, viewed from a spiritual vantage point the meaning emerges that if Man were to follow the dictates of his reason as Dante follows Virgil's difficult discussions and arguments, he can count on God's help which may appear in an infinite variety of forms.

Following a final series of trials that Dante undergoes on the last terrace of Purgatory, he is mysteriously transported to the Garden of Eden or Terrestrial Paradise situated at the very top of the mountain. At this point, Virgil's teachings concerning the correct use of human activity and human freedom come to an end. Under his guidance, Dante had achieved perfect control of his will. But while Virgil's intellectual journey had proven profitable, Dante now feels that as a Christian he can and must go further, far beyond the rational. This is why Virgil suddenly fades out at this point and why Dante's attention is drawn to a beautiful maiden who seems to be frolicking in the Garden. This young maiden, bathed in the light of pristine beauty and innocence, is the guardian of the Garden, and symbolizes the superior wisdom that awaits Dante's mind. She introduces him to an overview of such wisdom through her explanation of a mysterious and symbolic procession that unfurls before Dante — a procession full of extremely complicated meaning representing history as seen through God's eye and the complex relationships of Man to society and of society to God. This significant procession, the details of which are usually passed over by the reader, symbolizes history as

God intended it, as Man spoiled it, and as the true Christian should see it.

It is in the midst of this procession that Beatrice takes over as guide. Her entrance is very spectacular and recalls the second coming of Christ at the last Judgment. Here perhaps better than anywhere else in the poem Dante's technique for imparting both a human and divine meaning becomes clear. By using Beatrice who had been a very real woman and a very real love in his life as he does at this point, he makes the idea of Revelation a highly personal one. This is as it should be, for Revelation in the final analysis is a strictly individual experience. On the other hand, by placing her on a Chariot surrounded by signs indicating that she occupies a place to be occupied by Christ at His second coming, he also makes her a symbol for all Christians. In any case, Beatrice proceeds to lead Dante through a series of ritualistic experiences whose final outcome signifies the complete restoration of Man's original goodness and innocence. Dante is now completely weightless since he has been cleansed of even the memory of sin. As a result, Dante the pilgrim is now ready and disposed to rise to the stars and to commune with God. He has thus far flown backward in time; now he will fly upward in space.

It is a well known fact that, generally speaking, most readers of the *Comedy* stop with the Inferno, a few more struggle through the Purgatorio, but only a handful ever work their way through the Paradiso. This is a peculiar state of affairs inasmuch as experts generally agree that it is in the Paradiso that Dante's artistry achieves something very close to sublimity, both in technique and conception. Here too, perhaps, by standing back and trying to see the big picture, we can appreciate to a greater degree what Dante is trying to do and say in his last Cantica.

What we really have in the Paradiso is Dante the pilgrim acquiring a deeper and deeper understanding of non-material things, especially the mysteries of the Christian faith. In fact, we can say that it is here that he really begins to see as God sees. The pilgrim gains what might essentially be called divine knowledge, which is now imparted by Beatrice, just as human knowledge had been imparted by Virgil. In the Paradiso Dante truly immerses us in the world of the spirit by employing a technique whose main ingredients are light, music and color.

Perhaps his most striking device is the use of the moon, the sun and the other planets as stepping stones for following his beloved Beatrice in her heavenly journey. Here again we have what appears to be an apparently ingenious device assuming new dimensions of meaning if we would but step back and realize that the journey from one heavenly body to the next signifies the tremendous distances our minds and hearts must travel under the guidance of Revelation or Faith in order to get a mere intuition into the nature of God.

From the very first verse of the Paradiso we are made aware of the fact that the pilgrim is now approaching the ultimate goal of his journey—the actual sight of God. As Dante travels ever upward with his eyes fixed on Beatrice, everything becomes more transparent and spiritual. Even his discussions with Beatrice become further and further removed from the world of Man, the world as we see it. Thus, toward the very end we find Beatrice tutoring Dante on such subjects as the nature of form, spheres, and angels, as well as on such mysteries as predestination, degrees of blessedness and, most important, faith, hope and charity, In fact, Dante must be formally examined on these three virtues by their three great personifications, St Peter, St James and St John before being permitted to step over the threshold of the true Paradise. Upon Dante's passing this exam, everything seems to get rounder and rounder, brighter and brighter, sweeter and sweeter. Just as Hell reflected the disharmony and strife in Man, here we feel a strong sense of harmony and peace in God. What has really happened to Dante the pilgrim since leaving Eden is that he has "put on" God (to use a phrase from St Paul), and has, as it were, been viewing God from within. He has unconsciously been having his sights adjusted in order to be able to see from the top down. When through the efforts of Beatrice his sight is perfectly adjusted, St. Bernard takes over and intercedes with the Virgin Mary, petitioning her to give Dante's vision one final adjustment in order to enable him to withstand the tremendous brilliance of the simple point of light which is God. In the final vision, Dante for a split second distinctly sees in the point of light now become three concentric circles not only the triune nature of the Godhead, but, more importantly for the modern reader, how a human figure can fit perfectly into the circles. It is amazing how few readers grasp the full significance of the ending of the *Comedy* which in bold, clear strokes projects the powerful image of not only the humanity of God, but the potential divinity of Man.

The poem ends as abruptly as it had begun. This is as it should be, for there is really nothing more to talk about. Our poet-pilgrim has made us travel the entire universe, up, down, in and out, and has revealed to us the secret of eternal bliss, i.e. the realization that we as men, if we would but will it, are capable of participating fully in that almighty Love that moves the sun and the other stars. The *Comedy* is indeed a divine poem, written not only for the greater glory of God, but for the greater glory of Man, God's predilected Creature.

FEATURES OF THE POETIC LANGUAGE OF THE *DIVINA COMMEDIA*

HELMUT HATZFELD
The Catholic University of America

FOR URBAN TIGNER HOLMES, ON HIS SIXTY-FIFTH BIRTHDAY

A characterization of the poetic language of the *Divina Commedia* may receive sharper contours by the time-honored comparison of Dante with Giotto. Both represent a style which combines with the hieratic features of Romanesque art the realistic mobility of the Gothic, and impose on the fusion of these styles the geometrical forms of a freshly apprehended pre-humanistic classicism. Goethe had already recognized this when he said that both Dante and Giotto do not imitate nature but recreate it, thanks to "their imaginative eye." [1] Living in the time of the musical *Ars Nova*, moreover, they dropped many impersonal conventions. [2] By discovering space and plasticity, both became the founders of modern art and literature. [3] Those who have analyzed Dante's style did not fail to stress this imaginative realism in his language; thus Giulio Bertoni, mentioning new expressions like "l'aria impregnata di verde e di fiori," [4] thus Leo Spitzer struck by the imagined-realistic foliage of the wood of the suicides

---

[1] J. W. Goethe: *Dante* (1826) quoted in Martin Gosebruch, *Giotto und die Entwicklung des neuzeitlichen Kunstbewusstseins*, Köln: Du Mont Schauberg, 1962, p. 38.
[2] Pietro Toesca, *Giotto*: UTET, 1941, p. 143.
[3] Emilio Cecchi, *Giotto*, London: Oldbourne Press, 1960, p. 32.
[4] G. Bertoni, "La lingua di Dante," *Lingua e Poesia*, Firenze: Olschi, 1937, 27-50.

as "Non frondi verdi, ma di color fosco," [5] thus Luigi Malagoli startled by expressions of a magic spell like "ombre con manti" (*Purg.* XIII, 47). [6] Malagoli goes so far in maintaining the creativity of Dante's language that he denies realism as well as imagination to Dante's predecessors. [7]

Dante's resources were enormous. He alone was the poet who had read the whole of French literature together with the Bible, the Ancients (Aristotle, Cicero, Seneca, Virgil, Horace, Juvenal), and the Fathers and the Doctors (St. Jerome, St. Augustine, Albert the Great, Thomas Aquinas and St. Bonaventure). [8] We even know how Dante's imagination was kindled by a single Virgilian hexameter to expand it into a long *terza rima*. Thus Aeneas' famous beginning of the report on his adventures: "Infandum, regina, iubes, renovare dolorem" (*Aen.* II, 3), in the mouth of Count Ugolino (*Inf.* XXXIII, 4-6) becomes:

> Tu voi ch' io rinnovelli
> *Disperato* dolor, che *il cor mi preme*,
> *Già pur pensando*, pria ch' io ne favelli. [9]

Adjectival Segmentation

In Dante's particular imaginative realism, the first style feature that strikes us is what Malagoli calls, in a pertinent term, *Il scandimento delle cose*, i.e. the sharp separation of single elements within a well organized group. Giotto, in his fresco in the Arena Chapel of Padua, called "Jesus insulted by the Jews," pictured six young men surrounding and insulting Him, the one pulling his hair, the other his beard, the third lifting his hand to beat Him, the fourth somehow hesitating in the background, the fifth

---

[5] Leo Spitzer, "Speech and Language in Inferno XIII," *Italica:* 19 (1942), 91-104.

[6] Luigi Malagoli, *Linguaggio e poesia nella Divina Commedia*, Genova: Briano, 1949.

[7] Luigi Malagoli, *Aspetti dell' espressione letteraria negli scrittori religiosi delle origini*, Pise: Libreria Goliardica, 1953, 65 p.

[8] Felicina Groppi, *Dante traduttore*. 2.ª edizione notevolmente accresciuta. Roma: Tipografia Poliglotta Vaticana, 1962, 96-146.

[9] F. Groppi, *ibid*.

rushing forward to hit Him, the sixth kneeling and staring at Christ with an arguing gesture. That is the way Dante singles out individual souls from groups of sinners or saints. This type of composition by segments in Dante is even visible on the linguistic level. Here the adjectival segmentation gives to a scene, a person, or an object multiple facets by splitting up the overall qualification into different viewpoints, colorings, feelings and shadings; for a landscape for instance:

> *Dolce* color d'*oriental* zaffiro
> Che s' accoglieva nel *sereno* aspetto (*Purg.* I, 13-14).

or, by contrast:

> (La piova) *eterna, maledetta, fredda* e *greve* (*Inf.* IV, 7-8).

A character (Sordello) is seen from all angles:

> Come ti stavi *altiera* (sc. anima) e *disdegnosa.*
> E nel mover degli occhi *onesta* e *tarda* (*Purg.* VI, 61-63).

Professor Davie Carozza [10] has found that this visualizing *scandimento* concerns even the single but decisive adjective which is stressed and unduly extended by dieresis:

> Poi è Cleopatràs *lussurïosa* (*Inf.* V, 63).
> Non puoi fallire a *glorïoso* porto (*Inf.* XV, 56).

Scandimento is also achieved by the single, anteposited and, therefore striking, objective adjective: "*alpestre* rocce," "*fertile* costa," "*alto* monte;" [11] by adjective substitutes in negative qualifications for which Dante has become famous: "L'aer *senza stelle*" (*Inf.* III, 23) or "Quell' aria *senza tempo* tinta" (*Inf.* III, 29); or by synesthetic adjectival segmentation: "Loco *d'ogni luce muto*" (*Inf.* V, 28).

---

[10] Davie Carozza, *The Divina Commedia in French. A stylistic Study of Longnon's Translation.* Diss. Catholic University, Washington, D. C., 1964.
[11] Luigi Malagoli, *Saggio sulla Divina Commedia*, Firenze: La Nuova Italia, 1962, p. 52.

Gerund Constructions

Giotto uses a second means of giving the central element of a scene an emphatic accent by putting it not only in the foreground, but more drastically before the very eyes of the onlooker, by detaching it from a larger foreground scene. Such is the case of Mary embracing the body of Christ immediately after "The descent from the Cross" in the fresco of the same name in the Arena Church. The four other mourning women almost create a window for that pietà in the making. The art historians called this method "Solennità di inquadratura spaziale che può dirsi dantesca." [12] Malagoli speaks of such cases, in reference to Dante, as *frontalità*. I think it also involves a kind of framing of the action involved. Dante's language creates this frontal stress or framing primarily by the constant use of gerund constructions, which evoke space and depth for movement. [13] Therefore, I would like to add, Dante purposely invalidates the finite verb and doubles the gerund for this magnifying and visualizing presentation:

Venendo e *trapassando* ci ammirava
D'anime turba, tacita e devota (*Purg.* XXIII, 20-21).
Una donna soletta che si già
Cantando ed *iscegliendo* fior da fiore (*Purg.* XXVIII, 40-41).
La bufera infernal che mai non resta...
Voltando e *percotendo* li molesta (*Inf.* V, 31-33).
Così *benedicendomi cantando*
Tre volte cinse me... L'apostolico lume (*Purg.* XXIV, 151-153).

The choice of a strongly visualizing gerund has the same effect as a double gerund:

Menava io gli occi per li gradi
Mo su, mo giù, e mo *ricirculando* (*Par.* XXXI, 47-48).

Foregoing the many examples, which can be found in Malagoli, it may be said that Dante does not shrink from applying this frontalizing gerund to the most abstract cases:

---

[12] Cesare Gnudi, *Giotto*, Milano: Martello, 1959, p. 76.
[13] L. Malagoli, *Saggio, op. cit.*, p. 53.

L'alto padre *Mostrando* come spira e come figlia (*Par.* X, 50-51).

He does the same with the substantivized infinitive whose "frontalizing" function could not be assumed by the abstract noun:

> O *vero sfavillar* del santo Spiro (*Par.* XIV, 76)
> Che quella vivace luce (the Trinity)...
> Per sua bontade *il suo raggiare* aduna (*Par.* XIII, 55-58)
> Dio vede tutto e *tuo veder* s'inluia (*Par.* IX, 73)
> *Transumanar* significar per verba (*Par.* I, 70-71)
> Il dolce *frui* (*Par.* XIX, 2)
> Esto *beato esse* (*Par.* II, 79).

This solid substantivization of the infinitive occurs in concrete peasant languages where abstractions are rare, as e.g. in Rumanian.

KEY EXPRESSIONS

Expressions of steepness, climbing and falling not only come from Dante's topic. They seem rather to have preëxisted in Dante's mind and influenced his motives, structures and language, particularly the steep mountain of Purgatory. Dante actually speaks of "Il poggio sale più che salir non posson gli occhi miei" (*Purg.* IV, 86), and "temer cadere in giuso" (*Purg.* XXV, 117). If the motif existed in Christian mysticism (the ladder of St. John Climacus or a mountain to climb, for example), it certainly did not exist in Christian eschatology prior to Dante. Strikingly, for Giotto, too, steepness is a structural element. In the fresco of the "Miracle of the Spring" (Assisi) the thirst of a peasant, which is finally relieved, is explained by an intolerable heat, suggested by the reflection of the burning sun on a *steep rock* in the background.[14] Considering the arrangement of this picture together with the bird-like downward flight of the angels in the above mentioned "Descent of the Cross," Professor Gosebruch finds as the common structural principle in Giotto and Dante "Aufragen" and "Gefälle."[15] Common, too, are the symbolic implications, since in the "Miracle of

---

[15] M. Gosebruch, *ibid.*, p. 88 and 116.

the Spring" the second reason for the light-flooded steep rock is supposed to be the symbolisation of St. Francis' fervent prayer ascending to heaven.[16]

Dante's poetic language has in itself unusually numerous lexical elements of mounting and descending, not as *mots-thèmes*, but as *mots-clefs*:

> Che da *cima* del monte, onde si *mosse al Piano*
> (the avalanche of Trent) (*Inf.* XII, 7)
> *Montasi su'* n Bismantoa e in *cacume* (*Purg.* IV, 26)
> Che *cima* di giudizio non *s'avvalla* (*Purg.* VI, 37)
> E quell' amor che primo lì *discese* (*Par.* XXXII, 94)
> Dove il Po *discende* Per aver pace co' seguaci sui (*Inf.* V, 98)
> Quaggiù dove si *monta e cala* Naturalmente (*Par.* XXII, 103-104)
> Giù ogni stella *cade* che *saliva* (*Inf.* VII, 98)
> E il sol *montava sù* con quelle stelle (*Inf.* I, 38)
> Lo *scendere* e il *salir* per l'altrui *scale* (*Par.* XVII, 60).

What attracts Dante's eyes to moral heights and fascinates him are the eyes of Beatrice and those of Mary, "Gli occhi da Dio diletti e venerati" (*Par.* XXIII, 40). The contemplative eyes of Dante are lifted by the eyes of the Saints. Toynbee's *Concordance* contains about 300 entries of *occhi* and *occhio*. Giotto experts find this attractive fascination with the eyes of his Christs so different from the *numinosum tremendum* of the Romanesque *Majestas Domini*. Eyes can be seen as central in many of the scenes of the Arena Chapel, such as the "Wedding of Cana" and the "Awakening of Lazarus," and even in the treason scene where they appear as a sad reproach to Judas.[17] The transformation of Dante's own fearing and passionate eyes into loving and peaceful ones is a central aspect of the *Commedia*. At least Ulrich Leo[18] and Romano Guardini[19] would agree.

---

[16] Enzo Carli, *Giotto and his contemporaries*, New York: Crown Publishers, 1958, p. 14.
[17] E. Cecchi, *op. cit.*, p. 15.
[18] Ulrich Leo, "Sehen und Schauen bei Dante. Eine Stiluntersuchung," *Deutsches Dantejahrbuch* (1929), 183-221.
[19] Romano Guardini, *Vision und Dichtung; der Charakter von Dantes Göttlicher Komödie*, Tübingen: Wunderlich, 1946.

INDIVIDUAL RHYTHM

As to the individual rhythm after the schematic Romanesque and strict Gothic patterns of contrast, art historians hold that Giotto's pictures are willfully subdued to balanced masses and measurable rhythms which, they add, "is not different from Dante's poem," [20] or they call Dantesque his "eccezionale grandiosità e nitidezza di proporzioni." [21] To make the individual rhythm harmonize with the subject matter of the pictures, a critic has observed that in the "Renunciation of Earthly Goods" in the Assisi series an asymmetrical antithesis has been worked out in which there participate not only the small group of citizens behind St. Francis and the large group behind his father, but conversely also the small-low and the big-high houses in the background. Dante likes the same kind of asymmetry by his 6:4 scansion: "Non però qui si pente, ma si ride" (Par. IX, 103). In the fresco of the "Sermon to the Birds", a big tree on the right leans over as if to support the soft flight of the birds, as if it, too, would like to approach in order to listen. In the picture of the "Donation of the Cloak" to a beggar, the Saint is rhythmically put at the intersection of the lines of rocky hills in the background to stress his superiority, [22] his body remaining but his heart going with the beggar. Dante also knows this axis: "Che va col cuore e col corpo dimora" (Purg. II, 12). For Dante's rhythm proper we have the standard work by Martha Amrein-Widmer. [23] According to her findings Dante reserves the normal scansion, e.g. for the expression of iambic monotonous marching:

Poi fummo fatti soli procedendo (Purg. XIV, 130).

A sequence of short words marks abruptness, roughness, e.g. the blowing of the wind which pushes Francesca and Paolo around like leaves:

---

[20] M. Gosebruch, op. cit., p. 62.
[21] C. Gnudi, op. cit., p. 76.
[22] E. Carli, op. cit., p. 14.
[23] Martha Amrein Widmer, *Rhythmus als Ausdruck inneren Erlebens in Dantes Divina Commedia*, Zürich: Rascher, 1932, p. 34 ff.

Di qua, di là, di giù, di su li mena (*Inf.* V, 43).

An overlong caesura elicits pausing for, e.g. tasting bliss:

Io son Beatrice / che ti faccio andare (*Inf.* II, 70).

Liturgical solemnity is covered by the sapphic meter:

O Padre Nostro che nei cieli stai (*Purg.* XI, 1).

Thus Dante's texture of individual rhythms has produced 828 variations within his hendecasyllabic structure.[24]

CLASSICAL SOLEMNITY

This individual rhythm is, however, the outcome of a deeper rhythmical consciousness of classical geometrical distributions, as one very well knows from the one hundred cantos, the three cantiche, the terza rima, the divisions and subdivisions of the three eschatological realms. Giotto's pictures are constructed in rectangles and triangles on the two sides of a diagonal or a middle axis. These geometrical distributions are particularly visible on the Arena "Resurrection" and on the two sides of a middle axis in the fresco of the "Birth of St. John the Baptist."[25] The classical geometrical forms contribute solemnity to a style. In Dante there is first the solemn measured circumlocution of classical metonymies,[26] in which the Romanesque-Provençal periphrases[27] seem to have undergone the influence of a prose *cursus*. These metonymies particularly reveal Dante's periphrastical inventiveness. There are, e.g. the circumlocutions.

---

[24] Theophil Spoerri, *Dante und die europäische Literatur. Das Bild des Menschen in der Struktur der Sprache*, Stuttgart: W. Kohlhammer, 1963.

[25] Richard Seewald, *Giotto. Eine Apologie des Klassischen*, Olten: Walter, 1950, p. 128.

[26] E. R. Curtius, "Neue Dantestudien" in his *Gesammelte Aufsätze zur Romanischen Philologie*, Bern: Francke, 1960, 321-323.

[27] Gianfranco Contini, *Le Rime di Dante*, Torino: Einaudi, 1939, 2nd ed. 1946.

for Heaven:
Il chiostro nel quale è Cristo abate del collegio (*Purg.* XXVI, 128-129)
Quella Roma onde Cristo è romano (*Purg.* XXXII, 102)
La 've ogni ben si termina e s' inizia (*Par.* VIII, 87)
Dove Dio senza mezzo governa (*Par.* XXX, 122);
for Hell:
Là dove il sol tace (*Inf.* I, 60);
for God:
Lo rege per cui questo regno pausa (*Par.* XXXII, 61).
Lo imperador che sempre regna (*Par.* XII, 40).
L'amor che muove il sole e l'altre stelle (*Par.* XXXIII, 145);
for Christ:
L'agnel di Dio che le peccata tolle (*Par.* XVIII, 32);
for Maria:
Il nome del bel fior ch' io sempre invoco (*Par.* XXIII, 88);
for Beatrice:
Quel sol che pria d'amor mi scaldò il petto (*Par.* III, 1);
for Eve:
La piaga che Maria richiuse e unse (*Par.* XXXII, 4).

Classical in Dante is also the *figura etymologica* and *annominatio*, which in the vernacular was used only in a jocose or clumsy way. But for Dante the *annominatio* is another occasion of highest solemnity in harmony with the rythmical pattern of the verse:

Parer ingiusta la nostra giustizia (*Par.* IV, 67)
Amor che a nullo amato amar perdona (*Inf.* V, 103)
Cred'io ch' ei credette ch' io credesse (*Inf.* XIII, 25)
Si che l'un capo all' altro era cappello (*Inf.* XXXII, 126)
Tu fosti pria ch' io disfatto, fatto (*Inf.* VI, 42)
Siena mi fe', disfecemi Maremma (*Purg.* V, 134)
Il suo Fattore Non disdegnò di farsi sua fattura (*Par.* XXXIII, 5-6).

Dante extends in a similar way the classical *anaphora* at the beginning of consecutive tercets:

Amor ch' a cor gentil ratto s' apprende (*Inf.* V, 100)
Amor che a nullo amato amar perdona (*Inf.* V, 103)
Amor condusse noi a una morte (*Inf.* V, 106). [28]

---

[28] O. M. Johnston, "Repetition of Words and Phrases in the Beginning of Consecutive Tercets in Dante's Divine Comedy," *PMLA:* 29 (1919), 537-549.

Of classical solemnity, finally, are the many addresses and prayers, where in the second-person singular or plural of the past tense the Latin is transparent:

>Voi altri pochi che drizzaste il collo (*Par.* II, 10)
>O Buondelmonte, quanto mal fuggisti (*Par.* VI, 140)
>Per l'Evangelio e per voi che scriveste (*Par.* XXIV, 137)
>O divine virtù, se mi ti presti (*Par.* I, 22)
>E tu che se' dinanzi e mi pregasti (*Purg.* XXVIII, 82)
>Tu 'l sai, che col tuo lume mi levasti (*Par.* I, 75).

Why are these calculations and divisions not disturbing, still allowing for spontaneous artistic life? As to the art of Giotto again the technicians tell us that Giotto was not as yet in a position to comply with the later procedure of fresco painting so that his well chosen colors turned out pale. Whatever might have been his intentions, one of the characteristics of his final products is a pale spiritual coloring, "die unsinnliche Farbe". No better qualification could be found for the impression coming from the literary tableaux of the *Commedia*.

Verbal Metaphor

The central element producing this effect in Dante is the verbal metaphor which counteracts the sharpness of the contours of the design, *scandimento,* division and rhythm. The combination of an abstract substantive with an evocative verb is perhaps the strongest result of Dante's *inventio*:

>Io vidi sopra lei (Maria) tanta *allegrezza piover* (*Par.* XXXII, 87-88)
>Per li occhi fui di greve *dolor munto* (*Purg.* XIII, 57)
>La lena m' era del polmon si *munta* (*Inf.* XXIV, 43)
>L'uomo in cui *pensier rampolla* sovra pensier (*Purg.,* V, 16-17)
>Aveva *d'orror* là testa *cinta* (*Inf.* III, 31);
>L'*alito* di giù che vi s' *appasta* (*Inf.* XVIII, 107).

If the subject is not purely abstract, a personification at least will elicit a verbal metaphor in a superior way:

> Squilla di lontano Che paia il giorno *pianger* che si muore
> (*Purg.* VIII, 5-6)

If the subject is a poetical substitute for a concrete word combined with a frozen metaphor, the outcome is an awesome paradox:

> La rosa in che il verbo divino carne si fece (*Par.* XXIII, 73-74)
> Il bel giardino Che sotto i raggi di Cristo s'infiora (*Par.* XXXIII, 71-72)
> Quel sol (Beatrice) che d'amor mi scaldò il petto (*Par.* III, 1).

This abstract-concrete process can also occur in self-created single reflexive verbs: in*urb*arsi, in*lui*arsi, im*paradis*arsi:

> Quando rozzo e salvatico s' inurba (*Purg.* XXVI, 69)
> Dio vede tutto e tuo veder s' inluia (*Par.* IX, 73)
> Quella che imparadisa la mia mente (*Par.* XXVIII, 3).

FUSION OF THE REAL AND THE METAPHORICAL

The pale coloring of the verbal metaphor is only the nucleus of the principle of the indiscernible fusion of the real and the metaphorical which Malagoli calls *ondeggiamento*. This principle was similarly vindicated for Giotto as the penetration of the secrets of nature by a plastic evidence through which glows a deep Franciscan religiosity. [29] There is not the powerful throb of nature, but the feeling of nature as a function within a spiritual reality represented, as Pietro Toesca says, and he adds "as in Dante's *Divine Comedy*." [30] As far as Dante is concerned, one critic spoke about his giving the improbable the character of persuasive certitude. [31] And actually who would not be tempted to look in reality for the paradoxical "fiumana ove 'l mar non ha vanto" (*Inf.* II, 108)

---

[29] Achille Bertoni Calosso, "Giotto e lo stil nuovo," *Rassegna Italiana*: XX (1937).
[30] P. Toesca, *op. cit.*, p. 104.
[31] Leo Ferrero, *Appunti sul metodo della Divina Commedia*, Capolago, 1940.

before slowly realizing that such streams are to be found on the medieval moralistic "Carte du tendre," where there is also St. Augustin's *procellosum pelagus* and *fluctus concupiscentiae* or Richard of St. Victor's *fluctus maris* and Hugh of St. Victor's *lacus cordis*.[32] Likewise the readers of Dante, not capable of following him, are inexperienced sailors on the poet's sea, and he gives them advice: "O voi che siete in piccioletta barca... Tornate a riveder li vostri lidi" (*Par.* II, 1-4). And the visionary goes down to the level of the familiar.[33] Thus whoever cannot grasp the fusion of the whole skin of the thief Agnello Bruneleschi with the brownish skin of the serpent (*Inf.* XXV) which slowly absorbs him, is reminded of the process of burning paper:

> Come procede innanzi dall ardore,
> Per lo papiro suso un color bruno
> Che non è nero ancora e 'l bianco muore (*Inf.* XXV, 66).

Dante makes clear that the souls of the simonists protruding from the rocky holes, in which they were put topsy turvy are not burning entirely but in the same way that greasy objects burn along their margins:

> Qual suole il fiammeggiar delle cose unte
> Muoversi pur su per l'estrema buccia
> Tal era lì da' calcagni alle punte (*Inf.* XIX, 28-30).

The slow rain of fire in Hell is just like snow falling in the Alps on a windless day:

> Piovean di fuoco dilatate falde,
> Come di neve in alpe senza vento (*Inf.* XIV, 28-30).

In the highest of Heavens Beatrice brings Dante down to earth by her "pomological" explanation of the weakness of will:

---

[32] Hermann Gmelin, *Die Göttliche Komödie*. Kommentar I. Stuttgart: Klett, 1954, p. 31, and
Charles Singleton, "Sulla Fiumana...," *Romanic Review*: 39 (1948), 269-277.

[33] J. H. Whitfield, *Dante and Virgil*, Oxford, 1949, p. 84.

> Ben fiorisce negli uomini il volere:
> Ma la pioggia continua converte
> In bozzacchioni le susine vere (*Par.* XXVII, 124-126).

But it would be wrong to reduce to single examples the real metaphorical fusion which often is also a fusion of the styles of the troubadours, the Bible and Virgil. At issue here, as says Salvatore Battaglia, is a stylistic circle of necessary metaphors to cover a reality. Continuing Pascoli's way of studying Dante, Battaglia states:

> L'*hyle* o la *selva,* la quale, selvaggia a principio dell' Inferno, *frondeggia* al fine del purgatorio, mette, in certa guisa, il *fiore* nel paradiso, la candida *rosa* in cui forma si mostra l' umanità santificata, il *fiore* del volere quale il Cristo col suo sangue fece *germinare* dall' *albero* spogliato da Adamo. Ecco il *frutto* di santità... La selva è divenuto *giardino.* [34]

In other words, the fusion between reality and metaphor is based on the self-transformation of Dante's imagery, or as Malagoli has formulated it: "Si passa dall' espressione metaforica alla non-metaforica... senza il menomo iato." [35]

Paradox of Static Dynamism

Such a wholesale fusion is as much an artistic paradox as the psychological movement within a static expression. And yet this static dynamism was already seen by Vasari as far as Giotto is concerned. Vasari actually remarked about the "Annunciation" in the Bargello, "In this he [Giotto] has represented with extraordinary truth the fear and astonishment of the Virgin Mary [at the salutation of Gabriel] who in terror seems ready to run away." [36] Dante is his own critic:

---

[34] Salvatore Battaglia, "Linguaggio reale e linguaggio figurato in Dante," *Filologia e Letterature:* 8 (1962) 13-14, note 1.

[35] L. Malagoli, *Saggio, op. cit.,* p. 60.

[36] Giorgio Vasari, *The Lives of the Painters, Sculptors and Architects* (ed. W. Gaunt), London: Dent, 1963, v. I, p. 67.

> Dinanzi a noi pareva si verace
> Quivi intagliato, in un atto suave...
> Ed aveva in atto impressa esta favella:
> "Ecce ancilla Dei" (*Purg.* X, 37-44).

This dynamic touch, recognized by Vasari, is particularly visible in Giotto's animals in motion, as in the case of the sheep pushing against one another in the Arena fresco "St. Joachim among the Shepherds," or in the fluttering birds on the painting "St. Francis Preaching to the Birds" in Assisi. Dante selects, for such purposes, his development of homeric similes, stressing dynamic variations:

> (Come) le pecorelle escon del chiuso
> Ad una, a due, a tre, e l'altre stanno
> Timidette atterrando l'occhio e 'l muso... (*Purg.* III, 79-81).

or

> (Come) quando cogliendo biada o loglio,
> Li colombi adunati alla pastura ...
> Se casa avviene ond' elli abbian paura,
> Subitamente lasciano star l'esca (*Purg.* II, 124-128).

Dante challenges the painter with his literary condensations of so-called "transitory moments", e.g. ladies waiting between two melodies for the next dance without leaving the circle they had formed:

> Donne mi parver non da ballo sciolte
> Ma che s'arrestin tacite ascoltando
> Fin che le nove note ànno ricolte (*Par.* X, 79-81).

He challenges the sculptor by presenting the marching *envious*, groaning and bent under their heavy charges like caryatides, thus freezing their movement for explaining their attitude:

> Come per sostentar solaio o tetto,
> Per mensola talvolta una figura
> Si vede giunger le ginocchia al petto... (*Purg.* X, 130-132.)

CONCLUSION

Using Giotto's style as a projector, we have recognized in Dante's poetic language the same segmentation inherent in the adjectivation; the same framing incumbent in the gerund constructions; the same concept of steep heights and profound abysses revealed by key expressions; the same individual rhythm within classical geometrical divisions extended to striking metonymies, adnominations, anaphoras and *orationes,* producing solemnity together with scansions adapted to the situations. A subdued coloring that tends to efface the constructive design stems from the striking verbal metaphors, sign posts of a fundamental fusion of the abstract and the concrete or the metaphorical and the real, in which, paradoxically, not only does the familiar explain the metaphorically ineffable, but the movement also springs from the static presentation and the strange appears as self-evident.

METRICAL PATTERNS IN THE *DIVINE COMEDY*

GEORGE H. GIFFORD
Tufts University
President, Dante Society of America

Tennyson honored Virgil as "wielder of the noblest measure ever moulded by the lips of man." Dante presumably invented *terza rima*, and he wielded it in such a way as to compete with the glories of the dactylic hexameter.

For each canto the rime scheme is ABA, BCB — XYX, YZYZ. Furthermore a glance at the capitalization and punctuation on any printed page is sufficient to show that as a rule, each tercet is self-contained or relatively so. The tercet may be an independent sentence, or two may form the balanced parts of a simile. The first of a pair may be a temporal clause or its equivalent, an embroidered vocative (O animae grazioso e benigno, etc.), or the subject of the proposition to be balanced by the predicate. The second tercet may be a causal, final, or consecutive clause, or of course co-ordinated by *e* or *ma*. Longer sentences can be built by combinations of such decives, and the long sequences gain in frequency as the poem progresses. Each tercet is firmly bound together by the embracing rime of its first and third lines. This composition by tercets, whether or not it has any symbolic significance, produces an insistent ternary rhythm, which is the very ground swell of the poem. The fact that the rime word of the second line serves as an *amorce*, anticipating the embracing rime of the following tercet, holds the whole structure dynamically together, so that as Fubini points out, each tercet seems to blossom and unfold from what has gone before.[1]

So much for the rule, all of which is common knowledge. But no rule is adequately studied unless the exceptions are carefully considered. There are deviations from the seemingly relentless tercet rhythm; they are more numerous than is often realized, and perhaps deserve to be studied with a new approach.

In the following discussion I am taking the liberty of extending the meaning of the classic terms "thesis" and "arsis," indeed of giving them an abusive sense. Let us take as our starting point the original usage of the ancient Greek theorists, according to which "thesis" was the part of the metrical foot receiving the ictus, and "arsis" the unaccented remainder.[2] For present purposes I will distinguish *rimes* as thesis and arsis, i.e. more or less prominent. For example in the "common metre" quatrain ABAB, A is *in arsi* and B *in thesi;* so much so that the A rime can be neglected without greatly changing the effect. The hymns "Let saints on earth in concert sing" and "O God of Bethel by whose hand" are both sung to the tune "Dundee." The first has the A (or arsis) rime, the second dispenses with it. Has anyone in the congregation ever noted the discrepancy? So in the regular flow of Dante's *terza rima,* the rime words of the first and third lines of each tercet are *in thesi* and the intervening rime word *in arsi*. More than one English translator, despairing of the task of rendering *terza rima* complete, has retained only the thesis rimes, thereby sacrificing the subtlety of the pattern, but reproducing its gross effect.

Let us turn to a familiar canto, *Inferno* V. The smooth flow of the first tercet contrasts with the lapidary detachment of lines 4 to 6, but in each case the tercet comes to a full stop; the rhythm is regular. But in lines 7-12 the case is altered:

>   Dico che quando l'anima mal nata
>   li vien dinanzi, tutta si confessa;
>   e quel conoscitor de la peccata

---

[1] M. Fubini. *Metrica e Poesia* (Milano, 1962), I, Capitolo quarto, "Il metro della *Divina Commedia.*"

[2] The later Latin grammarians reversed the sense of these terms, and their practice is continued in the current use of *arsi* and *tesi* in Italian.

> vede qual luogo d'inferno e da essa:
> cignesi con la coda tante volte
> quantunque gradi vuol che giù sia messa.

If we read these lines without preconception, following the sense, they group themselves naturally in three pairs, and the ear will be struck by the threefold recurrence of the rime in *-essa*, which remotely recalls the rime scheme of the *Blessed Damozel*. Here is a new ternary effect which for the moment supplants the ternary rhythm of the single tercets. The new system may be compared to the *Aufgesang* — ABABAB — of the octave, a metrical pattern already in use by the *giullari* in Dante's life-time. Here we have ABABXB, with the B rime *in thesi*, just as in the octave. The X rime is intrusive, but since it is *in arsi* it is unobtrusive. It is in the proper place to serve as the *amorce* of the following unit, which will reinstate the normal pattern. In fact the lines of the following tercet are rhythmically quite on all fours with lines 4-6.

The next tercet, with its vocative, "Oh tu che viene," and "disse Minos" is followed, unexpectedly, by a pair of lapidary imperatives:

> "guarda com' entri e di cui tu ti fide:
> non t'inganni l'ampiezza del entrare!"

where *entrare* seems clearly *in thesi*. Virgil's response is a quatrain that falls naturally into two couplets, so that here again we have $2 + 2 + 2$ with the thesis rime *entrare, andare, dimandare*.

As generally printed — e.g. both in the text of the Società and Casella's, — with a colon after *spiriti mali*, (42) and *li mena* (43), lines 40-45 form two regular tercets, which balance nicely. But if we adopt Vandelli's second thoughts, no punctuation after *spiriti mali*, and *lì mena*, we are once more confronted with a $2 + 2 + 2$ system:

> E come li stornei ne portan l'ali
> nel freddo tempo a schiera larga e piena,
> così quel fiato li spiriti mali
> di qua, di là, di giù, di su lì mena;
> nulla speranza li conforta mai,
> non che di posa, ma di minor pena.

In any case, the following six lines show the 2 + 2 + 2 configuration, so that if we follow Vandelli here, two such systems are juxtaposed, built upon the rimes *piena, mena, pena,* and *riga, briga, gastiga,* each of the two similes — of the starlings and the cranes respectively — forming a quatrain.

Once more, near the end of the canto, Francesca's last words fall into the now familiar pattern:

> Quando leggemmo il disiato riso
>   esser baciato da cotanto amante,
>   questi, che mai da me non fia diviso,
> la bocca mi baciò tutto tremante.
>   Galeotto fu il libro e chi lo scrisse:
>   quel giorno più non li leggemmo avante."

In each case there is something like a shifting of gears, but the shift is smooth and noiseless. The statistical figures given below indicate that this pattern is more frequent than has been generally realized.

If we turn to A 4 31-36,[3] we find a somewhat similar case:

> Lo buon maestro a me: "Tu non dimandi
>   che spiriti son questi che tu vedi?
>   Or vo' che sappi, innanzi che più andi,
>   ch'ei non peccaro; e s'elli hanno mercedi,
>   non basta, perché non ebber battesmo,
>   ch'è porta de la fede che tu credi.

The break between the two sentences comes at the end of the second line, but since there is no corresponding break after *mercedi,* we will suggest here the formula 2 + 4.

In other cases the formula 4 + 2 seems appropriate, as in A 8 82-87:

> Io vidi più di mille in su le porte
>   da ciel piovuti, che stizzosamente
>   dicean: "Chi è costui che sanza morte

---

[3] This is the notation adopted in the new concordance to the *Divine Comedy,* shortly to be published under the auspices of the Dante Society of America by the Harvard University Press. A B and C indicate *Inferno, Purgatorio,* and *Paradiso.*

va per lo regno de la morte gente?"
E 'l savio mio maestro fece segno
di voler lor parlar secretamente.

In many cases where the formula $2+4$ or $4+2$ seems plausible one should hesitate before deviating from the regular $3+3$. Thus at A 7 115,

> Lo buon maestro disse: "Figlio, or vedi
> l'anime di color cui vinse l'ira;
> e anche vo' che tu per certo credi
> che sotto l'acqua ha gente che sospira,
> e fanno pullular quest'acqua al summo,
> come l'occhio ti dice, u' che s'aggira.

the syntax and punctuation would indicate $2+4$, but if we consider that *credi* marks a point or inflection — so to speak — before the influx of images that present the souls of the sullen, we may well consider the $3+3$ pattern to be the more expressive. Likewise at A 6 79:

> Farinata e il Tegghiaio, che fuor sì degni,
> Iacopo Rusticucci, Arrigo e 'l Mosca
> e li altri ch'a ben far puoser li 'ngegni,
> dimmi ove sono e fa ch'io li conosca;
> che gran disio mi stringe di savere
> se 'l ciel li addolcia, o lo 'nferno li attosca." [4]

the separation of the two clauses after *conosca* would suggest $4+2$, but if we observe that the first three lines are enumerative while the second three are expressive of the poet's *gran disio*, which erupts at *dimmi*, we shall give the preference to $3+3$. In the statistics given below I have indicated such cases by the notations $2+4$ (?) and $4+2$ (?). Judgement in such matters must be in part subjective, and I claim nothing definitive for the categories I have set up, hoping only that they may prove to be useful spade work.

Occasionally one meets with patterns still more complicated. The first canto of the poem follows the regular tercet rhythm

---

[4] Cf. A 27 25-30.

from start to finish with one striking exception, a shifting of gears which affects not six lines but nine (37-45). First comes a quatrain:

> Temp'era dal principio del mattino,
>   e 'l sol montava 'n su con quelle stelle
> ch'eran con lui quando l'amor divino
> mosse di prima quelle cose belle;

followed by a three-group:

> sì ch'a bene sperar m'era cagione
>   di quella fera a la gaetta pelle
> l'ora del tempo e la dolce stagione;

This may be described as an *ad hoc* tercet, shifted from the normal position, dominated and bound together by the rime words *cagione* and *stagione*, both of which are felt to be *in thesi*. Line 43 gives the *amorce* of the following tercet, and *leone* rounds out the system:

> ma non sì che paura non mi desse
> la vista che m'apparve d'un leone.

This underscores a dramatic turning point in the action, the encounter with the beasts. It is a moment of suspense. The ounce is playing cat and mouse with the poet, but the sun rising in Aries is an omen of hope. Hope is rudely shattered by the appearance of the lion, and what follows is a crescendo of terror. [5]

---

[5] Fubini's view (*op. cit.*, 202) is quite different. "in casi come questo vediamo come il periodo sintattico non si snodi insieme con quello ritmico, come il ritmo sintattico non coincida col respiro poetico e la terzina non venga fuori dalla precedente, ma riveli la sua funzione esclusivamente mnemonica; ... noi sentiamo in queste terzine alcunché di cascante: il metro ci appare qui qualcosa di estrinseco, sentiamo che c'è un'architettura che sostiene il periodo, ma che fuori di questo sostegno non ha, come dovrebbe essere nell'arte, un suo rilievo e valore." Vittorio Rossi, in his edition of *Commedia*, suggested, à propos of the similes in Cantos I and II, that in this part of the poem Dante was trying his prentice hand. The more I study what E. H. Wilkins has called "The Prologue of the *Divine Comedy*" the less I sympathize with such views. (v. *Annual Report of the Dante Society*, 1926, 1-7; reprinted with revisions in *The Invention of the Sonnet and Other Studies in Italian Literature*, 1959.)

A similar system of nine verses occurs at A 7 73, where Virgil, after the peremptory "Or vo' che tu mia sentenza n'imbocche," begins his discourse on the goddess Fortune. The simile developed in these lines is unusual in form. A quatrain tells about the heavens and the attendant angels assigned to them by their creator, and a five-group about the *ben vani* of this world, which are placed — *similemente* — under the ministry of Fortuna. This five-group is bound together and dominated by the rime *mondani, vani, umani*.

Again, at A 13 139, a quatrain is followed by the displaced tercet

> I' fui de la città che nel Batista
> muto il primo padrone; ond'e' per questo
> sempre con l'arte sua la farà trista;

The whole system may be represented as $4 + 3 + 2 + 3$. After it the final line of the canto stands out in stark detachment.

A system still more remarkable is found at the end of A 24. Vanni Fucci is speaking:

> Io non posso negar quel che tu chiedi:
> in giù son messo tanto, perch'io fui
> ladro a la sagrestia de' belli arredi,
> e falsamente già fu apposto altrui.

after the quatrain as in our other cases comes the displaced tercet, *ad hominem:*

> Ma perché di tal vista tu non godi,
> se mai sarai di fuor da' luoghi bui,
> apri li orecchi al mio annunzio, e odi:

and the prophecy begins with the distich

> Pistoia in pria de' Neri si dimagra;
> poi Fiorenza rinova gente e modi.

It continues with three more distichs, so that the whole system is $4 + 3 + 2 + 2 + 2 + 2$, followed directly by the last line of the canto, the Parthian shot,

> E detto l'ho perché doler ti debbia!"

Another clear instance of this configuration occurs at A 31 115, Virgil's interpellation of the giant Antæus. The 4 + 3 is an expanded vocative. The command comes in the following distich.

In addition to these five examples from the first *cantica* we may cite B 28 130-138.

The following statistics cover the occurrences of the patterns described in the preceding discussion. An asterisk before a verse number indicates that the sense runs on from what precedes. Following a verse number it indicates that the sense runs on into what follows.

2 + 2 + 2: A 5 7, *19, 40 (?), 46, 133; 6 58; 8 1, 13; 9 *67; 11 *4, 97*; 12 91, 133; 13 16; 14 61, 115; 16 82; 17 19, 70, 100; 18 73, 118, 127; 20 31, 106; 21 37; 22 79; 24 25, 37, 70, 145; 25 34, 145; 26 19, 79, 106, 112; 27 94, 106, 124; 28 28; 29 16, 46; 30 *16, 40, 58, 82; 31 10; 32 *61, 133*; 33 70; 34 28, 70, 76, 133.

B 1 *124; 2 25; 3 10, 136; 4 115; 7 16, 115; 11 61; 19 121; 20 112; 21 *10; 22 88; 24 106.

C 3 25; 32 145.

2 + 4: A 3 70, 88; 4 31 *49; 7 1 *34; 10 55; 11 55; 19 88; 22 * 100; 23 19, 112; 24 * 10; 27 34, 67; 28 * 13*, 76; 29 52, 112; 30 *7; 31 40; 33 127.

B 2 37 4 13, 121; 5 52; 17 64; 18 55.

C 7 *28.

2 + 4 (?): A 7 115; 12 127; 17 52; 21 1; 25 61; 26 88*; 28 46; 32 43; 34 37*.

B 1 7; 3 112; 5 1; 6 139; 11 109; 16 73.

C 8 22; 21 52*.

4 + 2: A 7 121; 8 82; 9 *37, 100, 106, 112; 12 *10, *40, 79*, 109; 13 46, 58, 118; 14 67, 124; 15 *16, 25, 61, *82; 18 10*, 58; 19 1; 21 25, 46, 79; 22 64, 112, 145; 23 133; 25 40; 28 37; 29 103; 31 *61; 33 55*; 34 64, 112. [6]

---

[6] Attention should be called to A 9 100-117, where three 4 + 2 systems occur in immediate succession.

B 4 1; 5 73, 115, 124; 10 13*, 49; 11 73; 16 109; 17 13; 22 100; 23 79; 24 19; 27 1, 10; 28 76, 97; 29 145; 31 70.

C 7 97; 8 67*; 9 37, 76; 10 55; 11 4*, *31; 12 82; 15 91; 16 136; 17 112*; 25 28; 30 10; 31 *37; 32 40.

4 + 2 (?): A 3 82; 4 19, *58; 6 79; 8 97; 12 22; 13 64; 17 85; 19 100; 20 52, 124; 22 25; 27 25; 28 85; 33 100.

B 1 13; 3 1; 4 91; 5 37; 6 *28; 10 1, 73; 16 85; 26 43; 27 70; 31 43.

C 2 1, *25; 3 109; 5 19, 34; 16 1, 115, 127; 20 118*; 22 64; 27 31; 30 46; 31 103*.

4 + 5 (or 4 + 3 + 2): A 1 37; 7 73; 13 139; 24 136; 31 115.
B 28 130.

At the end of a canto Dante had the possibility of two metrical patterns: a quatrain YZYZ, or a tercet YZY followed by an isolated line. He utilizes both possibilities and most of his endings can be ascribed to one or the other category, though there are a few borderline cases.

The effect of the detached final line is often very striking:

> Allor si mosse e io li termi retro. (A 1)
> Poi si rivolse e ripassossi il guazzo. (A 12)
> Io fei giubetto delle mie case. (A 13)
> Così tornò e più non volle udirmi. (B 16)
> Poi s'ascose nel foco che li affima. (B 26)
> poi alla bella donna torna' il viso. (B 28)
> quinci rivolse inver lo cielo il viso. (C 1)
> Poscia rivolsi li occhi a li occhi belle. (C 22)

When the final line follows a 2 + 2 + 2 system, this contributes to the effect of detachment, as in A 12, 24, 25, 34; C 32; similarly when it follows two balanced tercets as in B 8 and 20 and C 27, or a complicated system as in A 13.

In the *Inferno*, the detached final line seems to occur in a majority of the cases: in the *Purgatorio* in less than half; in the *Paradiso* in less than a third. Thus the final quatrain YZYZ is Dante's favored pattern and it becomes increasingly so as the poem progresses. The detached finals when they do occur in the latter part of the poem gain thereby in impressiveness. In nearly half the cases we have the configuration 2 + 2, plainly putting the firzt Z *in thesi*. So already in A 2:

> Or va, ch'un sol volere e d'ambedue:
> tu duca, tu segnore, e tu maestro".
> Così li dissi; e poi che mosso fue,
> intrai per lo cammino alto e silvestro.

In a number of cases the configuration is 1 + 3, which equally guarantees that both Z's are *in thesi*. So in A 8:

> Sopr'essa vedestù la scritta morta:
> e già di qua da lei discende l'erta,
> passando per li cerchi sanza scorta,
> tal che per lui ne fia la terra aperta".

also in B 1:

> Quivi mi cinse sì com'altrui piacque:
> oh maraviglia! che qual egli scelse
> l'umile pianta, cotal si rinacque
> subitamente là onde l'avelse.

The following statistics apply to canto endings:

Final line detached (the punctuation in the *Società's* text is indicated): A 1 .136 3 ;136 4 ;151 5 ;142 7 :130 12 .139 13 .151 18 .136 19 .133 20 :130 21 ;139 22 ;151 24 .151 28 .142 30 :148 32 ,139 34 ;139.

B 2 :133 3 ;144 8 ,139 9 ;145 11 .141 12 :136 13 ;154 16 .145 19 ;145 20 :151 26 .148 27 :142 (?) 28 ;148

C 1 :142 8 :148 12 :145 13 ;142 15 ;148 21 :142 22 .154 27 ;148 32 .151

2 + 2: A 2 139; 6 112(?); 9 130; 14 139; 17 133; 23 145; 27 133; 29 136; 31 144

B 7 133; 10 136; 17 136; 21 133; 22 151; 25 136; 32 *157.

C 4 139; 5 *136; 14 *136; 20 145; 25 136; 26 136; 28 136; 31 139.

1 + 3: B 1 133; 5 *133; 18 *142; 31 *142.

C 3 *127; 6 139; 33 142.

4: A 15 121; 16 133; 26 139; 33 153.
B 4 136; 6 148; 23 130; 24 151; 29 150; 30 142; 33 142.
C 7 144; 9 139; 10 *145; 11 *136; 16 *151; 17 *139; 18 133; 19 144; 23 136; 24 *151; 29 142; 30 145.

The explication of a canto will gain by taking account of the effect produced by the choice and placing of the metrical patterns that have been described, as well of course as by studying such structural features as the placing of similes and the repetition or parallelism of phraseology and vocabulary. Brief indication of the expressive value of such patterns have been given above in the case of A 1. 5, 7, 13 and 24.

Deviations from the normal tercet rhythm are most numerous in the earlier part of the poem. It will be apparent from inspection of our statistical tables that as the poem progresses they become progressively less and less frequent. Some apparently would conclude that they are blemishes due to negligence, scoriae that were gradually eliminated as the poet's art becomes surer of itself. I prefer to think otherwise, and suggest rather that they enhance the dramatic quality of the earlier cantos of the poem. In the *Purgatorio* and still more in the *Paradiso,* the clash of personalities gradually gives way to philosophical and mystic contemplation. More and more we meet with sentences that are longer, but wonderfully sustained and balanced. For such a purpose the tercet rhythm is ideally suited. At the same time a final quatrain rather than a detached final verse is increasingly favored. This, one suggests, is also an indication of the more meditative and less dramatic tone of the later cantos.

DANTE'S NOBLE SINNERS: ABSTRACT EXAMPLES OR LIVING CHARACTERS?

GLAUCO CAMBON
Rutgers - The State University

How to approach the *Divine Comedy* today: girt in the knightly armor of scholarship, or with the unarmed candor, say, of an Ike McCaslin vis-à-vis his bear-god of the wilderness? In Faulkner's story, the youth desiring to meet the forest's tutelary numen incarnate must first discard all weapons and man-made instruments; Dante's Dark Wood may, or may not be, another matter. Our trouble seems to be that neither the paraphernalia of "armed vision" by itself nor what Geoffrey Hartman would call "unmediated vision" alone can ensure proper access to the formidable poem. Overcommented as it is, and intricate in its own right, Dante's work discourages subjective ventures. But unless I, as reader, can have a personal meeting with the spirit of poetry that inhabits the *Comedy*, scholarship will not help, whatever its usefulness in defining the aesthetic revelation I shall have had to wrest from the poem itself in the teeth of history's reluctance. Thus I accept the risk involved in making scholarship secondary, that is, accessory to the primary experience of meeting the poem on my own terms. Ike McCaslin has to surrender to the elusive Old Ben before the ritual killing can be enacted.

For it is well to remember, in the face of the dominant structural-theological reading of recent decades, that theological or historical scholarship, beyond a certain point, may overgrow and stifle the poetry. The poetry as such, on the other hand, rescues its own cultural assumptions and makes them good in the texture of language. So much of the *Comedy* is available as given, in the staging of its dramatic action and in the very action of words and rhythms, that boldness can be justified in taking "texture" for a starting point rather than the structure per se and its cultural substructure. This much holds even for one who rejects Croce's aesthetic atomism and appreciates the structural defenders of the poem's unity (Singleton, Fergusson, Brandeis, Montano, among others) for having vindicated the protagonist's role as that of an objectified *dramatis persona* centrally relevant to the manifold epic, which would otherwise fall apart into discrete episodes of the Crocean kind.

But I cannot follow certain dogmatic inferences occasionally drawn from the structural-theological position to the detriment of the poetry. A dedicated, well informed and generally cogent scholar like Rocco Montano,[1] for example, develops such a certainty about Dante's preliminary certainties that, with all due respect for his labor of love, I am afraid he tends to become *plus royaliste que le roi* when confronting the interpretive problem of *Inferno*. His reductive argument goes that Francesca, like Farinata, Pier delle Vigne, Brunetto Latini and Ulysses, is a sinner *tout court* rather than a noble sinner, and that whatever sympathy or admiration Dante the Pilgrim may show for Hell's denizens is conditioned by the Pilgrim's temporary obfuscation: the latter is on the way to salvation, but still dangerously close to the passions of the damned, and one must not confuse him, the *dramatis persona,* with the author of the poem at the time of writing it. Montano concludes that all infernal figures are there only to exemplify how bad vice can be, and he would deny them any final dignity: witness Brunetto Latini's hasty leavetaking at the end of Canto XV, or Farinata's wrangling with Dante, which renews the earthbound factional strifes of Florence and is out of place in the final perspective of salvation.

The argument is so logical that it sounds unanswerable; in fact, it is just a puritanical reversal of De Sanctis' position, which saw only the glory and not the murkiness of Hell's inmates, since De Sanctis wanted to free them from their theological dungeon and thus make *Inferno* safe for democratic humanism. But poetry

---

[1] Rocco Montano, *Storia della poesia di Dante*, 2 vols. (Quaderni di Delta, Naples, 1962), passim.

is intangibly alive, and it refuses to be strait-jacketed by reductive logic, or enlisted in ideological disputes. Even if one admits that Dante's theology was so Manichean as to demand the moral annihilation of all sinners in his poetical world, can we not assume that the poet in him occasionally knew better than the theologian? that achieved vision overcame the dogmatic intentions and thereby, far from destroying the structural unity of the poem, made it subtler? Monolithic conformity only manages to stiffen or fossilize the work of art, whose life I see in an interplay of tensions and correspondences, as described, for instance, by Theophil Spoerri. [2]

To rob Farinata of tragic nobility [3] means to follow Virgil's warning against corruptive pity so literally that all we have left is an oversimplified abstraction instead of a crucial encounter and recognition in the Pilgrim's progress of Dante's *persona;* even Irma Brandeis, [4] for all her sensitiveness to the indwelling spirit of words, tends to see in the unreconstructed Ghibelline only the heretic. He is much more than that. True, Farinata and the others are embodiments of earthbound passion, and thus of what limits Dante must overcome if he wants to attain God-given peace. Dante shall leave them behind in his striving for harmony and completeness, but they are living figures, not one-dimensional, abstract examples of their respective sins, and as dramatic creations they transcend the ethico-theological scheme the poet used to bring them out.

How can we believe that the dispute between Dante and Farinata is utter vanity, when it concerns, beyond their factional antagonism, precisely that object of so much reiterated anger and love throughout the tripartite poem: Florence, the city, civilization, the focus of our destinies; the burning care of Sordello and Marco Lombardo and Cacciaguida? Neither the climbing of

---

[2] Theophil Spoerri, *Dante und die europaeische Literatur* (V. Kohlkammer Verlag, Stuttgart, 1963).

[3] For a recent vindication of Farinata's tragic stature, not unmindful of Francesco De Sanctis' nineteenth-century essay, see Kalikst Morawski, "The Tragic Aspect of the Farinata Episode in the *Inferno*", in *Books Abroad*, Special Issue: A Homage to Dante, May 1965, 58-68.

[4] Irma Brandeis, *The Ladder of Vision* (Doubleday, New York, 1960, 1962), 41-52.

Purgatory nor the flight into Heaven can divest Dante of this care.

> "Ma fui io sol colà, dove sofferto
> fu per ciascun di torre via Fiorenza,
> colui che la difese a viso aperto."

To have stood, alone among one's congregated allies and partisans, for mercy to Florence; to have saved Florence in the hour of Ghibelline victory, and thus to have risen above one's fiery partisanship; to have acknowledged the communal bond, at great cost to oneself and one's political future: "this is not vanity," to say it with Ezra Pound. The lines spoken by Farinata in Hell ring way beyond Hell, and they are enough to guarantee his tragic worth. He is not just "the Heretic" or "any heretic", he is dramatically individualized and larger than his sin; he is superhuman by contrast with Cavalcante, the all-too-human sharer of his flaming tomb. That his generosity did not suffice to save him from damnation enhances, rather than diminishes, his stature, even in the Christian clash of human with otherworldly values. For all his theme of exemplary salvation, Dante is also, as Auerbach has it, a poet of the secular world — and without the stormy drama of this world's scene, the heavenbound ascent and the (temporarily reached) heavenly perspective would collapse. Borgese has remarked [5] that Dante's wrath survives the purgative phase of *Inferno* and even of *Purgatorio* — luckily for the poem, I say, which lives on such dynamic contrasts to the extent that they mobilize for us the otherwise all-too-rigid architectural symmetry.

Far from discounting the essential contribution of scholars like Montano (or Singleton) to a unified reading of the *Comedy*, I propound a flexibly contrapuntal interpretation, which will allow us to grasp the tragic complexities of each climactic episode even while integrating it in the total process of Dante's fictional ordeal. Tragic dignity attaches to such figures as Francesca, Farinata, Pier delle Vigne, Brunetto Latini, Ulysses, because in each of

---

[5] G. A. Borgese, "The Wrath of Dante," now reprinted in *Essays on Dante*, Edited by Mark Musa (Indiana University Press, Bloomington, Indiana, 1964), 94-109.

them we witness the mystery of a lofty nature doomed by sin, and what could be more tragic to a Christian soul? We could also talk of the mystery of liberty and of the drama of temptation (and yet, if we cling to the theological argument, what choice did Francesca have? or how could Dante know that Ugolino was really damned? couldn't a last-minute repentance have saved him, and was the poet authorized to assume fictional omniscience concerning the secret intercourse between Ugolino and his God? isn't it, rather, that the poet claimed a poet's licence in placing those hypothetical damned in his Hell, since he needed them, and what's more, they needed him as an evoker and claimed their chance to speak through him?) At any rate, tragic or just pathetic (as Ciacco, Cavalcante and Ugolino undoubtedly are), these sinners are eminently human, with all that flesh is heir to. Our sympathy for them is not wasted, our appreciation of their suffering humanity can even survive the harsh theology that assigned them to everlasting doom — though this does not mean that we have to break up the poem into unrelated fragments.

Each sinner rehearses his life, or his catastrophe, for Dante, to whom they are stations in a pilgrimage, moments and instruments of a purification, of a self-recognition and eventual salvation. Yet they are all individual souls, God's highest work. In each of them Dante the pilgrim can mirror something of himself, at least their common fallible humanity, and more specifically some inclination which might drag him too into the abyss; but for the grace of God (and my watchful will) there go I... Paolo and Francesca ring a crucially autobiographical note for the Stil Nuovo poet who had wandered after several *donne dello schermo;* they are figures of his possible destiny, hence his response. Farinata, the heroic antagonist, is also what Dante might become if he heeded without restraint his own political and intellectual pride. Pier delle Vigne, as a wronged servant of his State, is in a way a counterpart of Dante, who through him purges the possible temptation of suicide in the face of injustice, and who without infringing on his Christian dogma vindicates Pier's memory on earth — Pier was not guilty of treason,

> per le nove radici d'esto legno
> vi giuro che giammai non ruppi fede
> al mio signor, che fu d'onor sì degno!

That cry "de profundis" is not meant to debase its utterer or to elicit snobbish condescension on the part of the reader. Brunetto Latini is a father figure, a momentary counterpart of Virgil as teacher, local embodiment and not caricature of the pervasive teacher motif on which so much of the whole poem's action is predicated; he is a *cara e buona immagine paterna,* and Dante acknowledges his debt to him. Again, there is something of the best of Dante's youth connected with him, and if the unity of the *Comedy* depends on despising Ser Brunetto, I have little use for that unity, and I invoke the poet's better knowledge against his dogmatic intentions.

Let us not forget that, if Brunetto is damned, so is Virgil; that Dante put to use Brunetto's *Treasury,* and that, if figures like Brunetto represent something to be left behind, they also embody or utter something which will stay with Dante: the prophecy of his exile, the auspice of literary and moral triumph, tragically proffered by him who could not triumph, and who, like a lesser Virgil, did as

> ...quei che va di notte,
> che reca lume dietro e sé non giova,
> ma dopo sé fa le persone dotte.

Even if we read an irony into Dante's touching avowal,

> ...ad ora ad ora
> m'insegnavate come l'uom s'etterna,

the irony is structural, not immediate, and moreover it is tragic; a reminder of how the living can use the dead, an example of the complex relation of an open present to a closed past. The "eternity" Ser Brunetto taught Dante to strive for was a humanistic immortality, thus not the true eternity, which only Beatrice can help him to secure. For himself, Brunetto Latini has only been able to gain the eternity of damnation. In Purgatory, Dante will formulate a memorable self-criticism in the humility of the artist who is learning to relativize the value of earthly fame from a higher perspective than Hell could afford:

> Oh vana gloria de l'umane posse!
> com poco verde in su la cima dura,

> se non è giunta de l'etati grosse!
> Credette Cimabue ne la pittura
> tener lo campo, e ora ha Giotto il grido,
> sì che la fama di colui è scura.
> Così ha tolto l'uno a l'altro Guido
> la gloria de la lingua; e forse è nato
> chi l'uno e l'altro caccerà del nido.
> Non è il mondan romore altro ch'un fiato
> di vento, ch'or vien quinci e or vien quindi,
> e muta nome perché muta lato.
> Che voce avrai tu più, se vecchia scindi
> da te la carne, che se fossi morto
> anzi che tu lasciassi il pappo e 'l dindi,
> pria che passin mill'anni? ch'è più corto
> spazio a l'etterno, ch'un muover di ciglia
> al cielo che più tardi in cielo è torto.
>
> (Purg. XI, 91-108)

Yet it is the vanity of conceitedness and not the value of art that Dante is here learning to reject; the intersection of history and eternity is his constant problem, and if with him, like the Christian he is, eternity emerges as the final judgment of history, it is not because history is irrelevant. Humanistic fame of the kind Brunetto taught him to acquire will still be on Dante's mind when, high up in Paradiso, he says:

> ritornerò poeta, ed in su 'l fonte
> del mio battesmo prenderò cappello.

Thus the valuable part of Brunetto's experience and teaching stays with Dante to the very end, and how could it be otherwise when we consider that in terms of his faith, earth is an arena and not a shadow, and that *Inferno* affords glimpses of the earthly values to be rescued from the wreckage of history, those very values which accrue to the theologically damned yet morally respected figure of beloved Virgil. When Beatrice takes over as Dante's educator (and as judge of history), she does what the Church did with the Roman Empire: she comes to integrate and save even while superseding, to raise and not to destroy. Just as Dante the narrating poet will never have to retract his tribute of affectionate esteem to Virgil, so he won't have to unsay what he so heartily says to the lesser mentor Brunetto. I find it hard to separate Dante the knowing poet from Dante the passionate pilgrim in Canto XV of *Inferno;* his warm words to Latini have the hindsight of Heaven, they are not spoken tongue in cheek. The chasm across which they are uttered defines the tragic scope of the whole episode.

This suggests a far more mobile and subtle relation between Pilgrim and Narrator (or between Persona and Author) than the rigid dogmatic separation of the two can admit; Dante the narrator relives certain crucial moments of his ordeal in unison with the naiver Dante he was while experiencing them, and they in turn were a reliving of certain decisive phases of his own earlier life, which the action of the poem, and the writing of the poem as such, bring to consummation. It would be wrong to believe that the privilege of otherworldly vision has definitively freed Dante from the burdens of earth. At the very moment of inditing his poem he has returned to earth, and the pathos of earth will intermittently assail him even while going through *Paradiso,* for the supreme vision was glimpsed and lost, and only death will bring final liberation. We could speak of several Dante *personae* (the bewildered pilgrim through Hell, by implication Dante's fiery youth; the serener visitor of Purgatory, by implication a wiser, sadder Dante of mature years; and the liberated traveller into Heaven, foretaster of permanent bliss), and of the changing relation of Dante the author to these personae, with each of whom he may momentarily identify even though he is wiser than they. A stable attitude does not prevail everywhere; the posthumous wisdom of the writer returned from the other world yields time and again to outbursts of passion, and these appear as *present* comment of the writer on the world he takes so much to heart, violent interjections of the imperious pen at its relentless task.

We have in the *Comedy,* then, both a self-transcendence and a frequent reimmersion of the author in his past experiences, which he can recapture in a kind of *historical present,* not only to judge, but also to respond, as Ishmael does with the crew of the vanished ship. Between Ishmael and his life on the Pequod, a whirlpool; between Dante and his earlier life, a light that failed, though it gave guidance. Did this hard-won wisdom make him harder or mellower? It is a post-exilic Dante we see at work, a man committed to his vision, not to an abstraction. I am not prepared to accept the closing lines of Canto XV, *Inf.*, as contemptuous of Brunetto and destructive of his dignity; "quegli che vince e non colui che perde," yes, an unseemly haste, forced by the circumstance of Hell, but conveyed by an image of victory, ironical though it may be. If we go by theology in the abstract, then Dante's placing Brunetto in Hell is a highly arbitrary gesture, founded on arrogant hypothesis; how could Dante know that the aged scholar had not repented his sin before death, in the sanctum of his soul? But of course Dante needed Brunetto in his ordeal, and even more in the rehearsing of his life — autobiography being one of the essential dimensions of the poem. The occasion for Ser Brunetto's damnation is not discussed at all in the episode; Dante is not really interested in showing us how bad a sodomite can be, because if that had been his concern, he could have easily picked some likelier candidate.

Florence and Florence's destiny, Dante and Dante's future, Ser Brunetto and the value of learning and teaching, these are the pressing concerns of our poet, and it is no use pretending that he is more insufferably righteous than he actually manages to be. Ser Brunetto's sin is a private affair; God took care of that, and how sad it is that such a fine man should have fallen! But to Dante the poet, that man is more than an abstract example of punished vice, he appears in his best aspect, he is almost incongruous in Hell, and this makes the meeting a more poignant ordeal for our pilgrim (and for the struggling writer). The whole situation reminds us that, whatever Mr. George Steiner may say, it is simply not true that Christianity made tragedy impossible. When the destiny of an immortal soul is at stake, beyond the horizons of earth, tragic possibilities deepen. Dante's "other world" brings this world into sharper focus; the tension between the two is part of Dante's challenge as a poet, the mainspring of his creativity.

And nowhere does this tension vibrate more keenly than in the Ulysses episode of Canto XXVI, where the damning sin furnishes a mere pretext for introducing a heroic figure whose bearing is anything but contemptible (as the alleged sin would require, instead, if the chief purpose of Dante in conjuring the much-travelled Greek warrior were to exemplify an abstract vice).

As John Nist has recognized in a very personal (and partly myopic) essay,[6] Ulysses mirrors something of Dante's own roaming life, Dante's leaving his family behind, Dante's intellectual curiosity and the dangers it once entailed. Unlike Dante's, of course, Ulysses' thirst for boundless knowledge will result in physical and metaphysical shipwreck. The horizon of infinity is not available to human effort, "argomenti umani," unaided by Divine Grace. And yet how grandiose is that hopeless effort! Ulysses' venture into the unknown may have blinded Romantic critics like De Sanctis to the non-humanist underlying attitude of Dante in evoking the twin flame, but the poem's unity gains nothing by demeaning the "virtue" of the pagan hero, a virtue Dante himself approves of within the larger framework of Christian revelation:

> fatti non foste a viver come bruti,
> ma per seguir virtute e conoscenza.

One must be temporarily deaf to poetry to misread the tragically inspired lines:

> e, volta nostra poppa nel mattino,
> dei remi facemmo ali al folle volo

as John Ciardi does (despite his other accomplishments as a translator) when he minimizes the value of "folle" (mad) the way a Sunday school teacher would:

> we made wings of our oars for our fool's flight [7]

The "madness" of Ulysses, no matter how self-judging that term can be, is no petty thing; Dante did not conceive a petty figure, indeed he showed in him the greatness of which the pagan world was capable, because only thus could the failure of Ulysses acquire its full significance in the context of a work which is engaged in

---

[6] John Nist, "The Impurities in Dante's *Commedia*," in *Books Abroad*, cit., 49-57.

[7] Dante, *The Inferno*, a new translation by John Ciardi (Mentor Books, 1954), p. 224. I also take exception to Ciardi's rendering of "virtute e conoscenza" with "manhood and recognition," which distorts Dante pitifully. This proves how a gifted translator of poetry can succumb to theological narrow-mindedness.

the search for ultimate values. Ulysses' destruction by the God-whipped maelstrom in sight of Purgatory's mountain confirms this view; the noble hero *almost* makes it, in defiance of the inviolable decrees emanating from what is to him "Altrui," an unknown and alien Power. Melville's Ahab will be one of his descendants.

If in Ulysses' fatally misguided thirst for world-wide experience, through an epically straightforward style that shuns all uncertainties, Dante portrayed something of himself, he symmetrically opposed to the Greek navigator Guido da Montefeltro, who is basically "other" than Dante, for Guido interests the poet as a real case of moral ambiguity, damning casuistry and devious weakness. With all due caution about clichés, one might see in Guido the prototype of the modern "Hamletic" anti-hero, as contrasted to the ancient hero who, Ahab-like, is lost through his overweening assurance and not through bad conscience. Theologically, Ulysses and Guido are on the same level, and they are meant to illustrate fraud; poetically, they are at the antipodes of each other, just like Farinata and Cavalcante, and they afford Dante a chance to wield language masterfully. The counterpoint of Guido's tortuous sentences —a moral portrait in themselves— to Ulysses' headlong utterance cannot be lost on the reader:

> S'io credessi che mia risposta fosse
> a persona che mai tornasse al mondo,
> questa fiamma staria senza più scosse....

The irony of Guido's self-deception with regard to his interlocutor is a dramatic touch of the first order, and his final perdition at the hands of the "logician devil" appropriately caps his story. Style evokes, style judges, style objectifies; there is no reason to discard De Sanctis' idea that European drama to be (especially Shakespeare's character study) was seminally contained in Dante's portrayals.

Style changes to suit each epic, or pathetic, or ironic portrait, and it can even mimetically descend to the bottom of abomination as in the episode of Mastro Adamo and Sinon; yet style retains its fundamental identity even while becoming other, just as Dante becomes somehow "other" (through compassion or fear, wonder or anger or disgust) only to become more fully himself. In every relevant figure he recognizes what is other and what is himself, and his poetry serves as both necromancy and exorcism. Thus his poetry is "experience," not of the unpeopled world as Ulysses would have it for himself, but of the other world, and of this world through the other. There is no need to reduce each heroic or pathetic figure to small size in order to save the coherence of the whole. This coherence is so strong that it thrives on the structural balance of thrust and counterthrust, as a Gothic cathedral does. Style decides, every time, style creates, and it creates by transcending the theological intention, by using it as a support, not by conforming to it as to a blueprint. This way a world is born —or reborn— in and around Dante's individual pilgrimage; and it is a full-sized world, not a parade of moralistic phantoms. Calvary and resurrection, Dante's ordeal culminates in a momentary recognition of the divine plenitude which every singular will, be it through strength or weakness, fatally had to miss by persisting in its isolation. Damnation is self-confinement in the singular form of existence; salvation is openness to communal infinity. Poetry is what accomplishes the impossible transition from the former to the latter pole, from the compressed and finally choked energy of Hell's funnel to progressively released energy, beyond the zero point where the first reversal of perspective occurs.

BEATRICE IN DANTE'S PLOT

ALLAN H. GILBERT
Duke University
Drew University

Like all great poets, Dante gave much attention to his plotting. Perhaps no poet has made his care clearer in the poem itself. Here are a hundred cantos, varying in length from 115 to 160 verses, but for the most part holding close to the norm of 145 for the *Pugatorio* and *Paradiso* and about six lines fewer for the *Inferno*. Moreover, the three cantiche are of almost the same length, being of 4720, 4755 and 4758 lines. As soon as the poet had settled on this uniformity, he could never have let it out of his sight. A legend says that he wrote part of the poem before his exile, and aonther that he hardly finished before he died. These hints of more than twenty years in composition are not contradicted by the passage on "the inspired poem to which heaven and earth lent a hand, so that it has made me thin for many years" (*Par.* 25, 1 ff.). The longer the period of writing, the more improbable that, before beginning, the detailed outline necessary for the present structure could have been made. Everybody knows the difficulty of producing something so slight as a paper that can be read in exactly fifteen minutes. That before writing any of the *Commedia*, its author planned ninety-seven verses of Paradiso 11 for Saint Francis demands foresight of poetical inspiration years in advance. Yet so far as he fell short of a plan revealing perfect foresight, he must as he composed have wrestled with not merely cantos but *cantiche* that were too long or too short. During the years when for his poem's sake he endured "hunger, cold and loss of sleep" (*Purg.*

29, 37) there will have been shifting of parts, large and small, and even modification of plan.

An early faint hint of a plan is the assertion at the end of the *Vita Nuova* that he intends to write worthily of Beatrice. If in any surviving poem Dante fulfilled this plan, it appears in the last four cantos of the *Purgatorio* and the first thirty-one of the *Paradiso*.[1] In the last of these, the visitor to Heaven speaks his farewell to her as she sits — her guardianship finished — with the other redeemed in the Rose, the only unhistorical visitor seated there.

Virgil first mentions Beatrice, though without her name, when he tells his charge that a worthier soul must act as guide in Heaven (1, 102). In his reply the traveler ignores any second guide:

> Poet, I ask you ... to lead me where you say, so that I may see the Gate of Saint Peter *(Inf.* 1, 130 ff.).

Though the traveler finds a gate at the entrance of Purgatory, this early speech alludes to Heaven.[2]

Virgil first names Beatrice when telling the traveler Dante of her intercession for him; there the Latin poet quotes her long explanation. Brief recognition of Beatrice is combined with thanks to Virgil:

> Oh compassionate she who rescued me! And courteous were you, heeding so speedily the true speeches she spoke to you (2, 133 ff.).

After Farinata has obscurely threatened his visitor with political misfortune, Virgil says to his pupil:

> When you stand within the sweet illumination of her whose fair eyes see the whole voyage of your life, from her you will learn of it *(Inf.* 10, 130 ff.).

The man concerned makes no answer. Virgil leading, the two go on their way. In the poem as it stands, this information is asked

---

[1] As though to do what can be done in carrying her to the end, Beatrice is incidentally mentioned in *Par.* 33, 38.

[2] In Dante's early plan, was this gate at the entrance to Heaven rather than Purgatory? To be sure, the gate of Purgatory admits only those finally to enter Heaven.

from Cacciaguida, with Beatrice's encouragement. The answer includes the famous lines:

> You will leave everything you have loved most dearly.
> This is the arrow that the bow of exile first shoots.
> You will experience how salty another man's bread tastes,
> and what a hard climb it is to go up and down another
> man's stairs. And what will burden your back most
> heavily will be the wicked and rascally company into
> which you will fall in the valley I speak of (*Par.* 17, 55 ff.).

This speech by Cacciaguida may replace lines in which Beatrice told of the visitor's future. If so, time for adjusting the passages in the *Inferno* was not granted to the poet.

Soon after leaving Farinata, the traveler mentions Beatrice's name in conversing with Brunetto Latini. Then the poet forgets her for twenty-two cantos, until he has brought his pilgrims part way up the mountain of Purgatory. There the traveler has cause for asking Virgil if in the *Aeneid* he did not deny the efficacy of mortal prayers in affecting heavenly decrees. Virgil explains that he was writing of prayers not properly addressed. Then follow six verses so easily detached that their omission does not break continuity. They contain the first appearance of the name Beatrice since Hell Gate was entered. Virgil says:

> Do not consider so important a doubt settled if she does not declare it to you who will be light between the truth and your intellect. I do not know whether you understand. I mean Beatrice. You will see her above, on the summit of this mountain, laughing and happy (*Purg.* 6, 43 ff.).

The pupil makes no direct reply recognizing that Beatrice has been named. He expresses a desire for haste such as we expect from Virgil (e.g., *Inf.* 17, 40; 24, 52; 34, 94; *Purg.* 12, 15; 27, 62). His speech is sometimes attributed to his desire to move on toward Beatrice, but that is an inference. It seems adequate to make his words a reference to Virgil's desire to hurry and to his own earlier fatigue and wish to pause (*Purg.* 4, 44; cf. *Inf.* 32, 82). Virgil's explanation of prayer needs no supplement. No commentator, within my notice, has made any attempt to show that Beatrice deals with the subject.

Beatrice is again mentioned by Virgil after passing through the first two terraces of Purgatory. Dante then wonders how heavenly things can be the more abundant the more they are given away. Virgil explains the eternal worth of love, concluding much as before:

> If my explanation does not satisfy you, you will see Beatrice, and she will completely relieve you of this and of every other longing. Make haste now so that quickly, like the other two, the remaining five wounds are healed, which are closed by being sorrowful (*Purg.* 15, 76 ff.).

The pupil pays no attention to this concluding part of Virgil's speech, with its reference to Beatrice. Of its earlier part, he wishes to say: "You satisfy me," but is kept from speaking. Thus the lines relating to Beatrice are so detachable that their absence would never be remarked. She does not in the *Paradiso* explain heavenly abundance.

Having gone through the terrace of wrath, the pupil asks Virgil about love, to be answered:

> As far as reason penetrates this I can tell you; further than that wait for Beatrice, because all beyond what I say is matter of faith (*Purg.* 18, 46 ff.).

Further, Virgil says that the noble virtue of right use of the reason is called by Beatrice free will, with the warning: "Be sure to keep it in mind, if she starts to speak with you about it" (18, 74 ff.). Both these references to Beatrice are disregarded by the hearer. On free will, Beatrice does speak, though with no questioning of her charge:

> The greatest gift that God in his generosity made as he created, and the one most in harmony with his goodness, and that which he most values, was liberty of the will, with which intelligent beings —all and each— were and are gifted (*Par.* 5, 19 ff.).

So incidental and so without demand on the traveler are Beatrice's words as hardly to justify the Latin poet's warning.

On the next ledge of Purgatory comes Virgil's most dramatic use of Beatrice's name. The timid traveler cannot be assured by

Virgil — after all his experience with his guide — that the flames punishing lust will not harm him. Having exhausted assurances and urgings, Virgil, a bit vexed, at last says:

> "Now look here, my son; between Beatrice and you stands this wall." As at the name of Thisbe, Pyramus when dying opened his eyes and looked at her, when the mulberry became scarlet, so —my hardness softened— I turned to my wise guide, hearing the name which in my mind always springs up afresh. At that he shook his head and said: "What, are you going to stand there?" Then he smiled, as is done to a boy who is won with an apple. So I entered the fire (*Purg.* 27, 35 ff.).

This persuasion through Beatrice, occupying four tercets, is essential to the action of the moment. If Beatrice's name had not been used, Virgil must have found some other strong inducement to move his timid pupil upward. Here too the returned traveler expresses his undying interest in her name. As they move through the flames, Virgil encourages his charge by talking still of Beatrice, saying: "I think I already see her eyes" (27, 54). But now, according to his earlier pattern, the hearer makes no reply. The narrative changes to the angel's guidance.

Having entered the Earthly Paradise with his pupil, Virgil gives over his task, saying:

> While you await the coming of those beautiful happy eyes which, by their weeping, made me come to you, you can sit or you can move about among the flowers (*Purg.* 27, 136 f.).

To this speech the hearer, according to his wont, makes no answer.

Though when Virgil mentions Beatrice, her supposed adorer never says a word in acknowledgement, he does twice mention her of his own volition. When Brunetto Latini refers to his visitor's troubled life, he is answered:

> What you tell about my course I am writing down, and am keeping it for explanation with other texts by a lady who will be able to explain them, if I get to her (*Inf.* 15, 90 ff.).

This again seems to allude to what Cacciaguida, not Beatrice, has to say. Since Brunetto died in 1294, he may have read the

Vita Nuova and had further knowledge enabling him to know who the "lady" is.

To Forese Donati, on the ledge of the gluttons, the traveler explains that Virgil has guided him through Hell and thus far up the mountain of Purgatory. Then he continues:

> He says he will give me his company until I reach the place where Beatrice is; there I shall have to be without him (*Purg.* 23, 128 ff.).

This recalls Virgil's early assurance of a "more worthy" guide to Heaven (*Inf.* 1, 121). No reference to Beatrice could be barer or briefer. Yet we may recall that Forese, a literary friend of Dante's, was more likely than Brunetto Latini to known of Beatrice. Did the author of the *Vita Nuova* mention her to these two because, historically, they could understand?

Thus, except for Virgil's story of Beatrice's mission to him, and the inducement to enter the flames on the topmost ledge of Purgatory, the references to Beatrice in *Inferno* and *Purgatorio* have a curious likeness. They tend to be short — even of one tercet — and to be detachable from the context. When Virgil makes them, his pupil expresses no interest. Suggestions that Beatrice will explain personal or doctrinal matters are hardly carried out. Some of this may come from an earlier plan in which Beatrice in the *Paradiso* spoke more fully or at least differently than now. They do not suggest a traveler eager to reach her. Their service seems structural, to keep before the reader that the poem has a sequence reaching forward. Moreover, the brevity and detachable quality of the passages alluding to Beatrice suggest their late insertion, when on revision the poet was striving to give an effect of unity and connection of parts to his work. Space for any comment by the traveler was then lacking, since Dante's plan did not permit much lengthening of cantos. Always, however, the difficulty of making insertions in the *terza rima* must be remembered. How many new rimes would the insertion of a tercet oblige the writer to find? His hundred cantos were convenient in that, at the worst, the revamping of rimes ended with the canto.

According to Virgil's last mention of Beatrice, his pupil is to wait in the Earthly Paradise for the beautiful and gracious eyes of the lady who for the lost man's rescue had come to Virgil with tears. Though ignored by his hearer, the Latin's words still prepare for a happy meeting with the Beatrice earlier mentioned in the poem, with the lady of the *Vita Nuova* for the relatively few of Dante's early readers who had perused the youthful work. The latter would expect her to be more accessible than she appears in the *Vita Nuova*.

But the writer interposes an interlude — shall we say an antidote? As the visitor looks with pleasure at the Earthly Paradise, especially at the rivulet of Lethe, he sees,

> appearing so suddenly as to turn from its path with wonder all other purpose, a lady alone, singing and gathering flower after flower among those coloring her path (*Purg.* 28, 37 ff.).

To her the stranger says:

> Oh beautiful lady, who warm yourself in Love's rays (if I can believe appearances that ever testify to the heart), be so kind as to move forward to this stream, so that I can make out what you are singing. You bring me to remember where and what Proserpina was at the time when her mother lost her, and she lost the spring.
> As a dancing lady turns with her feet on the ground and close together, and scarcely sets one foot ahead of the other, she moved toward me over the scarlet and yellow flowers, in virginal fashion lowering her chaste eyes, and satisfied my petition, coming so near that the sweet sound reached me with its sense. As soon as she stood where the grass was always wet with the ripples of the pretty stream, she did me the favor of raising her eyes. I do not believe so much light shone under Venus' brows when her son —by accident— pierced her with an arrow. The lady, close to the other bank, was laughing plucking with her hands more flowers, which the high land produces without seed. By three paces the stream parted us, but Hellespont, where Xerxes crossed —still a bit checking all human pride— was not more hated by Leander for spreading its waves between Sestos and Abydos, than I hated that brook for not opening me a way (*Purg.* 28, 43 ff.).

After Virgil's recent promise af Beatrice's "glad and beautiful eyes" (27, 136), this beautiful and laughing lady should be she, but, on the contrary, she is one who drives from the head of the visitor all other considerations. These thoughts are not specified, but after Virgil's words, what more natural than that they should concern Beatrice? So this lady displaces Beatrice. Is that heroine ever so charmingly described?

But quickly the episode of the lovely singer ends, though, as if to avoid change of atmosphere, she continues to be referred to as the "lady enamoured" and the "beautiful lady" (28, 148; 29, 1; 31, 100; 33, 121, 134). Her function, however, becomes instrumental in the action, whether to lecture on the garden, to answer questions or to act as guide (28, 88-144; 32, 86; 33, 128). As an expositor, she is beautiful like Beatrice when about to lecture on moon-spots or on Redemption (*Par.* 2, 28; 7, 17), and throughout her activity as guide through Paradise.

This lovely lady is at first unnamed, but later is called Matelda, so incidentally that one may guess that in an early state of Dante's manuscript her name appeared before (33, 119). In Dante's digressive poem her earlier actions seem a digression, but when further observed are functional in the narrative. The seeker for liberty is soon to come before Beatrice, who will rate him for deserting her (30, 126 ff.; 31, 1-63). Such lack of lover's stability gives a reason why, on the appearance of Matelda, the author, planning his plot, said that all other desire or thought by his chief character left its road (28, 38 f.). Virgil's recent invocation of Beatrice's beautiful eyes leaves the mind of the man who gazes on Matelda. She exemplifies the *pargoletta*, "the little maid or other emptiness of brief duration" (*Purg.* 31, 59 f.), for which Beatrice indignantly says, her lover forgot her. What the reader has just learned shows that Beatrice is right. Yet we are hardly to suppose that Beatrice consciously points to Matelda when she says *pargoletta*.[3] Matelda's relation to her as assistant probably forbids that. We are rather to think that Dante as author seized an opportunity not only to offer a charming interlude but to emphasize the susceptibility of his hero to feminine charm. After

---

[3] *Purg.* 31, 59 f. A *pargoletta*, evidently not Beatrice, appears in Dante's lyrics (*Rime* 87.1; 89.2; 100.72). We need not identify Matelda with them, even though —in the Garden— she may typify the pilgrim's wandering affections.

Matelda, how can his fickleness be doubted? Possibly the episode is an afterthought. Matelda may have been more prosaically conceived as an interim guide. Then as the author wrote he saw that her effect on the visitor could emphasize Beatrice's arraignment for infidelity soon to follow.

Soon after Matelda subsides from enamoured lady to prosaic demonstrator of the Garden's climate, Beatrice appears. In her manner there is nothing to justify eagerness to meet her at the cost of moving through terrifying flames or to recall Virgil's reminder of her tears when she came to him for the wanderer's rescue. When first in Beatrice's presence, the lover of ten years before suddenly trembles, as the result of a flame which he calls *antica,* from long since (*Purg.* 30, 48). If awakened now, for ten years his thirst has lain dormant (32, 2). Beatrice appears as an arrogant queen, an admiral efficient in directing his fleet, like the Venetian doge Dandolo at Constantinople. In reproaching the timid visitor, she is like a stern mother. As though jealous, she tells how he forgot her. Attempts to call him back "not at all affected him" (*Purg.* 30, 58, 70, 79). Confusion and fear so attack the culprit that he hardly can speak. "Present things" did turn him from her (31, 34). But reproaches for desertion still come. There is "poison" in her arraignment (31, 75).

The Virtues intervene for the cowering lover with the words:

> Turn, Beatrice, turn your holy eyes to your faithful [devotee], who to see you has taken so many steps (*Purg.* 31, 133).

The Virtues are making a favorable case; can the word faithful be reconciled with Beatrice's rebukes for infidelity? And that he has journeyed to see her is now first asserted, however we interpret most of the brief references to her in the course of the journey. Reasons for his expedition have been given, such as search for liberty (*Purg.* 1, 71), but not a meeting with Beatrice.

So there is a contrast. The traveler of the last terrace of Purgatory can be moved by the hope of meeting a welcoming Beatrice. The man who comes into her presence has forgotten her, must be shocked back into his emotion of long ago, *antica.*

Within the poem, save for Matelda, there is no reason for Beatrice's reproaches. Even biographical reasons are difficult to find. Professor Grandgent has written:

> This whole solemn and elaborate episode ... strikes one as having been devised by the author partly for the purpose of making real amends for past wrong, and setting himself right before the world. What may have been the nature of the guilt thus expiated ... by avowal? Was it a mundane love or an undue literary or scientific ambition? Our evidence is slight...
>
> Dante's conscience, apparently, was ill at ease; and here, in the *Commedia*, he at last tells the whole truth, admitting that his love for the *pargoletta* was not merely an innocent devotion to that "figlia d'Iddio, regina di tutto, nobilissima e bellissima Filosofia" (*Convivio* 2, 13), but also, and originally, a sentiment deserving reprobation. Now as far as we can see, Dante's devotion to Philosophy never ceased, his admiration never waned; throughout the *Commedia* ... she is the handmaid of religion and ... the guide to revelation (Edition of the *Commedia*, pp. 612 f.).

Thus finding no dramatic explanation for Beatrice's charges within the fiction, Professor Grandgent has turned to the writer's biography, without satisfaction. But are biographical explanations valid for an imaginative work, unless supported by passages within it? Can Dante even have expected from readers of the *Commedia* familiarity with the *Vita Nuova*? At least in the period after Dante's death it seems to have been little known. Above all, the scene is imaginative and fictitious, not one for Dante in his own person.

The traveler's penitence, which so breaks him down, is for vague transgressions. "Present things with their false pleasures have turned aside his steps" (31, 34). He accepts Beatrice's rebuke for leaving her for fallacious things, vanities (31, 56, 60). When on the terrace of envy, he had indicated his vice of pride, and he had later accepted the idea of sorrow for all seven of the deadly sins, and as returned from his experience, he had sins to weep for (*Purg.* 13, 136 ff.; 15, 81; *Par.* 22, 107). In mediaeval ethics, pride, what we call egotism, can lead to transgression, but the traveler's vices are not emphasized. Purification before ascending even for a brief visit to Heaven is not unnatural. Yet it seems incidental, or even a violation of the early conditions. Virgil told the candidate that for heaven he would need another guide, but not any special preparation. The structure of the *Commedia* makes easy the use of events not essential to the whole. Moreover, Beatrice's excoriation of the traveler is concerned chiefly with evident wickedness. Perhaps we can leave the episode of her attack on Dante as justified by its striking character, as an individual in a series of events not inevitably joined for Aristotle's pleasure.

The penitent's drafts from Lethe and Eunoe may be taken as passports to Heaven. Yet they too, like Beatrice's rebukes, seem limited to the experience of the moment. There has been an incidental suggestion that the souls of the dead wash in Lethe— not that they drink its waters — when their repented faults are removed (*Inf.* 14, 137). But the traveler is not a soul which has left its body on earth: he is a living man, yet to be purified in Purgatory. Such purgation would take many years, for which he expects to return, saying, just after leaving the terrace where pride is purged:

> Greater is my fear, which strains my spirit, of the torment on the terrace below, so that already the weight down there burdens me (*Purg.* 13, 136 ff.).

He has only observed for a few minutes the affliction which may endure for years of purification. Of Eunoe we hear nothing save in the Garden.

Of these drafts from Lethe and Eunoe, no affects appear in Heaven. The good Christian there is still of the Church militant (*Par.*, 24, 52; 25, 52). As not of the Church triumphant, he has no seat in the celestial Rose. Back on earth after his heavenly pilgrimage, the tourist was still an ordinary mortal, declaring:

> As I hope, reader, to return to that holy procession (of the blessed moving toward the Starry Heaven), so that I often weep for my sins and beat my breast (*Par.* 22, 106 ff.).

This perhaps emphasizes the dream-like character of the tourist's experience. Apparently Statius, going to a permanent place in

Heaven, drank of Eunoe with his companion (*Par.* 33, 135). So Lethe and Eunoe seem not unsuitable to the narrative, though their episode is not assimilated to the whole.

The puzzle of Beatrice's unexpected haughtiness does not exhaust the puzzles of the Garden. Much of the six cantos devoted to it relates the Biblical procession which shifts to a presentation of Church and Empire, the theme of Dante's *De Monarchia.* It uses the most striking traditional object in the Garden, the Tree of the Knowledge of Good and Evil. With its enormous importance in theology, it gives some fitness to the allegory of society in the setting of the Garden. Yet what Milton would have called "foul spirits," the giant, the harlot and the destructive animals, are unsuited to it. Dante indeed can bring in almost what he will at any time, permitted to do so by his structure, the visitor's observation of one scene after another, with a minumum of necessity or, in Aristotle's sense, probability. Such freedom was demanded by Dante's astonishing plan to write a hundred approximately equal cantos divided into three equal *cantiche.* He can do so only in a work in which the action of the chief character is without involution and the individual episodes are capable of shifting.

For the *Purgatorio,* Dante doubtless needed more matter rather than less. His main plan, founded on the seven sins, gave him seven sections, as compared with the ten allowed to Heaven by astronomy in that day, and with the twenty-four to be counted in Hell. Heaven, with its throng of free souls, allowed freedom of expansion so great as to make ten divisions enough. The four additional sections provided by the first eight cantos of the *Purgatorio* gave the cantica eleven parts, extending to twenty-seven cantos. Shall these be expanded to thirty-three? Instead, perhaps fearing to make the terraces over-full, Dante developed the meeting with Beatrice; to provide for this convergence is the Garden's only inevitable function, as in *Orlando Furioso* it is a starting point for Astolfo's voyage to the Moon.

So far as Beatrice's conduct is not easily reconciled with expectations, it may represent pressure for material. To develop an attack on Dante the old lover for such abandonment of her for Philosophy as is narrated in the *Convivio* demands more space and has more of novelty than his acceptance by a smiling spirit. If Dante meditated on Beatrice as a dramatic character, he may easily have come to see that she could not be left as shadowy as she appears in the *Vita Nuova*. There must be something positive. If she were to value a lover's devotion, she could not contentedly allow him to abandon her for even so splendid a mistress as Lady Philosophy. Yet such dramatic presentation —not easily reconcilable with the poem's ethical purpose— seemingly occurred to the poet late, too late to enable him to reconcile all parts of his poem with the concept of either a gracious or an exacting mistress.

When Beatrice appears lovely in white and green and scarlet, she still is *proterva* (*Purg.* 30, 70), as was Angelica when she chose to scorn such a lover as Orlando. She is like a haughty mother to a little boy. For more than forty lines she rates him (30, 103-145). She commands him to speak with a masterful "Answer me" (31, 11). Dante can hardly articulate "Si," when she sweeps on. He admits that present things concealed her face. In a speech of twenty-seven lines, she comes to her jealousy, with "a little girl or other brief vanity" (31, 59). Jealousy is always comic, though, as for Othello, it can also be tragic. With her unexpected outpouring, Beatrice reduces her former lover to the state of a small boy embarrassed, his eyes on the ground. But Beatrice goes on with poisonous words: "Lift your beard" (31, 68, 75). She has turned him from a man into a baby.

When carried in Virgil's arms like a child, the traveler is diminished to comic stature. When with a torrent of words Beatrice the virago overwhelms him, though he had relied on Virgil's promise of smiles (27, 136), he is still further put among the ineffective. In the *Convivio,* the author took credit to himself for turning from Beatrice to Philosophy. Here the lady's violence overrides any earlier plan of life. The weak and comic traveler, unable to defend his conduct, is at his greatest disadvantage, broken to helplessness by this woman he had expected to receive him gladly. This is the comedy, as in Falstaff's rejection by King Henry, of happy expectations defeated. As in most comic scenes, the situation in this one —with Beatrice standing solid (31, 100) in the chariot and shouting across the stream to this man dissolving in tears— must be brought before the mind's eye.

Before long, Beatrice abandons her arrogant condemnation of the man who forgot her beautiful limbs (31, 50). The transition, though not clearly indicated, perhaps comes when the Virtues beg

Beatrice to turn her holy eyes on her devotee (31, 133). She abandons her jealous role to act as a good adviser, exhorting the visitor to observe, that he may write on his return to earth (32, 104 f.; 33, 55). Soon, as good a guide as Virgil, she encourages questions, addressing her pupil as Frate (33, 23), as do Saint Benedict and Piccarda. Earlier his old friend, Corso Donati, had so spoken, and the humble Pope Adrian (*Purg.* 23, 97, 112; 19, 133). Though not quite forgetting to rebuke, Beatrice's geniality is evident as she jokes, saying with a smile: "If you cannot remember deserting me, remind yourself that you have drunk of Lethe's waters (33, 94), and later smiling with fuller-hearted amusement: "Turn and listen, for not merely in my eyes is Paradise" (*Par.*, 18, 20 f.). Her pupil speaks of her in terms to satisfy the most exacting mistress: her beauty is beyond a poet's strength; only her Maker fully enjoys it (*Par.* 30, 16 ff.; cf. 4. 39; 26, 113). Whatever part Beatrice plays as theologian or scientist, she is throughout the *Paradiso* the kind and smiling object of the traveler's devotion, justifying Virgil's most enticing speeches about her.

Thus Beatrice's jealous, admiral-like conduct when the traveler is rated from her chariot in the Earthly Paradise, is as little in harmony with what follows as with what precedes. There is, then, this block of impressive but almost intrusive high comedy in the thirtieth and thirty-first cantos of the *Purgatorio,* the pilgrim's arraignment.

Beatrice rules the poem for most of the *Paradiso.* Only in the Heaven of Jupiter does she fail to act. Later she disappears as abruptly as did Virgil. The traveler turns to address his beloved maestro, and sees no one. He turns to address Beatrice; he sees Saint Bernard (*Purg.* 30, 49; *Par.* 31, 68). Why was the "sweet guide and dear" not with him to the journey's end? Is she less devoted to the Virgin than Saint Bernard, less able to address a prayer to her? If Beatrice's influence is less, why does the saint say that she supports his prayer (*Par.* 33, 38)? We may answer that the substitution allows the formal leave-taking and thanks of the traveler to Beatrice, almost as though she were a saint, as she sits in the celestial Rose (31, 79-90). Farther on, Saint Bernard smilingly encourages his charge (33, 49). Then, with the abrupt end which the author gave his poem to match its abrupt introduction, this great saint is left unnoticed as the traveler tells of his own feelings, with which the poem stops. Was ever saint and kind guide so ignored? To avoid such treatment of Beatrice, she is removed early enough to permit a formal leave-taking not characteristic of the poem. Even from Cacciaguida, the Florentine departs without courteous words.

To Dante's sense that his poem should not appear to be made up merely of disconnected scenes on a journey, we owe the early narrative of Beatrice's appearance to Virgil. After the traveler has decided upon the journey (*Inf.* 1, 134), his reconsideration seems an author's afterthought to permit the introduction of Beatrice without rewriting the preceding canto (2, 31, 53 ff.). Can one suspect that the poet would have liked to present Beatrice in person rather than merely through Virgil's narrative, but found no easy way to do so? In the *Inferno* there are few later references to her; indeed she is ignored from canto 15 on to *Purgatorio* 6, as though the author's interest in details kept him from thinking of his whole sequence. In the *Purgatorio* the larger number of allusions to Beatrice binds that *cantica* more closely to its own later part and to the *Paradiso*, leading the reader to expect her appearance. For retrospective connection, the author feels less need, naming Virgil as guide but once in the Paradiso,[4] though there are other allusions to the earlier part of the journey.[5] Thus, though lacking Virgilian complexity, the action of the *Commedia* gains through the mention and presence of Beatrice, an effect of relation between its parts.

---

[4] *Par.* 17, 19. A reference to Virgil as poet rather than guide adds little if at all to the effect of narrative connection (15, 26).

[5] For Hell, see *Par.* 6, 74; 17, 21, 112, 137; 20, 48, 106; 26, 133; 31, 81; 32, 33; 33, 22. For Purgatory, see *Par.* 15, 93; 17, 20, 113, 137; 26, 139.

DANTE AND THE VIRTUOUS PAGANS

Gino Rizzo
University of North Carolina

Many studies have been devoted to an understanding of Dante's Limbo and the related problem of the fate of virtuous unbelievers. [1] These studies focus primarily on the theological basis of Dante's conception of Limbo, on whether his conception adheres to or departs from the position held on this question by Thomas Aquinas. At best, the scholarly works to which I am referring bring isolated and scattered passages in the poem to bear on the position taken by their authors with regard to the general question of Dante's orthodoxy. Because of this, they seem to disregard the context in which those passages appear. They overlook, that is, the progress of the pilgrim — the unfolding of the poem's "meaning" through the constant interaction of the cumulative experience of the pilgrim-poet with the various regions he traverses in his exemplary journey.

If we assume, as I think we should, that the structure of the poem rests on this interaction, rather than on a static depiction of

---

[1] Tito Bottagisio, *Il Limbo dantesco*, Padova, 1898; F. D'Ovidio, *Il Purgatorio e il suo preludio*, Milano, 1906 (especially on the salvation of Cato); E. Proto, "Nuove ricerche sul Catone dantesco," *Giornale storico della letteratura italiana*, LIX (1912), 193-248; Louis Capéran, *Le problème du salut des Infidèles*, Paris, 1912 (in particular the chapter, "La Théologie de Dante"); Emma Cavendoli, "Il Limbo dantesco dei pagani," *Giornale dantesco*, XXVIII (1925), 28-33; G. Busnelli, "La colpa del 'non fare' degl'infedeli negativi," *Studi danteschi*, XXIII (1938), 79-105. These are only some of the studies devoted to this problem; the bibliography on the subject is of course much more vast.

the "states of souls after death," we can view the problem of Limbo and that of the salvation of virtuous pagans, which is closely bound up with it, as an important element of thematic structure in the poem.

The theme of the virtuous pagans makes its first appearance with the introduction of Virgil as Dante's guide. In outlining the journey to be undertaken, Virgil explains to Dante his own limitation in this role and the need for "a more worthy spirit" to lead him into the heavenly city:

> con lei ti lascerò nel mio partire;
> chè quello imperador che là su regna,
> perch'io fu' ribellante alla sua legge,
> non vuol che 'n sua città per me si vegna.
> *(Inf., I, 123-26)*

That of having been "ribellante alla sua legge," is the most self-deprecatory statement Virgil makes on his relation to the Christian God. At this incipient stage of the journey, the distance which separates him from the heavenly city is a chasm — so much so that after having hastily minimized Virgil's shortcomings ("Poeta io ti richieggio/ per *quello Dio che tu non conoscesti,/* acciò ch'io fugga questo male e peggio,/ che tu mi meni là dov' or dicesti"), and having just as hastily accepted Virgil's offer of aid at the close of the canto, the pilgrim will need Virgil's reassurance that he has been sent by the "tre donne benedette" of Canto II in order to overcome his hesitation and entrust himself to Virgil's care.

It would be erroneous then to take Virgil's words literally, as Father Busnelli does,[2] and construe from them that Virgil and with him all the virtuous pagans of Limbo are guilty of a positive act of rebellion against God's law. For as soon as we reach Limbo in Canto IV, Virgil's account of those spirits' failure, as well as Dante's depiction of this circle of Hell, makes such an inference impossible.

But before we proceed with our examination of Dante's unfolding of this theme, it would seem imperative to survey briefly the theological background of the question of the *infideles negativi.*

---

[2] G. Busnelli, *op. cit.*, pp. 81 ff.

This must be done not so much in order to ascertain Dante's dependence on or independence of Aquinas, but to determine *why* Dante departs, as I think he does, from the position taken by the *Doctor Angelicus* in his conception and representation of Limbo.

As is well known, [3] Aquinas makes a sharp distinction between the fate of unbaptized infants and that of pagans who have reached the age of reason. As regards the infants, he finds Peter Lombard's *poena damni*, with its spiritual torments, much worse than the *mitissima poena* proposed by Augustine. In fact, from the premise that unbaptized children will not in any way suffer from the loss of God's vision, Aquinas comes to the conclusion that the *limbus infantium* is a state of perfect natural happiness — a happiness far inferior to the supernatural one enjoyed by the blessed, but perfectly commensurate with the limited capacity of human nature.

But Aquinas' assumption that human nature is of itself potentially directed towards the fulfillment of God's law proved quite detrimental to the fate of virtuous pagans — or, if not to their *fate*, then at least to the solution of the problem of their salvation.

The pagans who may be called "virtuous" must be adult, and this is the crux of the matter, since adults are endowed with free will. "If free will," Aquinas states (*Contra Gentiles*, 1, III, c. CLIX), "is not sufficient to either deserve or acquire God's grace, it may nonetheless prevent its acquisition . . . It is not without reason, then, that one is said to be at fault if he interposes an obstacle to the acquisition of grace. On His part, God is willing to grant His grace to everyone, because God, as it is written (I *Tim.*, 2, 4), '*omnes homines vult salvos fieri et ad agnitionem veritatis venire*'" ("God wants all men to be saved and to acquire the knowledge of truth"). [4] In other words, faith is a necessary — though not sufficient — requisite for justification, even though faith presupposes

---

[3] By far the most extensive historical study of the theological problem is to be found in Harent's *Dictionnaire de Théologie Catholique* ("Infidèles—Salut des"), VII (1923), cols. 1726-1930.

[4] "...licet aliquis per motum liberi arbitrii divinam gratiam nec promereri nec acquirere possit, potest tamen seipsum impedire ne eam recipiat... Et cum sit in potestate liberi arbitrii, impedire divinae gratiae receptionem vel non impedire, non immerito in culpam imputatur, ei qui impedimentum praestat gratiae receptioni. Deus enim, quantum in se est, paratus est omnibus gratiam dare: '*Omnes enim homines vult salvos fieri, et ad agnitionem veritatis venire,*' ut dicitur I *Tim.*, 2, 4."

knowledge of Revelation. God determines, without any merit on their part, those who are going to be born at a time and in a place where the light of Revelation is available; as well as those others who will be born in the midst of paganism and will be deprived of this light through no fault of their own. But if they are deprived of this "near" disposition to faith, they are nevertheless provided with a "remote" disposition, which is none other than God's will to save all men. Not to respond to such a call, thus moving from the "remote" to the "near" disposition to faith, is within the power of man's free will, and man's failure to respond amounts to a grave sin of omission.

This, it would seem, leaves the virtuous pagans without their virtue; or rather, their pursuit of the natural virtues, if anything, aggravates their failure in not disposing themselves so as to be worthy of God's grace and thus attain their supernatural end. As far as Aquinas is concerned, it would be improper, then, to speak of "virtuous" pagans, since *qua* pagans they are not only under bond of original sin, but also guilty of the grave sin of omission which has prevented them from coming withing reach of the truth of Revelation. As Aquinas explicitly says (*De Veritate,* q. 24, a. 12, ad. 2), "It is not possible for any adult to be without grace and live only in original sin; for as soon as he acquires the use of free will, if he prepares himself for God's grace, he will receive it; otherwise, this very negligence will be imputed to him as a mortal sin." [5] It follows that in his conception of Limbo Aquinas has no room whatever for pagans.

But as we turn to Dante's account in Canto IV of the *Inferno,* the first thing we see is that Dante's Limbo is precisely the dwelling place of adult pagans, side by side with what we take to be unbaptized children:

> Così si mise e così mi fè intrare
> nel primo cerchio che l'abisso cigne.
> Quivi, secondo che per ascoltare,
> non avea pianto mai che di sospiri,

---

[5] "...non est possibile aliquem adultum esse in solo peccato originali absque gratia; quia statim cum usum liberi arbitrii acceperit, si se ad gratiam praeparaverit, gratiam habebit; alias ipsa negligentia ei imputabitur ad peccatum mortale."

>   che l'aura etterna facevan tremare.
> Ciò avvenia di duol sanza martiri
>   ch'avean le turbe, ch'eran molto grandi,
>   d'infanti e di femmine e di viri.
> (Inf., IV, 23-30)

The word "infanti" is all that Dante has to say about unbaptized infants in his Limbo, which makes his variance from Aquinas all the more glaring and worthy of consideration.

Curiously enough, I owe this insight to Father Busnelli, who labored to prove precisely the opposite thesis, that is, the exact correspondence of Dante's thought to that of Aquinas. The correspondence, of course, is there, but only in so far as both Dante and Aquinas think that the infidels *failed* to attain the light of Revelation. Aquinas, however, sees in this failure a personal sin of omission to be added to original sin, and thus must exclude pagans from Limbo. Dante, on the other hand, represents this failure as the inability of human nature to attain Revelation without the help of divine grace, and thus confines his pagans to Limbo.

The "sighs" without laments, the "sadness" without torments, which make the eternal air tremble in this first circle, are the sensory counterpart of the spiritual condition implied by the *poena damni*, of which Peter Lombard spoke in his *Sententiae*.[6] The spiritual suffering of human nature in its privation of longed-for glory is translated in Dante's poetry as the tension between the affirmation of human values alone and the acknowledgement of their insufficiency in the light of the supernatural end of man:

>   Or vo' che sappi, innanzi che più andi,
> ch'ei non peccaro; e s'elli hanno mercedi,
>   non basta, perchè non ebber battesmo,
>   ch'è porta della fede che tu credi.
> E se furon dinanzi al cristianesmo,
>   non adorar debitamente a Dio:
>   e di questi cotai son io medesmo.
> Per tai difetti, non per altro rio,
>   semo perduti, e sol di tanto offesi,
>   che sanza speme vivemo in disio.
> (Inf., IV, 33-42)

---

[6] *Sententiae* II, xxxiii, 5, P. L. CXCII, 730.

It is obvious that only the inclusion of the virtuous pagans enabled the poet to present the drama of men, who "having merits" could not be saved because they lacked baptism; who could claim that the faith necessary to their salvation was not available to them because of God's inscrutable will; who find themselves lost for such defects and not for other faults.

In order to keep the pagans there — in the company of unbaptized infants — without departing from Thomas' premises, a modern theologian, Cardinal Billot, developed a novel theory which he presented from 1919 to 1923 in the authoritative Jesuit journal, *Études,* and which is still debated at least by Catholic theologians. The Cardinal's theory is based on this assumption: "The infidels are adult in age, but not in reason and moral conscience." Nothing could be further from Dante's spirit, but precisely because of this, it may serve to illustrate the distance which separates — at least in this matter — a rigorous and earnest interpretation of theological thought from poetic vision.

For Dante, the inclusion of the virtuous pagans in Limbo, or if you prefer, their exclusion from God's grace, as much as his choice of Virgil as his own guide, is a way of signifying both his continuity with and detachment from a civilization separated from his by the coming of Christ. As Dante scholarship has ascertained, the fate of the virtuous pagans is bound, in Dante's mind, with "the recognition of the essential historical function which he attached to the wisdom and literature of the Ancients. At the very top of the intellectual and moral progress attained by human and natural powers alone, there opens up the gate to supernatural perfection, to revealed truth and to the bliss of the chosen. The two worlds seem to be separated by one point only, and instead between the one and the other there is a chasm which is the mystery of divine grace." [7]

The value which Dante sees in the world of antiquity becomes even greater in the second part of Canto IV, for his representation of Limbo is actually twofold. In the first part, which I have examined so far, Dante conceives Limbo as a place of spiritual torment in keeping with the concept of *poena damni*. But the

---

[7] N. Sapegno, ed., *La Divina Commedia* (Firenze, La Nuova Italia, 1952), II, 249.

second part presents some considerable changes. Not long after his entrance into the first circle, the pilgrim sees a light that "dispelled a hemisphere of darkness," and comes with Virgil to a place occupied by notable people. "The deserved fame which still honors them in your life gains favor in Heaven, and thus promotes them," Virgil explains, and soon after, four imposing figures welcome the return of the Latin poet and include Dante in their "fair school," making him "sixth among such sages." As this honorable company of poets continues toward the light, they arrive at a castle wherein Dante sees people "dignified and grave of great authority in their semblance," speaking among themselves "seldom and with soft voices." From an open place, luminous and high, the great spirits of the past appear: Trojans, Greeks, and Romans; the philosophers, from the pre-Socratic down to the Arab Averroes, the scientists, mathematicians and doctors who have illustrated the genius of the non-Christian world, and more especially of classical antiquity.

One wonders if we are still in the same Limbo. The darkness is gone, the sighs and sadness are no longer to be seen or heard. As we progress from the throngs of infants, women and men who live in "longing without hope" to the castle inhabited by the poets, philosophers and heroes of the classical world we find "neither joy nor sorrow" in the appearance of these figures sorrounded by light. Obviously, if these sages display "neither joy nor sorrow" in their countenance, they can hardly be said to live "in longing without hope."

The analogy with the similar transition from Avernus to the Elysian Fields in Virgil's *Aeneid* is too clear to have escaped notice.[8] We cannot say, however, that Dante forgot his theology on this occasion. In fact, the first suggestion of a light burning in the darkness of Hell may well have come to him from Aquinas himself. It is Aquinas who unmistakably placed Limbo in the highest part of Hell, as Dante does. But in addition to this, Aquinas also saw a twofold Limbo for unbaptized children and for the Hebrew Fathers, which reminds one very much of the two parts of Dante's Limbo, even though the poet replaces the Fathers with the pagans. "Without any doubt," Aquinas says (*S. Th.*, III,

---

[8] Emma Cavendoli, *op. cit.*

Suppl., q. LXIX, 6), "the Limbo of the Fathers and the Limbo of children differ as to the quality of punishment or reward. For children have no hope of the blessed life, as the Fathers in Limbo had, in whom, moreover, shone forth the light of faith and grace. But as regards their situation, there is reason to believe that the place of both is the same; except that the Limbo of the Fathers is placed higher than the Limbo of children, just as we have stated in reference to Limbo and Hell." [9]

As he is not bound to forget his theology, neither is Dante likely to confuse the meaning of that light which shone forth in the Hebrew fathers. But once we accept the fact that Dante, contrary to Aquinas' views, does not attribute to virtuous pagans any personal sin of omission beside the original sin they share with unbaptized infants, it follows that in them, and especially in those among them who have most pursued both knowledge and the natural virtues, there shines forth the light of that *lumen naturale* which, according to Aquinas, God bestows on every human being.

But to have assured the virtuous pagans a place in his Christian Limbo poses a new kind of problem in Dante's mind. The twofold character of his depiction of Limbo of itself reveals the poet's uneasiness with the solution he has adopted. For, on the one hand, he sees the pagans in the first part as suffering the spiritual torment of the *poena damni* which is their retribution for original sin, and on the other, he grants the most worthy of them a serene and seemingly self-sufficient existence in the luminous castle of the second part. From a strictly logical point of view, if we accept Thomas Aquinas' premise that God has endowed even those who live outside of Christianity with a free will potentially capable of assuring their salvation, his conclusion that the pagans are guilty of not having allowed God to save them must be correct.

---

[9] "...limbus patrum et limbus puerorum absque dubio differunt secundum qualitatem praemii vel poenae. Pueris enim non adest spes beatae vitae, quae patribus in limbo aderat; in quibus etiam lumen fidei et gratiae refulgebat. Sed quantum ad situm, probabiliter creditur utrorumque locus idem fuisse; nisi quod limbus patrum erat in superiori loco quam limbus puerorum, sicut de limbo et inferno dictum est, art. praec."

Having placed in his Limbo men of reason, thirsting after truth, yet incapable of attaining it, and not attributing to them the sin of omission which would have plunged them into deeper Hell, creates a tension which is certainly greater than if Dante had accepted Thomas' corollary that all men through the exercise of their free will are either damned or saved.

Immediately after Virgil has described the condition of the souls in Limbo as one of longing without hope, the pilgrim is seized by great grief and presents Virgil with the question which must be on every reader's mind as he comes to this point:

> Gran duol mi prese al cor quando lo 'ntesi,
>   però che gente di molto valore
>   conobbi che 'n quel limbo eran sospesi.
> 'Dimmi, maestro mio, dimmi segnore,'
>   comincia' io per volere esser certo
>   di quella fede che vince ogni errore:
> "uscicci mai alcuno, o per suo merto
>   o per altrui, che poi fosse beato?'
> <div align="right">(<i>Inf.</i>, IV, 43-50)</div>

Dante's grief, the urgency of his double address to Virgil, the veiled reference to the quiver of a doubt, expressed by his "wishing to be assured of the faith that destroys every error," all concur to make us expect as direct and compelling an answer as the question which Virgil has been asked. Virgil's answer can be summed up in one word: Christ, or since Virgil now is not given to reveal as much, "A powerful One who, crowned with the sign of victory," stormed through Hell and came to deliver the souls of Adam, Abel, Noah and Moses — in short, all the Hebrew patriarchs who believed in His coming and thus were saved.

But what does Virgil's answer tell us with regard to the virtuous pagans in whose name the question seemed to have been asked? Virgil's answer points to faith in Christ as a means to salvation, thus implying that the pagans are confined to Limbo because they lack the Revelation of Christ. That is as much as the pilgrim, and through him his readers, are prepared to understand at this stage of the journey. The pilgrim's grief, his anxiety and doubt are countered by Virgil's solemn testimony to Christ's redeeming power. Granted that to a Christian of Dante's time Christ *is* the cornerstone in the unfolding of human history, still to a Christian of Dante's mind the fate of virtuous pagans is a matter far too important not to be more fully investigated in the course of the poem.

Indeed, no sooner have the two poets emerged from the horrors of Hell and set foot on the island where the mountain of Purgatory stands than the first spirit they encounter there turns out to be that of a pagan. This venerable old man, we learn in the course of Canto I of the *Purgatorio*, is the Roman Marcus Porcius Cato, who killed himself at Utica, after fighting for Pompey's cause, in order not to yield to the power of the triumphant Caesar.

Not only is Cato saved, but he is made by Dante guardian of the mountain, the very symbol of that moral freedom which the pilgrim hopes to attain by climbing its slopes. That Cato, a pagan, a suicide and an enemy of the Roman Empire, be chosen by the poet as an archetype of Christian salvation is certainly enough to arrest the reader and to justify the efforts expended by commentators, since Dante tells us nothing, in the poem itself, as to just how this Roman was saved.

It has been pointed out [10] that the Roman authors with whom Dante was familiar, and especially Cicero, Seneca and Lucan, exalted Cato as a staunch defender of civil liberties; that Dante himself, both in the *Convivio* (IV, v, vi, and xxvii) and in the *De Monarchia* (II, v), had seen in the stoic death of Cato a sacrifice made on the altar of his political commitment and moral freedom; that both Augustine and Aquinas had indeed condemned suicide, but "except when inspired by a divine instinct to show forth an example of fortitude," [11] very much as in the case of Christian martyrs, and finally that in the *Convivio* (IV, xxviii), the poet had found no other man more worthy of signifying God than the Roman Cato. That Dante admired and revered Cato as the epitome of moral virtue, there can be no doubt. But he was too strong in Christian doctrine to confuse the sacred with the profane, and

---

[10] The most thorough single study on Cato is, in my opinion, the one by E. Proto, *op. cit.*

[11] *Summa Th.* III, Suppl., XCVI, 6: "Ad sextum dicendum, quod secundum Augustinum (in I de Civ. Dei, cap. 17, 30 et 36), nulli licitum est sibiipsi manus injicere quacumque ex causa: nisi forte divino instinctu fiat ad exemplum fortitudinis ostendendum ut mors contemnatur."

if he says that Cato signifies God, he is certainly not confusing the two, but does so just as he so often sees in Jove an image of God, and as he once calls Christ, "Almighty Jove crucified for us." On the other hand, it is clear that Dante intends Cato's salvation to be taken literally as well as symbolically, for in the course of this episode he reveals three significant details.

The first is that Cato's body will be resurrected in the glory of Heaven ("la vesta ch'al gran dì' sarà sì chiara"); the second, that Cato possessed the four cardinal or moral virtues not by "acquisition," as is in the power of every virtuous pagan, but by "infusion," which would not be possible without the intervention of sanctifying grace through faith; the third, that Cato issued from Limbo at the time of Christ's Harrowing of Hell.

These three details clearly tell — at least to the reader of Dante's time — that Cato is saved, but still they do not reveal just *how* he received the sanctifying grace which he could not have possessed without baptism or faith in Christ. What is remarkable about Dante's silence on this point is that it is deliberate — a cirmumstance which Dante scholars have not seen so far. We know that Cato is saved, we also know *why* he is saved, but Dante finds it natural not to tell his readers *how*. As we will see presently, the poet remains silent because the pilgrim must see Cato's salvation as perfectly reasonable.

This may be easier to understand if we can prove that Dante himself thought so. In Chapter viii of Book II of his *De Monarchia*, which is of crucial importance for the light it sheds on this matter, Dante discusses different kinds of divine judgment and revelation. [12] "In order to arrive at the truth we are seeking," Dante

---

[12] I give here all the relevant portion of this chapter even though I shall refer to its various sections in later points of my discussion. (This and other references to Dante's "minor works" are from Moore's *Opere di D. A.;* the English translation is that of A. Henry, *The De Monarchia of D. A.* [Cambridge, 1904].)

"Ad bene quoque venandum veritatem quaesiti, scire oportet quod divinum iudicium in rebus quandoque hominibus est manifestum, quandoque occultum.

Et manifestum potest esse dupliciter, ratione scilicet et fide.

Nam quaedam iudicia Dei sunt ad quae humana ratio propriis pedibus pertingere potest, sicut ad hos: Quod homo pro salute patriae seipsum exponat. Nam si pars debet se exponere pro salute totius, quum homo sit pars quaedam civitatis, ut per Philosophum patet in suis Politicis; homo pro patria

says, "we must understand that the divine judgment in human affairs is sometimes revealed, sometimes hidden. It can be revealed in two ways: to reason and to faith. For, certain judgments of God can be arrived at by human reason standing on its own two legs — for example, the judgment that a man should give himself for the sake of his country. For if a part should give itself for the sake of the whole, and a man is part of some community, a man should give himself for the sake of his country as a lesser to a greater good... Now, this is a judgment of God; were it not so, man's right reason would not serve nature's purpose, which is impossible." To make his meaning even more clear, Dante goes on to examine other judgments of God to which man must be raised through faith and Holy Scripture. But of this more will be said later.

For the Florentine exile, who found solace in his bitterness in the contemplation of the "unspeakable sacrifice of the most austere Marcus Porcius Cato," [13] the suicide of the Roman is the religious fulfillment of God's judgment carried out through "a divine instinct," "to show forth an example of fortitude." As he seeks Cato's permission to enter Purgatory with his charge, Virgil significantly links the "Power from above" that moves him to the cause of Cato's suicide (*Purg.*, I, 68-75).

Both Cato and the pilgrim understand the meaning of Virgil's words, and there is no need for either the pilgrim or the reader

---

debet exponere seipsum, tanquam minus bonum pro meliori. Unde Philosophus ad Nicomachum: "Amabile quidem enim et uni soli; melius et divinius vero genti et civitati.' Et hoc iudicium Dei est; aliter humana ratio in sua rectitudine non sequeretur naturae intentionem, quod est impossibile.

Quaedam etiam iudicia Dei sunt, ad quae, etsi humana ratio ex propriis pertingere nequit, elevatur tamen ad illa cum adiutorio fidei eorum quae in sacris literis nobis dicta sunt; sicut ad hoc: Quod nemo, quantumcumque moralibus et intellectualibus virtutibus, et secundum habitum et secundum operationem perfectus, absque fide salvari potest, dato quod nunquam aliquid de Christo audiverit; nam hoc ratio humana per se iustum intueri non potest, fide tamen adiuta potest. Scriptum est enim ad Hebraeos: "Impossibile est sine fide placere Deo.'

...Occultum vero est iudicium Dei, ad quod humana ratio, nec lege naturae, nec lege scripturae, sed de gratia speciali quandoque pertingit, quod fit pluribus modis: quandoque semplici revelatione, quandoque revelatione disceptatione quadam mediante. Semplici revelatione dupliciter: aut sponte Dei, aut oratione impetrante."

[13] *De Monarchia* II, v: "Accedit et illud inenarrabile sacrificium severissimi verae libertatis auctoris Marci Catonis."

to know any more about the nature of this salvation than its exemplary function as an instance of divine judgment comprehended by reason. Of course, this is not to say that Cato may have attained salvation thorugh the power of *his* reason alone. We know from Limbo that this is not possible. But granted, as both Dante and his readers of course do, the existence of a purposeful plan in creation executed through God's judgment, what could be more reasonable than the salvation of this pagan who sacrificed himself in the interest of his commonwealth "in order to show forth an example of fortitude" so that others may overcome the fear of death?

In the chapter just quoted from the *De Monarchia*, Dante works a distinction between the divine judgments that are revealed to man's reason and those that necessitate faith in the Scriptures. "There are other judgments of God to which human reason by its own resources cannot attain," Dante says, "but to which it can be raised with the help of faith in what is told us in Holy Scripture. For instance, that none, however perfect in moral and intellectual virtues, in character and in deed, can be saved without faith, though he never even heard of Christ; for to human reason alone this cannot appear just, but when aided by faith it may appear so. For in the letter to the Hebrews it is written, "Without faith it is impossible to please God."

At first sight, Dante's statement that "none, however perfect in moral and intellectual virtues... can be saved without faith, though he never even heard of Christ," may appear as the most glaring contradiction to Cato's salvation — a contradiction all the more striking since the salvation of Cato must be apprehended by reason alone, whereas the exclusion of the virtuous pagans from Heaven demands faith in what is told in the Scriptures. But this contradiction may not be there at all if we make, as Dante certainly did, the important distinction taught by Aquinas with regard to the faith necessary for all in order to be saved.

To the question, "Whether it is necessary for the salvation of all, that they should believe *explicitly* in the mystery of Christ," (*S. Th.*, II, II, q. II, 7), Thomas makes faith in Christ mandatory for all, but then he adds: "Many of the Gentiles received revelations of Christ... If, however, some were saved without receiving any revelation, they were not saved without faith in a Mediator, for, though they did not believe in Him "explicitly," they did, nevertheless, have "implicit" faith through believing in divine Providence, since they believed that God would deliver mankind in whatever way was pleasing to Him." [14] This implicit faith, it would seem, is the faith possessed by Cato who pursued freedom and trusted in a liberator "in whatever way was pleasing to Him" — that is, he killed himself in order to free himself, just as Christ allowed himself to be killed in order to free mankind.

This distinction between explicit and implicit faith removes the paradox of an all-merciful God who cannot save any unbeliever through a gratuitous act of his will. This is, it may be well to recall, the problem which had beset Dante's mind since his exposure to Limbo and which demands now a more direct treatment, so that the pilgrim's faith may be further tested and fortified.

In keeping with the pattern of the whole poem, Dante unfolds his theme of the fate of pagans by steps and by degrees. Just as the progress of the journey shows us the path of Dante-*homo viator* as an ascending spiral, so the working of divine will is not revealed to him simultaneously, but through the cumulative effect caused by the juxtaposition of separate — yet related — moments of the pilgrim *in via*. It is in Canto III of the *Purgatorio*, not long after the encounter with Cato, that the demands on Dante's faith already implicit in Limbo are explicitly made.

Dante is confused when he sees only his shadow projected by the sun, and fears that Virgil may have left him. His ignorance in the properties of spirits such as Virgil, prompts the Latin poet to remind the pilgrim of the limitations of human reason:

> Matto è chi spera che nostra ragione
> possa trascorrer la infinita via
> che tiene una sustanzia in tre persone.
> State contenti, umana gente, al *quia;*
> chè se possuto aveste veder tutto,
> mestier non era parturir Maria;

---

[14] "...multis gentilium facta fuit revelatio de Christo ...Si qui tamen salvati fuerunt quibus revelatio non fuit facta, non fuerunt salvati absque fide Mediatoris; quia etsi non habuerunt tamen fidem explicitam, habuerunt tamen fidem implicitam in divina providentia, credentes Deum esse liberatorem hominum secundum quod aliquibus veritatem cognoscentibus Spiritus revelasset, secundum illum Job. 35, 11: *Qui docet nos super jumenta terrae.*"

> e disïar vedeste sanza frutto
>   tai che sarebbe lor disio quetato,
>   ch'etternalmente è dato lor per lutto:
> io dico d'Aristotile e di Plato
>   e di molt'altri;' e qui chinò la fronte,
>   e più non disse, e rimase turbato.
>   (*Purg.*, III, 34-45)

Virgil's avowal of the limitations of reason may seem at first no more than a restatement of the plight of the virtuous pagans in Limbo. But *there* the focus was on the condition of those spirits in suspense, while the cause of their condition was only indirectly suggested. Whereas here, through Virgil, it is Dante's reason that takes cognizance of its limited power, and thus acquires a new awareness of its distance from God's wisdom. Paradoxically, it is only by admitting its inability to penetrate the mystery of God's design that reason begins to conform to it, to adhere to its laws, in other words, to understand it in the only way in which it is possible for the human creature to understand its creator. This admission of its inadequacy is the very foundation of reason's useful role towards the enlightenment of God's grace. As Virgil bends his brow at the thought of Aristotle, Plato, himself and many others, the pilgrim is raised to the contemplation of a mystery which holds the key both to the fate of those virtuous men and to the purpose and outcome of the whole journey. The end of the canto, through the encounter with King Manfred, a heretic excommunicated by the Church but saved by God, provides the pilgrim with a tangible example of the infinite working of God's grace. Both Virgil's words and the *exemplum* offered by Manfred's salvation strengthen the pilgrim's humble acceptance of God's providence and encourage him to entrust himself to the inscrutable decree of His will.

Virgil's words in Canto III suggest also how the problem posed to Dante's mind by the fate of the infidels is not a mere theological question to be rationally solved by his intellect, but a test to be met through a heightening of his moral certainty. It is the very choice of Virgil as a guide which transforms the intellectual problem into a moral one, so that the exposition of this theme in the *Purgatorio* becomes an integral part of the pilgrim's process of purgation. Thus the assessment of Virgil's efficacy and limitations, as established in the course of the purgatorial journey, acquires the exemplary value that will gradually strengthen the pilgrim's will in his ascent of the mountain. This assessment of Virgil's fate is brought forth in the two encounters with Sordello, in Cantos VI and VII, and with Statius in Cantos XXI and XXII. The first of the two poets is linked to Virgil through Mantua, the second through Rome. The first is a Christian who embraces the pagan Virgil at the very mention of his birthplace, the second a former pagan who attempts to embrace Virgil because he owes him his life as a poet and his after-life as a Christian. Virgil reciprocates the embrace of Sordello, but the distance which separates the two Mantuans in the Christian context of their encounter could not be greater:

> Non per far, ma per non fare ho perduto
>   a veder l'alto sol che tu disiri
>   e che fu tardi per me conosciuto.
> Luogo è là giù non tristo da martìri,
>   ma di tenebre solo, ove i lamenti
>   non suonan come guai, ma son sospiri.
> Quivi sto io coi pargoli innocenti,
>   dai denti morsi della morte avante
>   che fosser dall'umana colpa esenti;
> quivi sto io con quei che le tre sante
>   virtù non si vestiro, e sanza vizio
>   conobber l'altre e seguir tutte quante.
>   (*Purg.*, VII, 25-36)

I see nothing in this passage to substantiate Busnelli's contention that Virgil's "non fare" corresponds to Aquinas' *peccatum omissionis*.[15] That Dante's language here follows closely that of Thomas may even be granted, but his meaning most certainly does not. If nothing else, in restating that his position in Limbo is next to the "pargoli innocenti," Virgil removes any doubt as to a possible disparity in the condition of unbaptized children and that of virtuous pagans. But of fundamental importance are Virgil's words in ll. 34-36. If, as a pagan, "ipsa negligentia ei imputabitur ad peccatum mortale," as Aquinas states, then Dante could hardly have Virgil say that he dwells with those not clothed with

---

[15] G. Busnelli, *op. cit.*, p. 91.

the three holy virtues, but who, *without vice,* knew the others and observed them all." Actually, unless Dante had thought Virgil (and consequently all the virtuous pagans) free from any mortal sin other than the original one, it is quite doubtful that he could have made him his guide in his own path toward Christian salvation.

But it seems time to turn our attention to the context in which this further statement of Virgil's condition appears. At first sight nothing more is said here that we (and the pilgrim) had not known since Limbo. But Virgil's account there stressed the negative side of the pagans' case ("Non basta;" "non ebber battesmo;" "non adorar debitamente a Dio"), whereas here the pagans' failure to be clothed with the "three holy virtues," is countered by the positive merit of having, without vice, known "the others and observed them all."

Coming as they do in the wake of Virgil's warning about the limitations of reason in Canto III, these words of his master leave the pilgrim to mull over the problem of the relation between "the three holy virtues," which he will not see until nightfall in the Valley of the Princes, and "the others" which he has already seen shining on the face of Cato. The pilgrim will have to witness the liturgical act of the first night, and then be taken by Lucia to the gate of Purgatory and be actively engaged in purging himself of the four sins of the will, before he is prepared to understand how the moral virtues can lead to the theological ones through the sanctifying grace of baptism.

This occurs in the encounter with Statius which, as I have suggested, parallels the one with Sordello. Statius, whom God has saved through Virgil's mediation, can pay him a solemn tribute of praise and gratitude:

> ... "Tu prima m'inviasti
> verso Parnaso a ber nelle sue grotte,
> e prima appresso Dio m'illuminasti.
> Facesti come quei che va di notte,
> che porta il lume dietro e sè non giova,
> ma dopo sè fa le persone dotte,
> ... ...
> Per te poeta fui, per te cristiano.
>
> *(Purg.,* XXII, 64-73)

The image of the pagan poet carrying a light which is of no avail to him, but helps those who follow, serves as an exemplary application of the value and function of the light in Limbo. Although Dante uses it in his own unique way, this image is not however altogether new with him. Also Augustine had used it, though not in relation to pagans but to the Hebrew Fathers: "O Jews, you carried in your hands the lamp of the law in order to show the way to others, while you remained in darkness!" [16] But it is precisely this adaptation of an image used by Augustine to symbolize the relation of Judaism to Christianity that is of extreme importance here. Not that Dante intended to replace the Jews with the pagans in the prefiguration of Christianity, which of course would be inconceivable. But in attributing to the classical world a function of unknowing prefiguration parallel to that of the Jews, Dante is following a long tradition of Mediaeval thought firmly established by Augustine and running through Aquinas. It is the force of this tradition which enabled Dante to put in the terraces of Purgatory *exempla* drawn from Graeco-Roman history side by side with those drawn from the Scriptures, and which prompts him here to find the image of the unknowing light bearer particularly fitting to the role played by Virgil in Statius' conversion.

This is perhaps as good a place as any in the poem to stress what is known as Dante's pre-Humanism. While using the general scaffold of Thomistic thought and the particular imagery of Christian literature, Dante injects into both a new meaning dictated by his love and admiration for the world of antiquity. Seen in this light, the problem of the virtuous pagans represents an element of psychological and esthetic tension in Dante's process of integration of Graeco-Roman culture into his Christian, Mediaeval context. The synchretism which allowed the poet to harmonize the great Christian tradition with the equally great classical tradition inherited by Christianity could not have been achieved without a gradual heightening of moral certainty, without the doubts and victories which mark the itinerary of the pilgrim-poet.

---

[16] Sapegno (*op. cit.* II, p. 250) indicates that this possible source for Dante's image was first pointed out by N. Tommaseo in his commentary to *La Comedia*, Venice, 1837.

But we would look in vain for a cleavage between the poet's obvious admiration for the wisdom of the Ancients and the certainty of his faith.

In Canto XXII of the *Purgatorio*, after he has witnessed the exemplary salvation of Cato, after Virgil's warning on the limitation of human reason in Canto III and his assertion in Canto VII that he had known and followed the moral virtues without vice, the pilgrim is finally shown through Statius' account of his own conversion to Christianity how the light carried by a pagan poet could be turned into God's intermediary in an instance of Christian salvation. But if the virtuous pagans can lead men who lived after Christ to the knowledge of Revelation, why can they not themselves be saved?

While the pilgrim continues in his ascent up the mountain of Purgatory and regains that perfect freedom of the will which will enable him to fly upward to Heaven, let us turn once more to that chapter of the *De Monarchia* that is so relevant to this interpretation. Its opening statement was that the divine judgment in human affairs is "sometime revealed, sometime hidden." We have seen how Dante applied judgments revealed through reason to the salvation of Cato, and those revealed through faith to the infidels' exclusion from salvation. We must now examine Dante's position with regard to those divine judgments which are hidden. "A hidden judgment of God," Dante writes, "is one which human reason cannot grasp either by natural law or by scriptural law, but only by some special grace. This may happen in various ways, which are all instances either of simple revelation or of revelation through ordeal." While "revelation through ordeal" turns out to be God's appointment of the Roman race as world ruler and falls without the scope of this study, let us consider Dante's definition of simple revelation, which he divides into spontaneous acts of God — such as God's direct calling to Samuel against Saul — and answers to human prayers. We need not go any further, since we already have all the necessary clues. God's judgments may be made manifest through reason or faith, as we have seen in the case of Cato and the exclusion of pagans from God's grace. But they may also be hidden, so that a special grace is necessary in order to recognize them. And these hidden judgments consist of simple revelations to man, either in the form of a direct calling from

God or of God's answer to prayers. To perceive these hidden judgments, neither reason alone nor reason aided by faith is sufficient. As they can be understood only through a special grace, we wonder whether the poet has ever claimed the aid of a special grace in his upward flight through the Heavens.

Indeed, in the very first canto of the *Paradiso*, as he recounts how he moved with Beatrice toward the Heaven of the Moon, Dante turns to his readers and says:

> Trasumanar significar *per verba*
> non si poria; però l'essemplo basti
> a cui esperïenza grazia serba.
> *(Par.,* I, 70-72)

After this, I am sure that no one will be surprised if, aided by that very same grace, he will be allowed to contemplate two instances of simple revelation of God to man; and if, moreover, one of these, the Trojan Ripheus, is an instance of direct calling from God, while the second, the emperor Trajan, exemplifies God's answer to human prayers.

But before we examine these two salvations in some detail, we must consider the context in which they occur. Fittingly enough, Dante and Beatrice are in the Heaven of Jupiter, where divine justice is unfolded and celebrated. It is here that the eagle formed by all the blessed of this heaven relieves the pilgrim-poet of "the great fasting" which had kept him hungry for so long, and finally formulates his doubt in no uncertain terms:

> ..."Un uom nasce a la riva
> de l'Indo, e quivi non è chi ragioni
> di Cristo, nè chi legga, nè chi scriva;
> e tutti i suoi voleri e atti buoni
> sono, quanto ragione umana vede,
> sanza peccato in vita o in sermoni.
> Muore non battezzato e sanza fede:
> ov'è questa giustizia che 'l condanna?
> ov'è la colpa sua, se ei non crede?"
> *(Par.,* XIX, 70-78)

It is the same question that must have been in the poet's mind since his first confrontation with virtuous pagans in Limbo. But there the question was put indirectly, Did anyone ever through his own merit or another's leave that place? And the answer, we have seen, was a statement of fact, in keeping with the limited capacity of human reason: A Powerful One came and delivered from Limbo the souls of the Hebrew Fathers. The question was then posed again in the *Purgatorio* —albeit still indirectly— through Virgil's admonition as to the limited power of human reason and the need for faith in Christ. This time the question involves the very nature of divine justice, and it is from this new perspective that part of the eagle's answer is first given in ll. 79-90. Rather than explained, the mystery itself is, of course, only reasserted. But through the imagery of the poet we move from the contemplation of God's hidden and manifest working to the motivation of his justice, which is his goodness. Thus, if in God's infinity justice and mercy are one and the same, we can see how the light of Revelation can reach just pagans in ways that are precluded to human understanding. And, at long last, after so much questioning of the pagans' virtue, we can now question with Dante, or rather, with the symbol of God's justice, somebody else's virtue, namely, that of Christians:

>   ..."A questo regno
> non salì mai chi non credette in Cristo,
>   *vel* pria *vel* poi ch'el si chiavasse al legno.
> Ma vedi, molti gridan 'Cristo, Cristo!'
>   che saranno in giudicio assai men *prope*
>   a lui che tal che non conosce Cristo;
> e tai cristiani dannerà l'Etiope,
>   quando si partiranno i due collegi,
>   l'uno in etterno ricco, e l'altro inope.
>   (*Par.*, XIX, 103-11)

The thorny question, Where is the justice that condemns virtuous pagans for not having known Christ?, is answered by Dante in the form of a paradox: No one can be saved without Christ, but God can nevertheless grant his grace to virtuous pagans and to withdraw it from those Christians who have proven unworthy of it. The paradox, however, is such only for the human mind, and not for the infinity of God's mind, which is above the contradictions of human reason and acts according to a superior principle of justice.

This is the context in which the extraordinary salvations of Trajan and Ripheus are introduced, as luminous examples of the inscrutable working of God's will. They are both instances of the "hidden" judgment of God in human affairs, which the pilgrim can directly witness thanks to the aid of a special grace. Ripheus, an obscure Trojan mentioned three times in the *Aeneid* but always in passing, knew and believed in Christ before His coming because of a direct revelation from God. The emperor Trajan, though dying a pagan, came back to life in response to the prayers of Pope Gregory the Great and was then redeemed through the same grace which brought him back to life. In Trajan's case, Dante follows a well established medieval legend, accepted also by Aquinas. The salvation of Ripheus, on the other hand, is due only to Dante and, of course, to God's will.

As we look more closely at Dante's conception of the kind of faith possessed by both Trajan and Ripheus, we find that it is not at all "implicit" faith as defined by Thomas Aquinas. The commentators refer in this connection to Aquinas' distinction between implicit and explicit faith, even though Dante clearly says that the two spirits now shining in the eagle's eye firmly believed in the passion and death of Christ:

> De' corpi suoi non uscir, come credi,
> Gentili, ma Cristiani, in ferma fede,
> quel de' passuri, e quel de' passi piedi.
> (*Par.*, XX, 103-105)

Moreover, God opened Ripheus' eyes to Christ's future redemption to such an extent that,

> ...ei credette in quella, e non sofferse
> da indi il puzzo più del paganesmo,
> e riprendiene le genti perverse,
> (*Par.*, XX, 124-26)

thus making of him an evangelizing Christian *ante litteram*.

My point here is that we cannot speak for either Trajan or Ripheus of Aquinas' implicit fait in divine providence which would only enable a pagan to believe that God will deliver mankind "in whatever way was pleasing to Him." This implicit faith may apply to Cato, of whose faith in Christ Dante says nothing more than what is suggested in the suicide of this Roman for the sake of freedom. But both Trajan and Ripheus must be instances of those revelations of which Thomas states that they were made to many of the Gentiles and which Dante defines in Chapter VIII of the *De Monarchia* as simple revelations of God, either in response to prayers, as exemplified by Trajan, or God's direct acts, as exemplified by Ripheus. The eagle had said that "To this kingdom no one ever rose/ who did not believe in Christ/ either before or after he was nailed to the cross." With exact correspondence, the symbol of divine justice will then say that Trajan and Ripheus issued from their bodies with firm faith in the feet of Christ "to be pierced or already pierced."

But if this is true of Trajan and Ripheus, how will Cato, without an explicit faith in Christ, rise to this kingdom? Cato is now at the foot of the mountain of Purgatory, but must eventually be one of the blessed in Heaven.

This is a question that cannot be answered, just as one cannot say why in the *Purgatorio* Dante cannot embrace Casella in Canto II, but Virgil and Sordello can embrace each other in Canto VII. These and similar questions cannot be answered because perhaps they should not be asked. As T. S. Eliot and others have rightly claimed, you must grant a poet what he asks to be granted within his frame of reference. In the frame of reference of the *Purgatorio*, Cato is saved because a divine instinct inspired him to a supreme sacrifice which shows forth the reasonableness of God's design in human nature. No direct mention of Christ and faith is necessary and the poet can leave the theological basis for this salvation in the background. In the *Paradiso*, on the contrary, it is the theological concept of divine justice itself that is in question, so that both the prerequisite of faith in Christ and the hidden working of God's grace are shown not as mutually exclusive but as integral parts of His divine Goodness.

There is still one more question —by far a more probing one— that may be asked at this point. Granted that baptism and therefore the Church of Christ, are a "portal of the faith," and granted also that in his infinite mercy God may see through that portal whomsoever he sees fit and in whatever way it pleases Him, doesn't the ultimate source of salvation rest in God's will rather than faith in Christ and baptism? If many who now cry, "Christ, Christ," will at Judgement Day be further removed from God than some who do not know Christ, doesn't this mean that predestination and not faith in Christ is the only objective mean of salvation?

This is, with remarkable coherence, the conclusion the eagle gives to its account of Trajan and Ripheus' extraordinary salvations:

> O predestinazion, quanto remota
> è la radice tua da quelli aspetti
> che la prima cagion non vedon *tota!*
> E voi, mortali, tenetevi stretti
> a giudicar; che noi che Dio vedemo
> non conosciamo ancor tutti gli eletti
> ed enne dolce così fatto scemo,
> perchè il ben nostro in questo ben s'affina,
> che quel che vole Iddio e noi volemo.
> (*Par.*, XX, 130-38)

The problem of *gratia Christi* ends, then, for Dante as well as for contemporary theological thought in the greater problem of *gratia Dei*, which examines the relation of God's predestination to human free will. Having made possible for pagans to receive the sanctifying grace of faith through a free act of God, rather than through faith and baptism, the salvation of pagans leads into the larger issue of individual salvation for all men.

After having both raised and confined virtuous pagans to Limbo, in a marked departure from Aquinas' thought, Dante presents a few instances of their individual salvation which are corroborated by Aquinas' views and follow the pattern laid down by the poet himself in the *De Monarchia*. We witness first the salvation of Cato, which shows an example of God's judgment made manifest to human reason. Later in the *Purgatorio* we are told how human reason can be raised by faith in the Scripture to accept the fact that pagans —albeit virtuous and bound to original sin through an invincible ignorance of Christ's revelation— must be excluded from the glory of God's vision. Finally, in Cantos XIX and XX of the *Paradiso*, while the symbol of God's justice restates the necessity of faith in Christ as a means to salvation, we can witness how the inscrutable will of God can bestow faith on pagans living outside of Christianity, but predestined to be saved.

Thus the question asked by the pilgrim in Canto IV of the *Inferno* finds its answer in the unfolding of the poem and in the completion of the pilgrim's journey. The problem of the salvation of virtuous pagans, at first only barely grasped by the pilgrim, is clarified and comprehended through a gradual process of formulations and resolutions. Only through the paradigmatic experience of the journey can the pilgrim move from his initial anguish and confusion in the *Inferno* through the moral growth of the *Purgatorio* to the enlightenment and firm possession of truth of the *Paradiso*. The theme of the virtuous pagans represents therefore an essential element of Dante's *itinerarium mentis in Deum*, giving substance and structure both to his spiritual experience and to the pattern of his vision.

THE *ALTRA VIA* AND GUIDO AS *ATTENDANT LORD*

JOHN MAHONEY
University of Detroit

The chief reason, no doubt, for the striking popularity of the episode of Francesca and Paolo in Dante's *Inferno* is the compelling and immediate basis for empathetic response which the story of the two young lovers evokes from whoever hears it. Such an immediacy of response is not so evoked from the episodes of Ulysses in Canto 26, and of Guido da Montefeltro, in Canto 27. Indeed, the reader seems to react rather with a puzzled and wondering response that Cantos 26 and 27 should present so deep in the malebolge, almost uniquely, two figures for whom Dante's own response should seem warm or favorable at all. It is one thing, even if not unfamiliar to students of Dante, that figures in the realm of the concupiscible should demand both the poet's sympathy and ours, but all that the reader has experienced prior to Ulysses, and all that his subsequent experience in the poem reconfirms supports the justice of his surprise not only in finding Ulysses and Guido presented sympathetically in their dialogues with the poet, but also in realizing that, in the last analysis, it is evident that Dante meant them to.

There are several aspects to the favor in which Ulysses stands. First, and probably of greatest importance, is that Ulysses seems for Dante, the poet, much what he seems for us. He is a figure ever mindful of the poet himself, one who followed a course of experience and of exploration similar, I think, in Dante's characterization of him, to Dante's own unchartered and fearsome decision to follow Virgil's lead into the region of the underworld. If the motives for the journeys for them were different, the timber of the human reaction and of the experience itself was much the same. As Mr. Logan has pointed out, [1] when Dante sees Ulysses appear as the larger flame in the twin fire, he seems to remember his own lines early in the poem.

> Ma io perchè venirvi? o chi'l concede?
> Io non Enea, io non Paulo sono:
> me degno a ciò nè io nè altri crede.
> Perche, se del venire io m'abbandono,
> temo che la venuta non sia folle:
> *(Inf.,* II, 31-35)

Yet it must be remembered especially that the identity of Ulysses which is presented in the *Divine Comedy* is only what Dante wanted to present, since the characterization of him in the poem proceeds directly and only from the poet's celebrated fondness for playing fiction on the unknown detail of the last minutes and hours of his figures' lives. That is to say, that regardless of the characterization Ulysses may have had in the specific tradition in which Dante may have known him, all the identity which the figure, Ulysses, owns in the *Divine Comedy* is the characterization of him which Dante provides within the limits of Canto XXVI.

The same may be said of the figure of Guido da Montefeltro. I have remarked elsewhere [2] of the special importance which this contrast in expectability about the figure of Guido in *Inferno,* and the figure of Buonconte in the *Purgatorio,* has on our understanding of the nature of the figures as correlatives in the poem as a whole. What we learn of Guido, and of course, of Buonconte, contrasts directly, and intentionally, with what the tradition about them bore to Dante. More specifically, Guido's appearance in the *Inferno* is a total surprise for another reason. The assumption about Guido (as a figure by far more contemporary to Dante's readers than Ulysses), was, in the public eye, that of a man who

---

[1] Terence Logan, "The Characterization of Ulysses in Homer, Vergil and Dante; A Study in Sources and Analogues." *82nd Annual Report of The Dante Society of America* (Cambridge, 1965), 19-46.

[2] John Mahoney, "The Living Poet and the Myth of Time: Dante's Christian Comedy," Dante Centenary Lecture, Dante Society of Toronto (Forthcoming, University of Toronto Press).

had chosen a course of repentance and of self denial, and whose death seemed the successful termination to the holy life of his latter days. The contrasts between what one might have expected for Guido and for his son —that is— to find Guido in *Inferno* when the world would have expected his salvation, and to find Buonconte in *Purgatorio* when the world might have expected his damnation, proceed as a direct result from the same fondness on the part of the poet to speculate his fiction on the last days and hours of men's lives. So we may be fairly certain in our surmise that these episodes isolate islands of artistic intention, ones which, upon analysis, seem to have much meaning for the whole structure of the poem. The result is that the figures of Guido and Buonconte contrast with the historical and contextual credibility of all the figures in their respective regions of the poem. Whatever we may know or not know of the rest of the figures of *Inferno*, it seems certain that they were included there because the world's opinion of them would support the likelihood and poetic credibility of the poet's meeting them there. And the same is true for the figures of *Purgatorio*. It is hard not to conclude, therefore, that Guido and Buonconte present two exceptions —exceptions not without risk for the poet's inclusion of them— which indicate that the rest of the figures, those against whom these are effective contrast, serve as correlatives, through the world's judgment of them, to their poetic purposes as exemplars of the vices or virtues which those *canzoni* are demonstrating.

To conclude so —rather, for Dante, to be able to assume that his readers would conclude so— was to remove from himself the stigma of judgment making. If the history of the criticism of the poem has been unmindful of this assumption from Dante, it is less a result of Dante's ineffective craft than it has been his readers' preoccupation with the historicity of the figures themselves.

But the same may be said of Ulysses. Ulysses falls, as a member of a class, into the same group as the figures of ancient times who appear in the earliest cantos of the *Inferno*. In part, of course, the reader's reaction to him must be the same as his reaction to these other figures—one of confusion over Dante's consignment of them all to the realm of *Inferno*. This has been explored, if not answered, in many places by many critics.[3] But the principle difference between Ulysses and the other figures is a difference so considerable that it is one which demands an altogether different and separate reaction to him by the reader: Ulysses is included in the malebolge. His inclusion there would seem to imply that some aspect of his characterization was worthy of inclusion in *Inferno*—an altogether more serious flaw than the kind of providential judgment placed on the figures of classical times as a whole, whatever that flaw may be. Mr. Logan's understanding of this flaw is that Ulysses' error derived from too great an attention on things of earth rather than things of heaven [4] and from a reliance on *esperienza* over the other parts of the virtue of *canoscenza*. Yet Ulysses' description of his own purposes in the last voyage he made —within the characterization of Ulysses presented in the *poem*, and with no respect to whatever classical context he may have— is that he undertook the trip to gratify, he says, the "passion to gain experience of the world and of the vices and of the valor of men."[5] It is important to remark, consequently, that Ulysses' purpose in his trip is identical to Dante's purpose in his poem, and to remember then also that Ulysses almost made it to the *Purgatorio*, which was, for Dante, to follow his experience in the *Inferno* of the vices of men and of the world. The point is, I think, that Ulysses emerges a figure all together admirable for Dante, if providentially damned, and that he must emerge equally so for the readers.

The result of this is that the reader and the critic are confronted with two figures, Ulysses and Guido, both of whom present critical impasses. Ulysses' life, under Dante's fictional play, is transformed from the historical context from which it emerged into the Christian and critical puzzle of wondering the nature of a Providence which could not remit that flaw, seemingly so admirable in men, and of determining the value of the "confession" on which Ulysses is to be judged, that he believed men are "not born to live as brutes but to follow virtue and knowledge." Similarly, Guido is

---

[3] A good example is John D. Sinclair's discussion in his edition (London, 1948), pp. 68-70.

[4] Logan, p. 40.

[5] Ibid.

transformed from the historical context from which he emerges —although one far more contemporary for Dante's original readers— into one who has been judged worthy of damnation because of excessive and unwise trust in the powers of the Holy Office. It seems not too much to say, therefore, that both Ulysses and Guido have been inexplicably condemned by possession of qualities for which common human reaction would have favored them. Ulysses' definition of man's purpose, if incomplete, is at least sound; Guido's assumption that absolution could precede offense is in no sense crass, but only simple, and neither Ulysses' nor Guido's "sins" are complicated by the same irascible involvements which characterize the errors of the rest of the *malebolge*.

Professor Fred Locke,[6] in his essay, "Dante's and T. S. Eliot's *Prufrock*," concludes that Guido of the poem is related to Dante as Eliot expects Prufrock to be related to the reader. The critical result of this observation is intended to justify the integral conclusion into Eliot's poem of the celebrated epigraph to it from Canto 27 of the Inferno: (line 61 ff.). If Professor Locke's remarks serve critical usefulness for our reading of T. S. Eliot, they seem to be not of much help to our reading of Guido. If, however, we assume for the moment that Eliot's *Prufrock* —of poetic importance in itself— originated in Eliot's mind instead as a comment on the nature and characterization of Guido da Montefeltro, other interesting aspects develop. Indeed, with this other pattern in mind, *The Love Song of J. Alfred Prufrock* may be seen as a comment on the minutes of Guido's life just prior to his encounter with the logician devil at the moment of death, and a comment

---

[6] Fred C. Locke, "Dante and T. S. Eliot's *Prufrock*," MLN, LXXVIII, 51-59. This is a highly interesting and valuable paper, but its main point is to establish the integration, by Eliot, of the epigraph with the poem he wrote. Though it is not relevant here in a paper whose point centers on the *Commedia*, my own remarks could be extended to include reference to the many recollections of the *Commedia* which *Prufrock* sounds. In addition to those cited in the main body of this article, one could, briefly, call attention to the themes of the "three beasts" from *Inferno*: luxury, avarice, and pride, or to Prufock's *nel mezzo del cammin di nostra vita* status, or the quite direct reference to one (Lazarus) returning from the dead. In general, it seems that a reading of Prufrock with the *Commedia* clearly in mind goes beyond the conclusion that the epigraph is integral to the poem and may even provide the suggestion that the epigraph serves to attach the poem and all that it means to the contexts of the *Commedia*.

related to Guido not unlike Tennyson's *Ulysses* is in its relationship to Dante's Ulysses. Just as Tennyson's *Ulysses* is poetic fiction inserted in time between the historical image of Ulysses and Dante's fiction about him, so *Prufrock* becomes a poetic fiction inserted between the world's understanding of Guido and Dante's extrapolation on it. If Tennyson's *Ulysses* serves only to reinforce the admirable qualities of Ulysses, especially his determination for knowledge and his willingness to risk human opinion for the sake of his intellectual cause, then Eliot's characterization of "Prufock-Guido" serves only to reinforce Dante's characterization of him as "the attendant lord." If Ulysses is capable of persuasion, neither by the "love of Penelope" or the natural timidity of his own companions, away from his human goal, neither is Guido able "to force the moment to a crisis," to identify the nature of his responsibility, nor, in the end, to deny that he is "an attendant lord," who serves to start the scene, "advise the prince, no doubt an easy tool..."

The effect, I think, makes it necessary to remark that Tennyson, as poetic critic and reader of Canto 26, and Eliot, as poetic critic and reader of Canto 27, have been far more accurate than the rest of us. Taken together, they serve to reinforce what seems Dante's intended reaction from his readers: that Ulysses and Guido contrast with one another, and that when taken together, they identify mutually the true nature of their own flaws. It must be remembered, after all, that Guido was remarking on his life to Dante in the context, not only of what we know, but in the context of what he had just heard Ulysses say. If this is true, then Eliot's characterization of Prufrock, with the character of Guido identified firmly by the epigraph, becomes one of the most accurate readings of Guido we have, especially against the outcast Ulysses' strong statement, which he, Guido, the "attendant lord" had just heard.

Nor does the extent of this judgment in anyway approach the extreme contrast already established by the inclusion in the same bolgia of two figures so much different from one another. On the face of it, Ulysses and Guido have nothing in common — neither stature of human opinion—similarity of historical context, nor identity of characterization. For whatever reason, Ulysses, a figure of strength, a man in search of experience and knowledge, not only almost accomplishes Dante's goal — Purgatory — but in the end stands firm in Dante's high opinion of him, and has remained firm in what he has earned from the poet's readers. Guido, on the other hand, has been transformed from an historical figure of relative indifference into a man victimized by the logic of church law. His victimization by church law serves only to thematize his whole identity. He is a man who served as the agent for another, who, unlike Ulysses, drew away from the moment of crisis, who, unlike Ulysses, did not lead but only followed, who, unlike Ulysses, did not approach, even in the human sense, the common human spiritual goal symbolized by the unattainable mountain. We do not know of Ulysses' reaction to his eternal state, except that he seems to bear it in character; we know, however, about Guido, that he "goes in bitterness." It is significant, too, that the very lines which comprise Eliot's epigraph for *Prufrock* characterize Guido as the only figure in the *Inferno* who is anxious that the "bright world's" opinion of him remain unchanged. This opinion — become in Dante's characterization a fraudulent one — has him resolute that no description of his ultimate state be allowed to reach the "bright world" through a living person. His fear of infamy is precisely that fear which Ulysses never felt. Human opinion, his wife's, his comrades', could not deter his heroic nature from his known human goal, a goal dictated to him by his understanding of men as "not brutes" but creatures determined to follow virtue and knowledge. For Guido, the choice since the day of his entry into religion had been the path of safety. If it turned out badly because he could not "force the moment to the crisis," he wanted to preserve at least the dishonor of his false reputation.

Something may be added in remark about the nature of the "roads" taken by Ulysses and Guido respectively, and about the road Dante the pilgrim took. In a certain sense, the road which Vergil tells Dante he must take at the very beginning of the *Inferno*, and before the journey itself has yet started, is one whose immediate destination is seen later to be the same as the last voyage Ulysses took. For Ulysses, however, the way to the mountain, however close he came, was blocked, and the idea of ascending it out of the question. When Dante and Vergil are first on the shores of the mount of Purgatory, however, Vergil describes that same "road" in other terms. The alternative he presented

Dante in the first canto of the *Inferno* became the experience of the Inferno:

> "A te convien tenere altro viaggio"
> rispuose poi che lagrimar mi vide
> 'se vuo' campar d'esto loco selvaggio:
> *(Inf.,* I, 91-93)

In the *Purgatorio,* the description is somewhat different, and the experience of the road ends far from the ultimate frustration it was for Ulysses. It now makes the prospect of climbing the mount easier, just as it has circumvented the unassailable trio of beasts which blocked "il dilettoso monte" and has brought the pilgrim and his guide to where the climb will be a joke. The lines echo one another:

> perchè non sali il dilettoso monte
> ch' è principio e cagion di tutta gioia?
> *(Inf.,* I, 77-78)

This is how Vergil describes for Dante the nature of the mountain which Dante has turned away from, and to which he must "take another road." But in *Purgatorio,* the prospects have changed:

> Dianzi venimmo, innanzi a voi un poco
> per altra via, che fu sì aspra e forte,
> che lo salire omai ne parrà gioco.
> *(Purg.,* II, 64-66).

Ulysses' attempt, by the road of experience and virtue, was denied, as was the attempt of each virtuous pagan denied, because he lacked the Christian status the fiction of Dante's vision demanded. If an order "dove si puote ciò che si vuole" could permit Vergil to guide Dante through successfully, it must be remembered that it was, after certain limits, a unique experience for Vergil as well as for Dante. But Guido's contrast of character to Ulysses, as described above, is a contrast of character with Dante too. And as Eliot has seen him in *Prufrock,* he is too cowardly either to confront the triple opposition of luxury, avarice, and pride or to choose the "altra via" that is his failure. He could not "dare / Disturb the universe..." he too had "... seen the Eternal Footman hold my coat, and snicker, And in short, I was afraid."

Unlike Ulysses, he need not fear the siren song of "the mermaids singing," he cannot face the threat of someone returned from the dead to "tell you all." The roads Ulysses and Dante eventually took were the same; the courses from which Dante and Guido-Prufrock turned away were the same. But Christian Revelation guided Dante on a course for which Ulysses had only human virtue to guide him. Guido turned away from that also, and settled into the insecure comfort of inaction. In the end, Dante's second attempt at the mount was the one Vergil saw, by contrast, as "a joke," Ulysses was barred by upset and drowning "com'altruì piacque," and Guido, in Prufrock's words, "lingered,"

Till *human* voices wake us, and we drown.

"THERE IS A PLACE DOWN THERE..." (*INFERNO*, XXXIV)

Mark Musa
Indiana University

After his harrowing passage along the body of Lucifer (the descent that became an ascent described so vividly in Canto XXXIV), the bewildered and distraught pilgrim asks of his guide three brief questions to which Virgil responds at length; the canto closes with the travelers' upward climb toward Purgatory. Virgil's elaborate answer has been the subject of much scholarly discussion dealing with cosmological and theological matters; the central problem with which this paper is concerned is of a more modest nature: at what point does Virgil stop speaking? Where, in the text that immediately follows, do the final quotation marks belong?

> Ed elli a me: "Tu imagini ancora
> D'esser di là dal centro, ov' io mi presi
> Al pel del vermo reo che 'l mondo fora.
> Di là fosti cotanto quant' io scesi.
> Quand' io mi volsi, tu passasti 'l punto   110
> Al qual si traggon d' ogni parte i pesi;
> E se' or sotto l' emisperio giunto
> Ch' è opposito a quel che la gran secca
> Coverchia, e sotto 'l cui colmo consunto
> Fu l' uom che nacque e visse senza pecca.   115
> Tu hai i piedi in su picciola spera
> Che l' altra faccia fa de la Giudecca.
> Qui è da man, quando di là è sera:
> E questi, che ne fè scala col pelo,
> Fitto è ancora sì come prim' era.   120
> Da questa parte cadde giù dal cielo;
> E la terra che pria di qua si sporse
> Per paura di lui fè del mar velo,

> E venne a l'emisperio nostro, e forse
>   Per fuggir lui lasciò qui 'l luogo voto   125
>   Quella ch' appar di qua, e su ricorse.
> Luogo è là giù da Belzebù remoto
>   Tanto quanto la tomba si distende,
>   Che non per vista, ma per suono è noto
> D'un ruscelletto che quivi discende   130
>   Per la buca d' un sasso, ch' elli ha roso,
>   Col corso ch' elli avvolge, e poco pende.
> Lo duca e io per quel cammino ascoso
>   Intrammo a ritornar nel chiaro mondo;
>   E senza cura aver d' alcun riposo   135
> Salimmo su, el primo e io secondo,
>   Tanto ch' i' vidi de le cose belle
>   Che porta 'l ciel, per un pertugio tondo,
> E quindi uscimmo a riveder le stelle.

If we take as sole criterion that of theme (and word material), we must assume that Virgil continues speaking until the narrative is resumed in line 133 ("Lo duca e io ...Intrammo..."). In answering Dante's question "...e questi com' è fitto / Sì sottosopra?", Virgil has occasion to mention, as a consequence of Lucifer's fall, the creation of the "luogo voto" (line 125) where the pilgrim and his guide are situated at the moment; the six lines that follow describe one of the features of the 'empty place' (the edge of the gorge cut into the rock by the "ruscelletto"). The second passage, then, is clearly a continuation of the first and, accordingly, should be seen as belonging to the same speaker. It would be absurd to imagine that after line 126 Virgil is interrupted by Dante who would proceed to round off the topographical description that his master had initiated: Virgil ending with "...qui ...di qua ...in su...", and Dante beginning with "...là giù... remoto..."!

Yet with one exception all commentators assume, without making the slightest attempt to justify their interpretation, that Virgil stops speaking with line 126.[1] And a number of them state that in the passage beginning line 127 we are meant to hear the voice of Dante the Poet who, transcending his role of simple narrator, would be exploiting the device of auctorial intervention to give

---

[1] The one exception is Benvenuto da Imola who comments as follows on line 127: "Hic Virg. facit topographiam idest descriptionem loci..."

us further information of a topographical nature. These commentators may have reasoned that since the existence of the "ruscelletto" was unknown to the pilgrim, it could not be referred to in the narrative proper: it is a fact that in the narrative proper of the *Divine Comedy* no event is related that does not take place before the pilgrim's eyes — no place is described that the pilgrim could not see.

Such an assumption, however, betrays absolute ignorance or disregard of the patterns established by Dante in his use of the rhetorical device of auctorial intervention. Whenever Dante chooses to interrupt his narrative it is always in order to offer a comment of a highly personal nature: the voice we hear will be either that of Dante the moralist (in which case we often find an apostrophe to some figure or abstract principle: "O Simon Mago..." [XIX, 1]; "O cupidigia..." [XII, 49]), or of Dante the artist,[2] who may now appeal to the Muses:

> O Muse, o alto ingegno, or m' aiutate;
> O mente che scrivesti ciò ch' io vidi,
> Qui si parrà la tua nobilitate.
> (*Inf.*, II, 7-9)

now to the reader; he may announce his subject-matter:

> O tu che leggi udirai nuovo ludo:
> (*Inf.*, XXII, 118)

urge the reader to find the correct interpretation:

> O voi ch' avete li 'ntelletti sani,
> Mirate la dottrina che s' asconde
> Sotto il velame de li versi strani.
> (*Inf.*, IX, 61-63)

ask for his confidence in the veracity of his report:

---

[2] I am limiting myself to what might be called "full-fledged" cases of auctorial intervention. There is always a suggestion of this device in similes, on the one hand and, on the other, in the use of verbs of saying and thinking in the first person (*dico, credo, io non so*, etc.). And there are numerous cases of this device enclosed in subordinate clauses ("...parlando cose *che 'l tacere è bello*," *Inf.*, IV, 104).

> Ma qui tacer nol posso; e per le note
> Di questa comedia, lettor, ti giuro,
> S' elle non sien di lunga grazia vote,
> Ch' i' vidi per quell' aere grosso e scuro
> Venir notando una figura in suso,
> Maravigliosa ad ogni cor sicuro,
> *(Inf.,* XVI, 127-132)

ask for his sympathy, now for the experiences of his pilgrim:

> Pensa, lettor, se io mi sconfortai
> Nel suon de le parole maladette,
> Ché io non credetti ritornarci mai.
> *(Inf.,* VIII, 94-96)

now for his self-imposed ordeal of remembering painful scenes:

> Finito questo, la buia campagna
> Tremò sì forte, che de lo spavento
> La mente di sudore ancor mi bagna.
> *(Inf.,* III, 130-132)

now for his problems as creative artist:

> Allor mi dolsi, e ora mi ridoglio
> Quando drizzo la mente a ciò ch' io vidi,
> E più lo 'ngegno affreno ch' i' non soglio,
> *(Inf.,* XXVI, 19-21)

Never does he exploit the device in question merely to offer us factual information that the pilgrim himself could not have known.

Thus, according to the distribution of speaking roles assumed by the commentators Dante would not only have shown absolute disregard for thematic unity but would have broken here the rhetorical pattern so carefully observed elsewhere throughout the *Commedia*. It has already been said that no justification has been offered for the traditional interpretation of our passage, and, indeed, it is difficult to imagine that anything of a positive nature could be adduced in its favor. We can only assume that the commentators were forced to take the stand they did by reasons of a negative nature: that they encountered difficulties, real or imagined, in the way of respecting the thematic unity of the passage 127-132 ("Luogo è ... e poco pende"). And it must be admitted that a somewhat closer examination of this passage and of the lines that follow seems to offer at least two such difficulties.

First, the resumption of the narrative in line 133 would be insufficiently motivated: Virgil, after mentioning the creation of the "luogo voto," would end his speech to Dante by describing a passage leading "to" and not "out of" the place where they are!), without giving the slightest suggestion that it would play any part in their itinerary, or any indication whatsoever that the moment had come to start on their way. Yet his words would be immediately followed by the narrative statement "My leader and I entered upon that path" as if this movement were the natural consequence of what has preceded. Surely a much smoother transition would seem to be guaranteed by the traditional interpretation according to which the whole section 127-139 is assigned to Dante: the poet, speaking directly to the reader, would first inform us of the location of a certain passage-way (and he would have no reason to do so unless this were related to his story), then, as narrator, announce the entrance into that passage.

Secondly, the word *là giù* ("Luogo è là giù...," 127) in the mouth of Virgil may well have represented a problem to the commentators: since the place mentioned in the preceding line, "quella ch' appar di qua..." could not possibly be the antecedent of *là giù* (if only because the Mount of Purgatory is not 'down'), they have evidently assumed that our adverb is used absolutely in the sense '(somewhere) down there,' that is in the southern hemisphere or in the center of the earth — where Virgil and the pilgrim were at this moment. In that case *là giù* could not possibly be uttered by Virgil who is already *là giù;* it must be said from the point of view of one who is above. Hence the supposition that in line 127 we are meant to hear the voice of Dante who would be speaking from his position in our world looking from his vantage point upon the scene 'down there.' But if with this conjecture the commentators were satisfied that they had solved the "spatial problem," surely they were over-hasty in arriving at their solution: the Dante of this world (seated at his desk!) looking down upon the fictional characters of his fictional underworld! What could be more absurd than the supposition that an author can have a spatial relationship to the characters of his own artistic creation?

Thus, because the antecedent of *là giù* in line 127 could not be found in line 126, the commentators have chosen to interpret this adverb in an absolute sense in spite of the absurd consequences of such an interpretation — when they might have looked one line farther back (it is not said that the antecedent of a word must immediately precede it) and found the word on which *là giù* depends:

> E la terra che pria di qua si sporse
> Per paura di lui fè del mar velo,
> E venne a l' emisperio nostro, e forse
> Per fuggir lui lasciò qui 'l *luogo voto*   125
> Quella ch' appar di qua, e su ricorse.
> Luogo è *là giù* da Belzebù remoto...

The *luogo voto* is surely the antecedent of *là giù*: "there is a place down there in the *luogo voto* as far away from Beelzebub as his tomb extends."[3]

Now the reader may say: but the *là giù* is still impossible in the mouth of Virgil! He is, after all, in the *luogo voto* with the pilgrim; how then can he say: '*down there* in the *luogo voto?*' How has the discovery of an antecedent changed the nature of the problem which the commentators faced (Virgil saying 'down there' of the place where he is)? No, the discovery of an antecedent is all-important. Whereas the absolute use of the adverb of place is determined by the spatial position of the speaker, no such limitation obtains when the adverb has an antecedent, for it is this antecedent which determines the reference. No matter where "I" may happen to be, I can say 'down there' of a place already referred to as below another place. Where do I have to be in order to say: "There once was a hermit who lived on top of a mountain in the southern Appenines who every week would come down to the valley for provisions. One day when he got down

---

[3] I agree with Barbi that by *tomba* is meant the "natural burella," and that the "luogo voto" of line 127 must be somewhere at the edge of this cavern — not, for example, as Grandgent would have it, that the *tomba* is all of the passage emptied by Satan's fall and that the *luogo* is "just beneath the crust of the earth's surface that supports the island of Purgatory."

there..." The spatial relationships of the storyteller's world need have no connection with those of his story.

Now it may occur that the two worlds overlap, as when the storyteller happens to be in one of the places mentioned in his story; then he must choose between the perspective of his world, of his situation, and that of his story. This is the case in our passage. What Virgil does is to choose first one then the other: with the "nostro emisferio" of line 124 and particularly the "qui" of 125 he has adopted the first perspective, that of his situation at the moment; then, after having mentioned the Mountain of Purgatory ("quella ch' appar di qua...") he shifts to the second, to the perspective of his story — the story of Lucifer's fall ("Da questa parte..."). The "luogo voto" can now be called *là giù* because it is seen from the perspective of Purgatory.

With the establishment of "luogo voto" as the antecedent of *là giù*, which makes possible the attribution of lines 127-132 to Virgil, thematic unity is reestablished and the grotesque consequences of the theory of auctorial intervention for the same lines are avoided. Moreover, with the establishment of Purgatory as point of view we now understand the apparent abruptness mentioned earlier of the shift to narrative in line 133: the mention of Purgatory, which now becomes the pilgrim's goal, must be immediately followed by his entrance into the path that leads thereto, as if in obedience to the laws of movement of attraction that come into play with the sudden evocation of Purgatory. By the same token, with the establishment of Purgatory as the point of view we can understand the brevity with which the journey upward is described: almost 34 cantos were necessary to relate Dante's passage from the surface of the earth to its center; the return to the surface is covered in seven lines. In fact, it is tentatively summarized in the two lines 133-134 in which the goal of the journey is anticipated:

> Lo duca e io per quel cammino ascoso
> Intrammo a ritornar nel chiaro mondo.

And in the seven-line description it was necessary to make only two (independent) statements: "intrammo" and "salimmo su" — the actual arrival at the goal being mentioned in the result clause "tanto ch'...", as if it were an inevitable consequence; and the only indication of haste or speed is expressed entirely in terms of repose negated: "E *senza cura* aver *d'alcun riposo.*" Indeed, the closing lines of the *Inferno* seem to anticipate the spirit of tranquility, of refreshing ease with which the *Purgatorio* will open.

IL *PEREGRIN* E I *NAVICANTI* DI *PURGATORIO*, VIII, 1-6
SAGGIO DI LETTURA DANTESCA

Giovanni Cecchetti
Stanford University

> *Era già l'ora che volge il disio*
> *ai navicanti e 'ntenerisce il core*
> *lo dì c'han detto ai dolci amici addio;*
> *e che lo novo peregrin d'amore*
> *punge, se ode squilla di lontano*
> *che paia il giorno pianger che si more...*

1

Com'è universalmente noto, queste due terzine hanno sempre esercitato, ed ancora esercitano, un fascino del tutto particolare sui lettori. Nella tradizione critica più antica, i commentatori tendono a restringersi e limitarsi all'esegesi, chiarendo le varie espressioni senza mai cedere ad osservazioni di natura più personale. Ma in tempi relativamente recenti si è di solito insistito sul loro carattere emotivo, sull'elegia dell'esule, sulla nostalgia per la patria lontana, e si è perfino cercato di trarle fuori del contesto vedendole come lirica indipendente e come esempio insorpassato di poesia indefinita ed evocativa. Forse anche il modo insolito in cui Dante dà l'ora, in termini, si direbbe, psicologici, anziché astronomici, ha un po' contribuito a far dimenticare che cosa veramente significhino e quanto in realtà lunghe e complicate siano le loro ramificazioni e il loro peso.

La tendenza romantica a dare speciale risalto ai "sentimenti" si può dire sia confluita nella "Lectura Dantis" di *Purg.* VIII di

Eugenio Donadoni, che pure era studioso molto serio, pubblicata nel 1919, ma da allora ristampata varie volte, sia in volume che in antologie di critica dantesca.[1] Ecco quel che in proposito dice il Donadoni:

> Versi, nei quali circola il sangue e palpita il cuore del Poeta: dei non pochi che attestano la sua condizione di esule. Ma il dolore qui è superato: l'uomo ha pianto... l'esilio ha perduto la sua asperità, universalizzandosi e sublimandosi in quelle due figurazioni di sperduti nel mare e sulla terra, con alle spalle la patria dolce e scomparsa e davanti l'ignoto e il terrore, nella immagine eternamente significativa del sole che cade, del giorno che muore: figurazioni indefinite, che, per la loro indefinitezza medesima, vengono a significare assai più che non dicano; e ci parlano dell'uomo irrequieto ed efimero, prostrato nel suo anelito verso l'infinito: e domanderebbero il commento della musica più che quello della parola.

E aggiunge, quasi condensando ciò che ha scritto prima: in questi "pochi versi" "suonano le prime note di quella poesia dell'indicibile, di quel lirismo puro, che sarà la gloria e il tormento dell'età romantica". Ove le due terzine son trasferite in una zona sentimentale e indeterminata che con Dante non ha nulla a che fare, e di conseguenza vengono chiaramente fraintese e travisate. Riprendendo ed annacquando il Donadoni, così scrive Aleardo Sacchetto in quella che è forse la lettura più recente dello stesso *Purg.*, VIII:

> Struggente elegia, in cui i motivi, pensieri e sentimenti confluiscono, fondendosi e sciogliendosi nella soavità delle armoniose terzine. Terzine le quali — fu già osservato con finezza — domanderebbero il commento della musica, più che quello della parola.
> Una struggente elegia, il cui fascino più segreto e profondo è, forse, questo: un 'irreale sospensione fra la terra

---

[1] E. Donadoni, *Il Canto VIII del Purgatorio*, "Lectura Dantis", Firenze, s. d. (ma 1919), ristampata in *Scritti e discorsi letterari* dello stesso autore, Firenze, 1921, e, recentemente, in *Studi danteschi e manzoniani*, Firenze, 1963. I passi citati qui sotto derivano da quest'ultima edizione, p. 4.—La stessa "Lectura" appare in due antologie dei nostri giorni: *Letture dantesche*, a cura di G. Getto, Firenze, 1956, vol. II, pp. 161-180, e G. De Feo-G. Savarese, *Antologia di critica dantesca*, Messina-Firenze, 1958, pp. 196-199.

e il cielo, l'una ancor "presente e viva" e l'altro già imminente, ma solo intravveduto e non ancora attinto.[2]

Non cito di più, ma devo pure osservare che nella seconda parte di questo brano il Sacchetto contamina il Donadoni con il Momigliano, della cui interpretazione riporto subito la parte principale. Il Momigliano ed il Sapegno sono senza dubbio i due commentatori più interessanti del Novecento, e cercano ambedue di tenersi più direttamente al contesto. Dice il Momigliano:

> Spontaneamente le impressioni della verità e del mondo s'infondono in quelle dell'oltremondo, e sull'esordio del canto aleggia una nostalgia insieme terrena e celeste, che unisce in una medesima malinconia le anime che aspirano alla patria celeste e il pellegrino che ha in cuore la lontana patria terrena.

Qui c'è senz'altro del giusto. Ma bisogna pur ammettere che lo sforzo per superare la posizione romantica vi produce uno sdoppiamento fra le anime e il pellegrino. La doppia nostalgia, "terrena e celeste", è accettabile soltanto se si restringe a "celeste" e si aggiunge che è espressa in termini terreni. Ma non è questo che il Momigliano voleva dire. Ed ecco come commenta il Sapegno:

> Ma anche qui ogni nota è funzionale e si lega alla struttura, preannunziando e riportando a un'unità tonale la varia e sapientemente concertata materia del canto. L'elegia dell'esule, che qui risuona con un pathos tanto più intenso quanto più è indeterminato ed impersonale, è riecheggiata e ricondotta alle sue segrete ragioni autobiografiche dalla profezia del Malaspina con cui il canto si chiude. Ma il tema dell'esilio si arricchisce di molteplici significati e si dilata a configurare tutta l'atmosfera religiosa

---

[2] A. Sacchetto, *Il Canto VIII del Purgatorio*, Torino, 1961, p. 6-7.—Per le altre citazioni (dal Momigliano e dal Sapegno) basterà avvertire che derivano dai commenti.—Per ciò che riguarda i commentatori antichi si è tenuta presente la monumentale edizione in folio di G. Biagi, G. L. Passerini, e E. Rostagno, *La Divina Commedia nella figurazione artistica e nel secolare commento*, voll. 3, Torino, 1924-1939.—Per l'esegesi linguistica si rimanda al saggio di A. Pagliaro, *Ritmo e sintassi nel linguaggio dantesco* (in *Altri saggi di critica semantica*, Messina-Firenze, 1961, pp. 287-295).—Dopo queste indicazioni non ci sarà più bisogno di appesantire il testo con riferimenti bibliografici.

> e morale di una situazione d'attesa e d'inquietudine, che coinvolge ad un tempo l'atteggiamento delle anime dell'Antipurgatorio e i sentimenti del pellegrino d'oltremondo...

Qui l'osservazione migliore indica la situazione "d'attesa e d'inquietudine" delle anime. Ma nel complesso non si supera di molto il Momigliano.

Per poter veramente capire tutto il valore di quelle terzine, e delle due immagini importantissime su cui sono centrate, bisogna poter andare molto più lontano, oltre i loro immediati confini psicologici e contestuali, e quindi bisogna tener presente il canto, o piuttosto i canti, a cui appartengono, e insieme tutto il *Purgatorio*.

2

L'autore delle *Chiose anonime* e il Landino, un trecentista e uno scrittore del pieno umanesimo, nonostante si limitino anch'essi all'illustrazione esegetica ed allegorica, davanti alle due terzine citate parlano l'uno di "similitudine" e l'altro di "comparazione". E vero che nessuno dei due sembra avvertire la possibile portata della definizione (né del resto lo avrebbe potuto), ma il fatto che la diano è già di per se stesso notevole. Noi possiamo raccoglierne il nebuloso suggerimento non tanto per esaminare quelle terzine stesse nella loro struttura interna, quanto invece come stimolo a considerarle da un punto di vista assai più ampio.

Si tratta in verità d'una metafora composita, costituita di due metafore complementari che confluiscono e si fondono in una sola. Ma ancora più importante è che ciascun membro del doppio ordine di rapporti analogici su cui si basa ritorna varie volte nel *Purgatorio*, propagginandosi in un complesso di diramazioni che ne approfondiscono e ne precisano la validità, ed appare inoltre anche nelle altre Cantiche.

Per quanto io sappia, non si è fatta mai troppa attenzione alle immagini ricorrenti della *Commedia*, e vanno riconosciute invece come un elemento costitutivo fondamentale. Ogni poeta degno di questo nome fa leva su certe espressioni ricorrenti, su certe immagini, e non per sforzo o per volontà, ma perché in esse spontaneamente si prefigura, e si raffigura, il mondo che egli va creando; esse rappresentano, in altre parole, ciò in cui prendono sostanza i miti della sua fantasia. In Dante ce ne sono moltissime, disposte più o meno in serie, con richiami nei punti cruciali del poema. E se vanno intese nel loro molteplice significato strutturale, allegorico, morale, eccetera — ne va anche sentito il continuo accrescersi e complicarsi, che procede insieme con la crescita del poema stesso, contribuendo non poco alla sua straordinaria pienezza. Allora, mentre acquistano una grande complessità, in qualche caso assumono addirittura un valore chiave, pressoché definitorio, confermando quello che, in un modo più o meno concretamente identificabile, i lettori hanno sempre percepito in un brano, in una Cantica, o perfino nella *Commedia* intera.

Tutto questo implica, s'intende, una lettura totale: perché non si può dimenticare lo sfondo da cui quelle immagini sono scaturite, il terreno su cui son germogliate — ossia le premesse storiche, religiose, culturali, i dati dell'esperienza personale del poeta, quello che egli intende dirci, e nello stesso tempo il vasto complesso dell'opera. Così l'immagine singola sarà vista come anello di una catena, e soprattutto in rapporto a un gran numero di fatti, a un nucleo centrale, metaforico e insieme determinante, di cui è parte inevitabile — e non quale espressione isolata, non importa quanto sembri fascinosa di per se stessa.

Enorme è senza dubbio il peso del "peregrin" all'inizio di *Purg.*, VIII, e dei "navicanti" che al "peregrin" fanno da introduzione e premessa, anzi da componente essenziale. E dato che ambedue le parti della doppia metafora appartengono a una lunga rete di immagini simili, bisogna osservarle quando ricorrono, ora l'una ora l'altra, nei momenti centrali della Cantica.

Ma prima sarà bene accennare al contesto immediato da cui nasce l'inizio di *Purg.*, VIII. Siamo, si sa, alla fine dell'Antipurgatorio, nella valletta dei principi negligenti. Sta per calar la notte, e Dante deve fermarsi, perché di notte, come gli dice Sordello, non si può salire. Sia lui che le anime hanno un intenso desiderio di andare avanti, per passare attraverso la purificazione e raggiungere il porto supremo — la visione di Dio. Dante vaga per la valletta per parlar coi principi e vede, cosa che mi pare assai rilevante, un gruppo di anime che cantano il *Salve Regina*, la preghiera degli esuli anelanti alla patria: "ad te clamamus, exsules filii

Hevae, ad te suspiramus, gementes et flentes in hac lacrimarum valle", dicono i versetti più caratteristici, che servono a introdurre il finale: "et Jesum, benedictum fructum ventris tui, post hoc exsilium ostende". In tal modo, le anime dell'Antipurgatorio, non ancora ammesse nel regno dell'espiazione, esprimono il loro intenso desiderio per la vera patria, o per il "ritorno". A questo punto viene ad inserirsi nel racconto l'indicazione dell'ora, con il "peregrin" e i "navicanti".

3

L'umanità dantesca è concepita, secondo il pensiero cristiano e cattolico, come un coro a cui, per attitudine naturale, tendono tutti gli individui. L'*Inferno* è il regno degli esclusi: per questo ognuno vi resta inchiodato alla sua rabbia, al suo gesto, che costituisce anche la sua disperazione; e ognuno vi parla in termini personali, col rancore dell'espulso, sempre in opposizione al coro. Perfino quelli che sono animati dalla passione politica, la quale di per se stessa avrebbe un senso collettivo e corale, non si esprimono mai in termini collettivi, bensì in termini che si riferiscono unicamente a loro stessi, al loro "Io" isolato e protervo.

Nel *Purgatorio* non si può avere altro che la situazione opposta, e sebbene il coro supremo non sia ancora raggiunto (lo è soltanto in quanto le anime san con assoluta certezza che vi arriveranno), ognuno vi si sente potentemente attratto, in una specie di gravità rovesciata. Questa spinta ascensionale, connaturata e istintiva, attrae tutti verso il luogo a cui appartengono fin dalla nascita, come dirà Beatrice al principio del *Paradiso*:

> ma folgore, fuggendo il proprio sito,
> non corse come tu ch'ad esso riedi.
> (*Par.*, I, 92-93)

Il Paradiso è dunque "il proprio sito", la vera patria a cui ognuno ritorna o vuol tornare. Dante aveva espresso lo stesso concetto in *Convivio*, IV, XII, 14: "lo sommo desiderio di ciascuna cosa, e prima da la natura dato, è lo ritornare al suo principio". Nella *Commedia* lo mette anche sulle labbra di Tommaso d'Aquino, il quale dice che San Francesco con la morte ritornò "al suo regno"

(*Par.*, XI, 116), e lo ripete nel linguaggio immaginoso di Piccarda: Dio e la sua volontà è "quel mare al qual tutto si move" (*Par.*, III, 86), è il porto in cui si placa ogni ansia e si appaga ogni desiderio. Tale appagamento, che è la meta ultima della creatura insoddisfatta, Dante, seguendo la teologia e la liturgia, lo chiama "pace".

Non ci sarà bisogno ora di citare, come fonte e come sostegno, i padri della chiesa, i teologi, o il rituale, perché si tratta di cose notissime a chiunque abbia un minimo di familiarità con le tradizioni del cristianesimo. Basterà invece riferirsi ad alcuni dei moltissimi casi della *Commedia* in cui la parola "pace" ritorna in questo senso e in modo più o meno accentuato. "Pace", intesa come unione con Dio, sarà il saluto biblico-liturgico di Stazio, quando dice ai due pellegrini: "Frati miei, Dio vi dea pace" (*Purg.* XXI, 13), e sarà anche la risposta di Virgilio ("nel beato concilio / ti ponga in pace la verace corte", *Id.*, 16-17), il quale sentendosi escluso dal coro e riconoscendo l'impossibilità di potervi essere mai ammesso, si dice relegato nell' "eterno esilio". E sarà la definizione che l'angelo dell'astinenza potrà dare del Paradiso nel penultimo girone del *Purgatorio:* "quinci si va chi vuole andar per pace" (*Purg.*, XXIV, 141). Più notevole ancora è vederla ricorrere in due versi di struttura pressoché identica, il primo dei quali si riferisce non solo all'appagamento paradisiaco, ma all'esilio terreno, che a quell'appagamento dovrebbe preludere: "e da esilio venne a questa pace" (*Par.*, X, 129), dice Tommaso d'Aquino di Boezio, offrendoci nel frattempo una doppia definizione; ed "e venni dal martiro a questa pace" (*Par.*, XV, 148) afferma Cacciaguida di se stesso e del luogo in cui ora si trova. Anche Francesca aveva pronunciata quella parola, sentendovi lo scopo unico della vita umana, e insieme avendo chiara la coscienza di doverne restar per sempre priva: "noi pregheremmo lui de la tua pace" (*Inf.*, V, 92). Ma se "pace" è il risultato dell'unione totale con Dio e con la sua volontà, comporta anche il totale annullamento della propria personalità: "e 'n la sua volontade è nostra pace" (*Par.*, III, 85; ma si vedano anche i vv. 79-81 dello stesso canto) dice Piccarda, con parole simili a quelle con cui l'Aquila chiuderà il suo discorso (*Par.*, XX, 138), affermando implicitamente che il Paradiso consiste nel dimenticarsi in un coro che a sua volta si dimentica in Dio. Allora il pellegrinaggio del Purgatorio non servirà a liberare le anime soltanto dalle tendenze peccaminose ma anche dai loro atteggiamenti individuali, rendendole capaci di quell'annullamento, di quella "pace", ottenibile nella patria celeste.

In *Vita Nuova* XL Dante aveva definito "peregrino" "chiunque è fuori della sua patria". Nella *Commedia* egli estende la lontana definizione attribuendole un largo significato religioso e teologico; per cui "peregrino" diventa chiunque sia incamminato verso il coro finale, tanto se si trova ancora entro i limiti dell'esistenza terrena che nell'Antipurgatorio o nel Purgatorio. Si pensi infatti alla risposta di Sapia, quando Dante domanda a un gruppo di anime se c'è nessun italiano fra loro:

> O frate mio, ciascuna è cittadina
> d'una vera città: ma tu vuo' dire
> che vivesse in Italia peregrina.
> (*Purg.*, XIII, 94-96)

La "vera città" è naturalmente quella patria di cui ho parlato, quella "Roma onde Cristo è romano" (*Purg.*, XXXII, 101), alla quale tutti appartengono, perché ogni anima, chiosa il Landino, "essendo creata da Dio di niente, a sua imagine e similitudine et immediate, non può avere altra patria che la celeste". Il resto è pellegrinaggio. Dante insisterà su questo significato di "peregrino" in tutta la seconda Cantica. Già all'inizio, quando le anime, scese dal "vasello snelletto e leggiero", si sentono smarrite nel nuovo ambiente, e chiedono a Virgilio e a Dante se conoscono "la via di gire al monte", il Maestro risponde:

> Voi credete
> forse che siamo esperti d'esto loco;
> ma noi siam peregrin come voi siete.
> (*Purg.*, II, 61-63)

Un continuo senso di transito domina in tutto il *Purgatorio*, l'unica Cantica immersa nel concetto di tempo, dove ognuno si sente in cammino verso l'alta "città" ed espia con gioia ("io dico pena, e dovria dir sollazzo", precisa appunto Forese in *Purg.*, XXIII, 72). L'immagine del "peregrin", che contribuisce non poco a crearlo, dopo essere apparsa nella grande metafora dell'inizio di *Purg.* VIII, ed avere assunto un peso tutto particolare, ritorna proprio mentre ci si avvicina alla sommità della montagna. Passando accanto a Dante, Virgilio e Stazio, la turba "tacita e devota" dei golosi li guarda con meraviglia

> sì come i peregrin pensosi fanno,
> giugnendo per cammin gente non nota,
> che si volgono ad essa e non restanno.
> (*Purg.*, XXIII, 16-18)

E vien ripresa subito dopo con un significato ancor più comprensivo. È mattina; Dante ha sognato Lia che raccoglieva i fiori cantando:

> e già per li splendori antelucani,
> che tanto a' pellegrin surgon più grati
> quanto, tornando, albergan men lontani...
> (*Purg.*, XXVII, 109-111)

Siamo nel Paradiso Terrestre, ove il "peregrin", tutt'altro che "nuovo", è ormai vicino al "proprio sito", sta per finire il suo viaggio di ritorno, secondo quanto dice, come s'è visto, San Tommaso in *Par.*, XI, 116, per arrivare nella sua patria, o nella sua "città".[3] Le parole "tornando" e "men lontani" hanno qui un peso fondamentale, e confermano il senso di viaggio verso il coro supremo implicito nell'immagine del "peregrin". Ora Dante, come le anime che raggiungono la vetta, potrà secondare la gravità ascensionale senza frapporre ostacoli di sorta: "Ond'io leva 'mi" (*Purg.*, XXVII, 113); tale forza di attrazione verso l'alto si affinerà sino al punto di non farsi nemmeno più sentire durante la salita verso l'Empireo, perché nel clima fermo dell'eternità beatifica lo

---

[3] Per questo concetto di "ritorno", su cui mi son trattenuto allo scopo di mettere in risalto la natura e l'importanza di un'immagine, si potrebbe esser tentati a una discussione sui possibili precedenti platonici della cultura dantesca. Ma Dante stesso, in *Par.*, IV, 49 e ss., confuta la teoria platonica della preesistenza delle anime nelle stelle, donde discenderebbero per incarnarsi e dove risalirebbero dopo la morte del corpo, considerandola inconciliabile con la dottrina cristiana. È molto meglio tenersi alla tradizione biblica e patristica. Infatti, già in *Eccle.*, 12, 7, dell'uomo e della sua morte si dice: "et revertatur pulvis in terram suam unde erat, et spiritus redeat ad Deum qui dedit illum". E si sa come un concetto simile sia sempre stato parte integrante del pensiero cristiano, perché indissolubilmente legato con il principio dell'anima creata direttamente da Dio e perciò immortale.

scorrere da un cielo all'altro non sarà il risultato d'un movimento fisico bensì di una purissima inclinazione spirituale. Ma proprio lassù Dante si sentirà finalmente arrivato. Allora anche l'immagine del "peregrin" riapparirà per l'ultima volta, ricca di tutto il senso che aveva sempre racchiuso:

> e quasi peregrin che si ricrea
> nel tempio del suo voto...
> (*Par.*, XXXI, 43-44)

Ora egli è in patria, misticamente "tornato". —Tale specie di coronamento paradisiaco dell'immagine in questione è quanto mai significativo. Si sa che il *Paradiso* è la Cantica dove tutto si chiarifica e si definisce. Neppure le più semplici e appariscenti linee direttive del poema (dagli intenti polemici di Dante alla missione di riformatore politico e sociale che si è imposta) si possono capire senza il *Paradiso*. Per cui sarà giusto allora che proprio lassù anche le immagini principali —o i concetti-miti della *Commedia*— vengano a trovare la loro soluzione.

Quel che si è detto finora, o quel che si dirà più avanti, non deve far pensare che si vogliano ricercar delle simmetrie nell'interno di una o più Cantiche. Le simmetrie per se stesse son cosa di poco rilievo; in Dante ce ne sono moltissime, e semmai il compito di chi le nota dovrebbe esser quello di dimostrare se rimangono o meno puramente esterne e strutturali. Qui si vuole invece mettere in luce il cammino di un'immagine chiave, che si trasforma in una specie di terminologia, in un nodo espressivo tutto particolare, e che contiene uno dei filoni centrali della *Commedia*. Nel corso di tale cammino è quanto mai notevole veder passare il "peregrin" per l'inizio di *Purg.* VIII. Si tratta del punto cruciale dell'Antipurgatorio: le anime tese alla purificazione non posson procedere, e per conseguenza son costrette a reprimere l'aspirazione e la spinta verso l'alto. Sentono il pungolo del "proprio sito", e non possono incamminarvisi. Le coglie allora una profonda nostalgia, espressa da Dante per mezzo di un densissimo rapporto analogico; ma non è la nostalgia dei commentatori moderni, la nostalgia del passato, del pellegrinaggio terreno ormai finito, bensì la nostalgia del futuro, della patria vera a cui desiderano "tornare".

È stato scritto ripetutamente che *Purg.* VIII è il canto dell'esilio. Senza dubbio; senonché l'esilio è il tema di tutta la seconda Cantica, sebbene qui sia svolto in modo assai più diretto e insistito a causa della speciale situazione delle anime e di Dante stesso, e a causa dei dati dell'esperienza personale del poeta, che (come vedremo più avanti) vi son richiamati ad esprimere, di riflesso, il nuovo esilio, e perciò vengono a trasformarsi essi stessi in corrispondenze espressive, ossia in rapporti analogici. In *Purg.* VIII, in altre parole, non si vuol cantare nè l'esilio delle anime dalla terra nè l'esilio di Dante poeta, non questo *doppio* esilio, come potrebbe sembrare a prima vista, ma un *altro* esilio.

4

Ho detto sopra che l'immagine dei "navicanti" introduce e rincalza quella del "peregrin" (che va considerata centrale) finché non vi confluisce come componente; che non sono due immagini ma una sola, distribuita in due parti, e anzi ripetuta. L'unica maniera di render convincente un'asserzione simile è dimostrare che per Dante le due immagini sono affini e hanno un significato sostanzialmente identico.

Si sa che il viaggio della vita è stato tradizionalmente espresso con la metafora della navigazione. Dante l'adopera già in *Convivio* IV, XXVIII, 2, immettendovi anche il concetto di ritorno che abbiamo incontrato illustrando il "peregrin": "la nobile anima... ritorna a Dio, sì come a quello porto onde ella si partio quando venne ad intrare nel mare di questa vita". Nella *Commedia* uno degli esempi più memorabili s'incontra nell'episodio di Guido da Montefeltro: "quando mi vidi giunto in quella parte / di mia etade ove ciascun dovrebbe / calar le vele e raccoglier le sarte" (*Inf.*, XXVII, 79-81), in cui si allude non a una fine ma a un principio, non a un arrivo, ma alla preparazione per una nuova partenza — quella del "vasello snelletto e leggiero". Nel *Purgatorio* questa immagine occorre ripetutamente; e prima di tutto ad indicare il poema stesso ("per corer migliori acque alza le vele / omai la navicella del mio ingegno, / che lascia dietro a sé mar sì crudele", *Purg.*, I, 1-3), ripetuta all'inizio del *Paradiso* nello stesso senso ("dietro al mio legno che cantando varca...", "l'acqua ch'io prendo già mai non si corse", *Par.*, II, 3 e 7). Ma il poema ed il viaggio coincidono, sono la stessa cosa. Per cui ritornerà come metafora del cammino della purificazione. —Da questo punto di vista si potrebbe dire che fosse prodotta dalla geografia stessa della montagna del Purgatorio, circondata da ogni lato dall'acqua— un'acqua che non fu mai navigata da "omo che di tornar sia poscia esperto" (*Purg.*, I, 132), dice Dante con evidente riferimento ad Ulisse —come chiosa, fra i commentatori antichi, Benvenuto (e si noti a prova anche la corrispondenza verbale fra questo "esperto" e quello di "ch'i'" ebbi a divenir del mondo esperto" di *Inf.*, XXVI, 98)— e insieme con la coscienza di mettere il proprio viaggio in diretto contrasto con quello dell'eroe greco.

Se la metafora della navigazione indica il cammino della vita e il poema-viaggio di Dante, non dovrà sorprendere vederla spontaneamente diventare uno dei modi costanti per esprimere il pellegrinaggio del Purgatorio e l'ansia delle anime verso il porto della pace suprema. Gioveranno ancora gli esempi. All'ingresso dell'Antipurgatorio Virgilio spiega la natura della montagna, "che sempre al cominciar di sotto è grave; e quant'uom più va su e men fa male" (*Purg.*, IV, 89-90), e aggiunge:

> Però, quand'ella ti parrà soave
> tanto, che su andar ti fia leggero
> com'a seconda giù andar per nave,
> allor sarai al fin d'esto sentero.
> (*Purg.*, IV, 91-94)

Ora l'immagine viene a comprendere in sé anche la gravità ascensionale di cui si è parlato. Sulla soglia del quarto Girone, nel centro della Cantica, costretti ancora alla sosta perché il sole sta per tramontare, Dante e Virgilio rimangono

> affissi
> pur come nave ch'a la piaggia arriva.
> (*Purg.*, XVII, 77-78)

E presso la cima del monte, quasi alla fine della purificazione, alleggerito dal lungo cammino, Dante mentre parla con Forese (e proprio poco prima era ritornato il "peregrin"), si sentirà esattamente come quella nave che, a detta di Virgilio, seconda la corrente:

> ma, ragionando, andavam forte,
> sì come nave pinta da buon vento.
> (*Purg.*, XXIV, 2-3)

Allora, anche immagini a prima vista diversissime, assumono un'affinità insospettata. Nel Paradiso Terrestre Dante dice: "al volo mi sentia crescer le penne" (*Purg.*, XXVII, 123), che potrebbe esser benissimo il risultato di una contaminazione fra le metafore di navigazione che si riferiscono al viaggio-poema e il volo d'Ulisse ("dei remi facemmo ali al folle volo", *Inf.*, XXVI, 125). Il nuovo volo, attraverso il Paradiso, a cui Dante si sente pronto dopo la purificazione e dopo le ultime parole di Virgilio, a suo tempo sarà chiamato "alto" (*Par.*, XV, 54 e XXV, 50). Si potrebbe dire che così egli intenda continuare il raffronto fra i due viaggi — l'uno ("folle") che senza l'aiuto della Grazia vorrebbe oltrepassare i limiti dell'umano, e l'altro ("alto") che raggiunge la trasumanazione proprio in virtù della Grazia. È certo che l'immagine del "volo", anche se non si accetta questa contaminazione, nel *Paradiso* sostituisce, per il personaggio-autore, l'immagine della "nave" e dei "navicanti" che caratterizza invece il cammino del *Purgatorio*. Ma di contaminazione si è tentati di parlare anche per altre immagini, come per il caso di "acque della pace" (*Purg.*, XV, 131), in cui la parola "pace" ha il senso che abbiamo visto, e "acqua", di evidente derivazione biblica, rientra in tutto un ciclo di metafore affini.

In maniera diversa, ma non meno notevole, per ritornare a noi, la navigazione ricorre ancora in uno dei canti di Forese. A un certo momento Dante afferma che le condizioni politiche attuali (e si sa la fondamentale importanza che il fatto politico ha in tutta la *Commedia;* tale da suggerirci che proprio in esso risieda la molla remota da cui scaturì il nucleo primo del poema) gli danno il desiderio di morire al più presto possibile, di abbandonare una volta per tutte la speranza di veder riformata una società corrotta:

> "Non so", rispuos'io lui, "quant'io mi viva;
> ma già non fia 'l tornar mio tanto tosto,
> ch'io non sia col voler prima alla riva..."
> (*Purg.*, XXIV, 76-78)

A parte la profonda tristezza racchiusa in questi versi, spiegabile con il fatto che il personaggio Dante sta parlando con un intimo amico, e tenendo a mente che la "riva" è quella del secondo canto del *Purgatorio,* là "dove l'acqua di Tevero s'insala", non si può tralasciar di notare che nemmeno qui si tratta d'un arrivo, ma d'una partenza, cioè dell'inizio di una nuova navigazione e di un nuovo pellegrinaggio, e quindi il riferimento si riconnette alla stessa serie purgatoriale che son venuto illustrando.

Le immagini di navigazione sono per Dante un altro modo di definire il suo viaggio. E i "navicanti" del secondo verso di *Purg.* VIII fan parte, dunque, insieme al "peregrin", di una lunga metafora a indicare il camino verso il coro celeste, verso il "ritorno", o verso l'annullamento della propria personalità in Dio; dicono cioè il desiderio di arrivare in patria, o in porto, al più presto possibile. Ed è indicativo che questa metafora così composita appaia in tutta la sua ricchezza proprio nel momento in cui, come si diceva, le anime son costrette al ritardo. Qui i "navicanti" e il "peregrin", che nel resto della Cantica saranno sempre separati (quasi il riprendere di un solo capo del doppio filo di cui è costituita la catena), s'incrociano e s'annodano per la prima e l'ultima volta, dandoci uno dei nuclei metaforici del *Purgatorio*. Va da sé allora che il loro valore, nel vasto contesto a cui appartengono, diventa davvero paradigmatico e definitorio.

5

Se, con quel che si è detto finora, non si è inteso in nessun modo di risolvere l'inizio di *Purg.* VIII in una determinazione puramente ed esclusivamente concettuale, ma piuttosto di metterne in luce la straordinaria ricchezza, bisogna, d'altro lato, riconoscere che il fatto concettuale esiste, e che le varie situazioni create dalla fantasia del poeta si configurano in origine come esemplificazioni dei concetti di cui è costituito il suo mondo. In Dante non esiste mai né il descrittivo né il puramente lirico; tutto ha una funzione precisa e si genera dai fatti rappresentati. Ogni parola, ogni immagine deriva da una particolare situazione e insieme dalle necessità dell'intero poema. Ci son poeti che cominciano da un'immagine, intorno alla quale costruiscono il loro edificio, elaborandola, sviluppandola, circondandola d'altre immagini, finché non arrivano a un quadro più complesso. In Dante questo non avviene mai. In lui nasce prima il quadro da rappresentare (ossia il concetto da esemplificare — due cose sempre concomitanti), e le immagini non sono altro che la materia naturale in cui esso spontaneamente prende sostanza. Di qui la forza e la grande unità del suo poema; di qui la mancanza di ogni compiacenza verbale; di qui l'impossibilità, per noi lettori, di staccare dalla *Commedia* una terzina, un verso, o finanche una singola parola. E di qui anche le ragioni per cui le immagini principali —essendo ciò in cui si concretano e si rappresentano i concetti centrali— vengono riprese e richiamate, o variate, lungo tutto il poema, quasi creando un'altra struttura, in apparenza completamente diversa da quella a cui ci si riferisce di solito, ma in realtà inevitabilmente congiunta ad essa, e forse anche piú significativa.

Un punto su cui bisogna insistere è quello relativo all'esperienza personale di Dante. Molti commentatori moderni, per *Purg.* VIII, e soprattutto per le due prime terzine, che si ricollegano, in uno dei parallelismi comuni a moltissimi canti, alle ultime (ma hanno anche un loro perfetto parallelismo interno: l'una dedicata interamente ai "navicanti" e l'altra al "peregrin"), hanno parlato di motivi autobiografici. Qui c'è senz'altro del vero. Perché non c'è nulla nel mondo interiore dell'uomo, a cominciare dalle opere poetiche, che non derivi, seppure in modo assai distante, dall'esperienza personale. Quel che importa è vedere se il risultato, cioè il fatto creato, rimanga autobiografico o meno. Senza dubbio Dante provò la nostalgia dell'esule, l'amarezza di chi è stato strappato ad "ogni cosa diletta" (*Par.*, XVII, 55). Ma qui tali sentimenti si tramutano, come s'è visto, nello stato d'animo dei pellegrini dell'Antipurgatorio che anelano alla vera patria ("Et Jesum, benedictum fructum ventris tui, post hoc exsilium ostende"). E il fatto autobiografico puro e semplice viene respinto da tutto il contesto e diventa, per riferirmi di nuovo ad affermazioni precedenti, parte di una vastissima trama di rapporti analogici. Perché in Dante, come non esiste mai né il descrittivo né il puramente lirico, non esiste mai nemmeno il puramente autobiografico. Anche per le invettive politiche si potrebbe dire che nascono dalle sventure personali di Dante, eppure in realtà queste sventure non furono mai più di uno stimolo alla riflessione che lo condusse a formulare un generoso quanto illusorio disegno per riformare la società contemporanea. Ed i risultati nella *Commedia* sono talmente alti che si può dire che col fatto personale non abbian più alcuna relazione diretta. Lo stesso vale per tutto il resto — e particolarmente per quei passi che hanno sempre esercitato tanto fascino sui lettori. Si pensi ai "ruscelletti che de' verdi colli / del Casentin discendon giuso in Arno" (*Inf.*, XXX, 64-65). Certo Dante li aveva visti, e li aveva amati; ma nel poema diventano la sete di Maestro Adamo, anzi un modo di esprimere quella sete; e così lo stormire delle foglie della Pineta di Ravenna, in *Purg.*, XXVIII, 19-21, si cambia per analogia espressiva nel moto della foresta del Paradiso Terrestre.

Lo stesso avviene all'inizio di *Purg.* VIII, dove Dante presenta in termini terreni la tensione delle anime costrette alla sosta durante l'ultimo cammino verso la patria. La nostalgia dell'esule si transforma nella loro stessa ansia. È per questo che il tema dell'esilio continua per tutto il canto, con Nino Visconti, esiliato in terra e nell'Antipurgatorio, e con Currado Malaspina, che, esilato nello Antipurgatorio, parla a Dante di esilio. Tali corrispondenze danno ancor maggior risalto alla condizione delle anime. E perciò, anziché a "ragioni autobiografiche" (per citare il Sapegno), sarà meglio riferirsi, come in tanti altri punti della *Commedia,* a remote radici di carattere personale, le quali diventano parte integrante del poema e perciò si traducono in qualcosa di totalmente spersonalizzato.

Ma qui si voleva dar soltanto un rapido saggio di lettura dantesca, partendo dalla premessa che un'immagine, anche quando appare isolata, va vista nel suo scorrere e diramarsi per l'ampio contesto di un'intera Cantica e possibilmente di tutto il poema. Perché è proprio attraverso queste diramazioni e legami che essa acquista una vitalità e una rirchezza assai maggiore di quanto si sarebbe potuto sospettare. Così, se ce n'era bisogno, si è avuta insieme una riprova della straordinaria compattezza e coerenza, non solo strutturale ma espressiva (due cose che in Dante coincidono sempre), della *Commedia.*

E nel frattempo si è cercato anche di mostrare che l'inizio di *Purg.* VIII va letto come un'analogia. Dante vi presenta non il pellegrino e i naviganti in terra, ma l'inquietudine delle anime tese nel desiderio nostalgico del ritorno al "proprio sito". Per cui i sentimenti —se vi vuole usare questa parola— terrestri, su cui fa leva, appartengono a una terminologia, che va intesa in senso metaforico, adoperata a dire la condizione di quelle anime nel loro attuale pellegrinaggio.

DANTE AND ISLAM: HISTORY AND ANALYSIS OF A CONTROVERSY

VICENTE CANTARINO
Indiana University

> A me, che morto son, convien menarlo
> per lo 'nferno qua giù di giro in giro.
> E quest'è ver così com'io ti parlo.
>   *Inferno* XXVIII, 49-51
> e quello "non è una fandonia
> come quella che si conta di te" [1]

The question of the Oriental influences on the *Divine Comedy* has been one of the most controversial aspects of Dante scholarship during the last century. The influence of Muslim eschatology on Dante's conception of the Other World as presented by Miguel Asin Palacios in 1919 and the discovery and publication of the *Liber scalae Machometi* in 1949, containing the Mohammedan legend of the prophet's journey to the infernal regions and subsequent ascension to heaven, are the cornerstones in this controversy.

The publications written on the subject since Asin Palacios' publication of his work, and even before, amount today to a substantial bibliography. Glancing through it the reader is struck by the extent of the polemic throughout the republic of letters and the passionate tone and divergence of opinions. It cannot be denied that this controversy helped scholars to a better understanding of Dante's eschatological background in the conception of his

---

[1] A. de Fabrizio (26), *Il "Mirag,"* p. 312. See bibliography.

Divine Comedy, although it degenerated, at times, into a crusade to defend the glory of the *altissimo poeta* against allegations of Mohammedan influence.

Even though complete agreement was never reached and probably never will be, a survey of the controversy should be valuable as an effort to separate issues which are frequently confused and to provide a clear understanding of an important section of the huge Dante bibliography.

As early as 1740, the Spanish Jesuit, Juan Andres (1),[2] in a remarkable book on the origin of literature, expressed his opinion that Dante might have been inspired by Arabic traditions in the composition of his *Divine Comedy*. In the 19th century, Francesco Cancellieri (17), Charles La Bitte (41) and Pasquale Villari (77) studied the forerunners of Dante and pointed to Christian legends of the Other World as sources for the *Divine Comedy*. Alessandro d'Ancona (25) called attention to the similarities between the *Divine Comedy* and Indo-Iranian eschatological legends. Only with E. Blochet (11), at the turn of the century, did the research on Oriental sources gain more ground.

In 1901 Blochet investigated the question "s'il n'y a pas dans la Divine Comédie et dans les legendes antérieures qui appartiennet au même cycle qu'elle des traces de cette Oriental influence."[3] Blochet believed that the origin of most eschatological legends lay in Indo-Iranian sources, from which they migrated to Christian Europe, where they received form and content.[4] One of these legends was that of the *Mi'raj*, Mohammed's ascension, which "Dante a pu entendre de la bouche d'un des chevaliers qui entrèrent à Jerusalem avec l'empereur de l'Allemagne,"[5] for Dante "ne connaissait les lettres arabes."[6] This tradition, however, was considered by Blochet as a very secondary source, "il faut chercher ses [Dante's] véritables sources dans les formes occidentales de cette légende qui ont été répandues dans le monde chrétien durant

---

[2] This number and the following refer to the bibliography which follows at the end.
[3] E. Blochet, *Les Sources Orientales...*, p. xv.
[4] Ibid., p. 155.
[5] Ibid., p. 160.
[6] Ibid., p. 11

tout le Moyen-Age."[7] By this he meant the Christian legends of the Other World which he also derived from Indo-Iranian sources. He points out that some of the episodes in the Christian legends are also found in the Arabic eschatology.[8] He had previously studied, in *L'Ascension au Ciel du Prophète Mohammed* (1899),[9] the Oriental origin of the Greek form of the eschatological legends. The idea of a translation of the Mohammedan legend of the *Mi'raj* did not occur to him although it had already been mentioned by Steinschneider in his studies on the Medieval translations. For Blochet, "la gloire de Dante consiste moins à avoir inventé le cadre de la légende, qu'à y avoir fait entrer des épisodes qui n'ont de correspondants dans aucune autre littérature et surtout dans les formes orientales de la Légende de l'Ascension."[10]

Only a few years later Marcus Dods (28) published eschatological legends from Egyptian and Babylonian up to medieval times. He introduces some of Jewish origin, but he does not mention any Muslim ones. Dods, unlike Blochet, cautiously states "that references to the *Divine Comedy* will be made, but they must be taken as quite gratuitous, merely incidental illustrations."[11] He actually gives credit to Dante for having not only composed, but invented, the various scenes of the *Divine Comedy*.

In 1905 Francesco Torraca (76) brushes aside Blochet's opinions. "Egli [Blochet] ragiona così: Dante conobbe le narrazioni occidentali di altri viaggi al mondo di là; ma queste narrazioni derivano dalla leggenda orientale; dunque è la fonte prima della Divina Commedia."[12] In his opinion "Dante non ha precursori perciò non al tenebroso Medio Evo europeo appartiene la Divina Commedia, ma alla nuova complessa varia luminosa civiltà italiana."[13]

In 1907, A. de Fabrizio (26), referring to Blochet's *L'Ascension au ciel* and to Alessandro d'Ancona's *La leggenda di Maometto*,

---

[7] Ibid., p. 19.
[8] Ibid., p. 32 ff. Blochet also recognizes the fact that Muslim eschatology had Hellenistic elements: ibid., p. 54 ff.
[9] See bibliography.
[10] Ibid., p. 195.
[11] M. Dods *Forerunners*, p. 3.
[12] Cit. by M. Asín Palacios, *Islam*, p. xiv fn.
[13] F. Torraca (76), *I Precursori*, p. 30.

takes this legend of the *Mi'raj* as the Muslim contribution to Dante's inspiration for the *Divine Comedy*. He bases his argument on *Lo specchio della fede* by Roberto de Lecce (1425-95), in which Mohammed's ascension is told "molto sommariamente, come se si tratasse di cose già note al lettore" [14] and which he believes to be also preceded by a long oral tradition. In his opinion "che i Visionarî medioevali conoscessero il Mirag è probabile; che lo conoscesse Dante pur essendo amissibile, non si può allo stato odierno degli studî affermare... esclusa l'ipotesi d'una imitazione diretta, consapevole... rimarrebbe la possibilità d'una impercettibile efficacia che nell'orditura della Commedia la leggenda avrebbe avuta, confusa con altre più importanti narrazioni affini, se non assorbita da esse." [15]

A few years later, in 1910, Raffaele Ottolenghi (64) turned from Muslim traditions as alleged sources of Dante's eschatology to the traditions of the Spanish Jews, especially in Ibn Gabirol's religious poem *Keter Malkut*, 'The Royal Crown.' And in 1911 Paolo Amaducci [16] claims to have found the source of the *Divine Comedy* in the Biblical narration given in the *Book of Numbers*, chapter XXXIII according to St. Peter Damian's mystical exegesis.

What Dante scholars thought about the preceding discussions of the possible sources for the *Divine Comedy* can be readily seen in Bruno Nardi's comments on Amaducci's work: "Ad agitare le acque della letteratura dantesca, che da alcuni decenni insigni maestri s'adopravano a purgare da elementi torbidi e a ricondurre entro gli argini d'una sana critica, furono improvisamente gettati, alla fine dell'inverno 1911, due volumi — dove Paolo Amaducci dava il sensazionale e alquanto chiassoso annunzio di avere scoperta la 'fonte della Divina Commedia.'" [17]

This 'sensazionale annunzio' was quickly forgotten when Asin Palacios' (2) work on Muslim eschatology appeared in 1919, arousing a great commotion among scholars of Romance and Oriental literatures alike. His *Escatología musulmana y la Divina Comedia* was not a restatement of former theories. The presentation was

---

[14] A. de Fabrizio, *Il Mirag*, p. 309.
[15] Ibid., p. 313.
[16] Amaducci, Paolo. *La fonte della Divina Commedia*, 2 vol. Rovigo, 1911.
[17] B. Nardi, *Pretese fonti...*, p. 1.

new, and so was the emphasis on the Muslim legends of the Other World, which are recorded and analyzed with uncommon mastery.

Previously, Asin Palacios had shown Dante to be a follower — through Christian filterings — of the neo-Platonic mysticism of the Cordovan philosopher Ibn Masarra. He had also called attention to the resemblance between the ascent of Dante and Beatrice into Paradise and the ascent of Ibn ʿArabi, the Murcian mystic. [18] Taking this as a starting point, Asin Palacios asserted that Ibn ʿArabi's ascension was a mystical-allegorical adaptation of Mohammed's ascension, the Miʿraj. In the Muslim lore, the Miʿraj was preceded by an Isra, a nocturnal journey of the Prophet, during which he visited the infernal regions of the Other World. The tradition, widely spread in the Muslim learned and semi-learned writings, was, according to Asin Palacios, the prototype of Dante's journey in the *Divine Comedy*. He then turned his attention to medieval Christian legends that antedated Dante's work. His research "not only confirmed that in Moslem sources there were to be found prototypes of features in the *Divine Comedy* — it further revealed the no less Moslem origin of many of those mediaeval legends themselves." [19]

Asin Palacios adopted the main aspects of Blochet's theory of the Oriental sources. [20] He objected, however, that in Blochet's presentation too little attention was paid to "los conductos más próximos, constantes y estables de comunicación entre la cultura oriental y occidental" [21] and criticized Blochet's lack of documentation.

Asin Palacios' main contributions to this problem were therefore his extensive and well documented presentation of Muslim eschatology and the emphasis he put on Spain as the most constant and stable area of communication between the two cultures. The Muslim tradition was not conceived by Asin Palacios as the origin

---

[18] M. Asín Palacios, *Abenmasarra y su escuela. Orígenes de la filosofía hispano-musulmana*. Madrid, 1914; p. 160. Reprinted in *Obras escogidas*, I: *Ibn Masarra y su escuela*... Madrid, 1945; p. 158.

[19] M. Asín Palacios, *Islam*, p. xiv; *Escatología*, 2nd ed., p. 3.

[20] Asín Palacios claimed (in a note added since the publication of the Spanish original, *Islam*, p. xiv fn.) not to have known of Blochet's work.

[21] Asín Palacios, *Escatología*, 2nd ed., p. 371 fn.

[21] Asín Palacios, *Islam*, p. 253.

of all human interest in eschatological themes. Nor did he deny the possibility of other ways for the diffusion of Oriental legends. But he emphasized throughout his works the idea of cross-cultural communications that took place in Spain.

The ensuing controversy was caused by implications of Asin Palacios' theory: the importance given to Muslim influence, if accepted, necessitates a re-interpretation of the relationship between Christian lore and Muslim lore as well as between Medieval Christian folklore and its classical and early Christian models. The militant tone, however, which the controversy assumed was initiated by Asin Palacios' overly confident presentation. For his book is certainly polemical; it tries to convince more than to explain. It is therefore hardly surprising that the following dispute had, at times, a tone of violent dissention.

Not everything in Asin Palacios' *Escatología*, however, is written in such a confident tone. His chapter on the transmission of Islamic models to Christian Europe and in particular to Dante is, confessedly, based on assumptions. In the chain of transmission of the legend of the *Mi'raj* to Europe and to Italy, there is a link missing. Asin Palacios tries to solve the problem in three different ways. The first is through Dante's teacher and friend, Brunetto Latini, who during his service as ambassador of Florence to the court of Alphonse the Wise "was in a position to acquire his knowledge of Arabic at first hand." [22] "Everything thus would seem to bear out the suggestion that the master of Dante Alighieri received more than a merely superficial impression from his visit to Spain, and may well have been the medium through which at least some of the Islamic features apparent in the *Divine Comedy* were transmitted to the disciple." [23] Another way in which Dante could have become aware of the Muslim tradition was through his Jewish friends such as Emmanuel Ben Salomo or

---

[22] Ibid., p. 254.
[23] Ibid., p. 255, note added since the publication of the Spanish original: *Escatología*, 2nd ed., p. 586 fn. On this see Levi della Vida, *Fonti islamiche*, p. 404 fn. "Dopo gli studi di U. Cassuto (p. es. *L'elemento italiano nelle Mehabberoth* in *Rivista Israelitica*, I-II, 1905-1906; *Dante e Manoello*. Firenze, 1921), è fuor di luogo continuare a parlare di relazioni culturali tra Dante e gli Ebrei suoi contemporanei." This argument however — of Dante's Jewish friends — was used again by G. Cattaui, *Les Sources*, I, p. 163.

Hillel of Verona.[24] Finally, Dante himself might have had "a certain leaning" towards Islamic culture. Moreover "if it cannot be proved from Dante's writings that he knew Semitic languages, neither can it be proved that he was ignorant of them."[25] Later, Asin Palacios would say on the same subject "en la Divina Comedia existen ideas e imágenes escatológicas que son específicamente islámicas y cuyo conocimiento exige el de la lengua árabe en Dante o en quien se las hubiera traducido."[26] As to the connection between the Muslim models and the Christian legends of the Other World, Dante's work included, Asin Palacios can only offer probable channels. Thus the 'missing link' in the transmission will become a very important focal point in the later controversy.[27]

The polemic around the *Escatología musulmana* was surveyed and analyzed by Asin Palacios himself a few years later. His replies to the objections (there was not a single case of self-correction) were published in four different journals as "Historia y crítica de una polémica." It contained a comprehensive bibliography of about eighty articles to which Asin Palacios added the short comments of 'favorable,' 'undecided' or 'adverse.'[28] Of the scholars, Dantists, and philologists listed, the forces seemed to be rather equally divided. Among the Orientalists, leading authorities like Massignon, Levi della Vida, and G. Gabrieli, are considered by Asin as being undecided. The Dantists who did not agree with Asin Palacios — and they were the majority — answered in passionate and often nationalistic tones.

---

[24] Asín Palacios, *Islam*, p. 259.
[25] Asín Palacios in *La Escatología*... *Giornale Dantesco*, XXVII (1924), p. 15.
[26] However, about the importance of this documentary evidence Asín Palacios said: "El testimonio histórico, el documento escrito, caso de existir, comprobaría las inferencias basadas en los hechos, pero no añadiría ni un adarme de fuerza a la convicción científica engendrada por las inferencias antes que el testimonio fuese descubierto." *Escatología*, 2nd ed., p. 387 (*Islam*, p. 255 is somewhat milder in the translation).
[27] In the bibliography appended to this article, only the most important reviews of Asin Palacios' book are mentioned. See numbers 9, 10, 16, 32, 33, 58, 65, and 75.
[28] The second edition of Asín Palacios' *Escatología* appeared in 1943. Appended was the survey of the polemic he had previously published: this latter was cursorily brought up to date (1941). Since it was a reprint of the first edition, it failed to contribute to the polemic or to stir up new interest.

The main objections raised against Asin Palacios can be summarized as follows: (a) The Muslim texts are taken from different sources and various authors and geographical areas, and they differ chronologically; (b) The same analogies can be found in classical and in Biblical and early Christian models; (c) The undeniable similarities found between Dantean and Islamic eschatology could be explained in several other ways: Christian and Muslim eschatology coincide in many aspects because they developed in parallel but independent fashion from a remote source older than Islam. Or they coincide, in autonomous evolution, because of a certain parallelism between the two cultures, or because of a certain universal similarity in the psychology of man in conceiving themes of the Other World.

With this, the controversy over the extent of Muslim influence on the works of Dante remained in a deadlock for almost three decades.[29] A survey of the controversy up to the time of Asin's review shows that the main points used in the discussion were: (a) The possibility of Dante's having been aware of the Muslim legends of the Other World and of the allegorical interpretations of the Muslim eschatology by Muslim mystics. (b) Dante's personal attitude toward Muslim lore and things Arabic in general.

Asin Palacios' theory, although rejected almost unanimously and without any qualifications by Dante critics, did not fail to leave a deep influence on subsequent research of which, however, Dante scholars have not always been fully aware. Although the controversy still seemed to be contered mainly on Dante's *Divine Comedy*, strictly speaking, the problem of the 'sources' had shifted to that of our basic interpretation of the European Middle Ages. It postulated, namely, a re-examination of our conception of medieval European lore and culture in their relation to the classical and early Christian background on one side, and to the Muslim contributions and participation in the so-called 'Western' tradition on the other.

Another aspect of Asin Palacios' theory which has had to be taken into consideration ever since by later investigators, was the undeniable role of Muslim Spain in the transmission of Arabic lore to the West.

---

[29] Ibid., p. 65.

In his article "Dante e l'Oriente" (1936), Olschki (61) seems to have had in mind the importance of "il contributo musulmano alla scienza ed alla filosofia cristiana di quei secoli." [30] He certainly rejects the claims of those who interpret the Dantean eschatology as "emanazione diretta" from the Muslim eschatology as conceived by mistic *Sufis* and especially Ibn 'Arabi, as well as the exaggerations of those who "per reazione tendono ad annullarla, ritenendo Dante del tutto ignaro delle cose d'oriente e poco curioso di esse." [31]

However, he evades the main issue when saying "nella universale sinossi di dottrina e di storia che fu presente alla mente di Dante come fonte di meditazione e d'ispirazione, l'oriente ebbe la sua parte." For his idea of the Orient and, in his opinion, Dante's in the *Divine Comedy*, is a very vague and romantic one. It is *l'Asia favolosa*, "quegli immensi territori già inaccessibili agli Occidentali" [32] under the rule of Genghis Khan, that he is talking about. Olschki rightly acknowledges the importance of the Greek and Christian background of Muslim culture. In his opinion: "Le dottrini dei filosofi arabi furono accolte in Occidente in virtù del loro puro contenuto speculativo... come eredi di quella tradizione antica cui si riconnettevano per le loro stesse origini e per la loro stessa dialettica i padri e i dottori della Chiesa... Questi autori arabi erano, dunque, studiati e seguiti in occidente in virtù della continuità spirituale che essi rappresentavano." [33] He rightly stresses also the fact that the purely religious aspects as such never took any real part in the cultural exchange. Here, "Mahometto non ha parte alcuna; e se Algazali, Averroè e altri autori d'oriente tentarono l'accordo sostanziale, dialettico, allegorico, teologico e mistico col Corano, nulla di tutto questo potè entrare e penetrò nel pensiero occidentale, così come rimase del tutto escluso da esso ciò che faceva parte della 'legge' di Mahometto e della morale pratica e religiosa dell'Islam." [34] Olschki, however, does not mention, along with the cultural one, another exchange, perhaps more

---

[30] Ibid., p. 65.
[31] Ibid., p. 65.
[32] Ibid., pp. 69 and 72.
[33] Ibid., p. 89.
[34] Ibid., p. 89.

difficult to define, yet always present whenever peoples come in contact. The mutual influence and impact of this exchange — folklore should be included here — is only too often disregarded. However it is precisely in this exchange, at a learned, semi-learned and popular level, that the problem lies, not in the romantic interest Dante might have had in things Oriental.

In 1944 Ugo Monneret de Villart (54) tried to show that medieval interest in Islam was a Spanish trait, scarcely found in France and to an even lesser degree in Italy, a fact which has been used as a serious refutation of another of Asin Palacios' premises. The reader, however, must bear in mind that in this book Monneret de Villart uses *Islam* as a religious term, and the medieval study of Islam which he analyzes is only the purely theological, missionary interest shown by the orders of the time, which was understandably greater in Spain, where the Muslim influence was also greater. He admits, however, the possibility of Dante's having been aware of Muslim eschatology, particularly of the *Kitab al-mi'raj*.[35] His findings, therefore, enlightening as they are, cannot be used as arguments in the case of Dante, whose contact with Islam, as pointed out by Asin Palacios, was not on the religious level.

August Rüegg (70) in his book *Die Jenseitsvorstellungen vor Dante*, published in 1945, presents a thorough study of concepts of the Other World prior to Dante. However, only classic and early Christian visions are investigated. He has, to be sure, a chapter 'on the question of Islamic influence on Dante,' but his analysis of the Islamic questions is the least convincing in an otherwise excellent study.

With regard to the problem of the similarities between the Christian and Muslim legends of the Other World, he finds it "selbstverständlich, dass Mittelalter in der Arabischen wie in der germanischen Welt kulturell, weil auf demselben Traditionsboden erwachsen, in der Haptsache ähnliche Gründzüge aufweist, wenn es auch im Norden des Mittelmeers mehr römisch-germanisch-

---

[35] Ibid., p. 54. Monneret de Villart is due credit for having called attention to the mss. of the French translation and the Latin translation of this work existing repectively in the Bodleian and the Bibliothèque Nationale de Paris. Ibid., p. 53.

keltische und im Süden mehr orientalisch-griechische Färbung hat." [36] Rüegg does not ask whether Dante knew the Muslim eschatological legends. Moreover, he wrongly attributes to Asín Palacios the claims that all Muslim forerunners of Dante are direct sources for his *Divine Comedy*. Hence his argument that in such a case "wären wir gezwungen anzunehmen, Dante hätte eine ganze Bibliothek aus verschiedenen Jahrhunderten stammender Schriften arabischer Mystiker, Philosophen und Dichter zur freien Benutzung gehabt." [37] He also brings up the argument of the 'missing link' in the transmission: "wenn Dante alle diese Muslim Vorbildsmotive so massiert und geordnet, wie sie bei Asín figurieren, bequem in einer Schrift vorgefunden hätte, dann musste man fast an eine Mohammedanische quelle denken." [38] Rüegg obviously demands of the Arabic source a similarity which he hardly expects from Christian models.

In 1949, an Italian and a Spanish scholar, E. Cerulli (22) and Muñoz Sendino (57), working independently and unaware of each other's research, published the Latin and French version of a Hispano-Arabic book containing the legend of Mohammed's journey to the infernal regions and his ascension to the heavens. [39] The book, called *Libro della Scala* — or *Liber scalae* and *Livre de l'eschiele Mahomet* in the Latin and Old French versions — was translated at the order of Alphonse the Wise by the Jewish physician Abraham into Romance and by Bonaventura de Senis (Siena) into Latin.

---

[36] Ibid., I, p. 436.
[37] Ibid., I, p. 440.
[38] Ibid., I, p. 440.
[39] The two scholars offer, however, a different approach to their work. Muñoz reproduced the French and Latin texts. Cerulli attempted, not always with great fortune, to correct the text found in the manuscript. As for the authors' commentaries on the *Book of the Ladder*, Levi della Vida (44) says: "il lavoro di Muñoz, benchè condotto con grande zelo e con evidente fatica di ricerca, è troppo ingombro di digressioni non pertinenti all'argomento, troppo debole nell'analisi storica e letteraria e troppo viziato da errori e distrazioni (here we could add also "too prejudiced in favor of Asín Palacios' theories') per poter essere collocato sullo stesso livello di quello di Cerulli, il quale sarà certamente completato da ricerche ulteriori... ma è, e rimarrà, un poderoso e mirabile contributo allo studio della penetrazione della cultura ispanoislamica nell'Europa cristiana e all'intelligenza del complicato processo della formazione ed elaborazione della *Divina Commedia*." *Fonti islamiche*, p. 406.

Besides the edition of the texts, Cerulli adds in his book a thorough study of the diffusion of the *Libro della Scala* in the West, including quotations from Muslim eschatology used by medieval authors. In the last chapter, "Dante e l'Islam," he examines Asin Palacios' statements in the light of the *Libro della Scala*. Cerulli does not attempt a restatement of Asin Palacios' theories, but rather in a conscientious and moderate manner tries simply to analyze the similarities and parallels between the *Libro della Scala* and the *Divine Comedy*.

Nevertheless the *Libro della Scala* caused the controversy to flare up again. In spite of the objections which were made against Cerulli's edition from the linguistic point of view, by Levi della Vida (44) and by Groult (40), the *Libro della Scala* was hailed as the 'missing link.'

Levi della Vida (44) in his review of both Muñoz' and Cerulli's editions, published in *Al-Andalus* (1949), says "Oggi non è più possibile dubitarne, che il Libro della Scala reso accessibile all'Occidente latino in duplice se non triplice versione, fosse rimasto ignoto a Dante sarebbe fuori di ogni verosimiglianza. La tesi di Asin intorno alla possibilità, ma alla realtà di relazioni tra Dante e l'escatologia islamica rimane dunque definitivamente confermata." [40] F. Gabrieli (30) in *Diogenes* (1954) also wrote: "Cultural nationalism — or, as I prefer to interpret it, mental laziness put together with diffidence and the lack of positive proof — can no longer deny that the brilliant hypothesis of thirty years ago has at last a splendid confirmation, at least in the intuition on which it was based." [41]

Bruno Nardi (59), on the other hand, in his article "Pretese fonti della Divina Commedia" (1935), heatedly rejects the above-mentioned statements: "Poichè sembra che da parte di taluno si sia dimenticata la vecchia regoletta del loicare: a posse ad esse non datur illatio," and requests a more positive proof: "Una simile affermazione non può esser fatta se non dopo un attento e accurato essame comparativo, per il quale sono stati apportati

---

[40] Ibid., p. 392.
[41] *New Light on Dante and Islam*, p. 66.

molti materiali, ma che a me sembra non sia ancora stato fatto come doveva esser fatto." [42]

The controversy had already been centered since the publication of Cerulli's book on the comparative analysis which Nardi requested. Cerulli himself had already reduced considerably the number and extent of the similarities between the Muslim schatology and the *Divine Comedy*. Cerulli's more moderate tone and the less numerous points of similarity offered in his book were frequently referred to as a retreat from Asin Palacios' first position, but wrongly so, for the similarities and coincidences pointed out by Asin were still valid, and so were the objections concerning the diffusion of the Muslim traditions throughout Christian Europe. Cerulli's approach was different and so, therefore, were his conclusions. He simply compares the *Divine Comedy* with the Muslim eschatology as it appears in the *Libro della Scala*, this book being the only literary source so far discovered which could in all probability have been known by Dante.

Cerulli's comparative study brought very little agreement beyond the statement that Dante did not directly copy from the Muslim legend as found in the *Libro della Scala*. Levi della Vida, for example, says "Il libro della Scala ... ha fornito alla Divina Commedia alcuni elementi importanti, sia nel disegno generale o sia nei particolari." [43] M. Porena (68), on the other hand, "Circa la relazioni fra il libro della Scala e la Divina Commedia l'unica cosa che a me par quasi certa si è che in Dante non si abbiano non dico imitazioni ma neanche riecheggiamenti o reminiscenze sicure del libro musulmano." [44] The diametrical opposition expressed in these two comments is characteristic of the divergence of opinion among commentators after the publication of the *Libro della Scala*.

It becomes clear to the reader that we are dealing here no longer with an evaluation of the similarities found in both traditions, Christian and Muslim, but of those found in the two works, Dante's *Divine Comedy* and the anonymous *Libro della Scala*. Dantists frequently require the relationship between the *Divine*

---

[42] Ibid., p. 356.
[43] Levi della Vida, *Fonti islamiche*, p. 401.
[44] In *La Divina Commedia...*, p. 58.

Comedy and the *Libro* to be proved by similarities which can only be explained as reflections of the influence of the *Libro*. They in fact require not only a similarity but a faithful copy, and this they rightly say is not to be found. U. Bosco (13) says in this respect, "qui dobbiamo ammettere che per ciascuna di quelle analogie si può legittimamente restare in dubbio; ciascuna, forse, può essere spiegata con una fonte comune o con la comune fondamentale esperienza umana. Ma resta il loro complesso, che è imponente." [45] This has not yet been studied.

It should be pointed out (Levi della Vida had already mentioned this fact) that the *Libro della Scala*, if considered as the only source for Dante's acquaintance with Muslim eschatology, necessarily confines Asin Palacios' arguments from a general Muslim influence to the influence of this book. In this respect, the nature of the book seems to be the greatest objetion against Asin Palacios' theories, because, in the *Libro della Scala*, there is nothing of the mystical and allegorical interpretation of the legend as we find in Ibn Masarra or Ibn 'Arabi. Nor is there anything of the doctrine of light which was Asin Palacios' starting point in his search for the Muslim sources of the *Comedy*.

This, however, cannot be used as a definite refutation of Asin Palacios' theory. On the contrary, the diffusion of the Mohammedan legend in Christian Europe has been proved by literary documents, namely the *Libro della Scala*. To reject a priori any other contacts between Christian and Muslim lore, through literary or oral channels, would be to adopt a position that can hardly be considered reasonable. [46] For we know now that toward the end of the 12th century, there was written an allegorical and philosophical treatise on the soul's journey into the Other World. [47] It was composed in either Sicily or Catalonia, and shows an obvious and deep influence of Avicenna's philosophy and also of Ibn Gabirol. This

---

[45] In *Contatti della cultura...*, p. 101.

[46] G. Soulier *Les Influences orientales dans la peinture toscane*, Paris, 1924. He illustrates the relationships between Tuscany and the Levant and shows the knowledge and interest by Italians in Muslim art from the eleventh century.

[47] M-Th. d'Alverny "Les pérégrinations de l'âme dans l'autre monde d'après un anonyme de la fin du XIIe siècle" in: *Archives d'histoire doctrinale et littéraire du Moyen-Age* XIII (1940-42). See also Cerulli, *Il Libro...*, p. 519.

proves that by the beginning of the 'Duecento' such philosophical allegories of Arabic descent were known in Christian Europe.

It is generally accepted that Dante was not particularly inclined towards, or showed any special liking for, things Arabic as such. But it should be pointed out that Dante lived, worked, and composed his *Divine Comedy* in a world where Arabic thought was omnipresent in learned circles. Dante admittedly drew from a Latin translation of an Arabic book, the *Liber de Causis*, fundamental elements for his theory of earthly and mystical love and the metaphysics of light which permeates his vision of Paradise.[48] The *Libro della Scala* has shown that this was also the case with the eschatological themes of Mohammed's legend. This is a fact we must admit in spite of the apologetical and missionary efforts of the Church. In fact, it was this importance given to things Arabic which aroused the missionary zeal of the Church against them, with the consequent creation of an image of Islam as the "vilissima religio."[49] It is under this perspective that an evaluation of things Arabic is still to be made.

The most impressive *a priori* argument against any influence of Muslim eschatology is the contrast between Mohammedan and Dantean attitudes. This, however, should not be overemphasized since there are many parallel cases of borrowing and even of translation with radical changes in spirit and form during the Middle Ages.

Olschki (62) in his article "Mohammedan Eschatology" (1951) intimates correctly that Muslim eschatology drew from Jewish, Christian and Parsi sources. He could have also added that these are not the beginning of human interest in eschatological themes. He also points to the Christian-Mozarabic influence on the development of Mohammedan eschatology in the Middle Ages, which

---

[48] Dante might not have been aware that the *Liber de Causis* contained Arabic philosophy; see Cerulli, *Il Libro...*, p. 513. On the *Liber de Causis*, see Murari, Rocco: "Il *De Causis* e la sua fortuna nel Medio Evo" in: *Giornale storico della letteratura italiana* XXXIV (1899), pp. 93-117, and Manuel Alonso, S. J.: "El *Liber de Causis*" in: *Al-Andalus* IX, (1944), p. 43, and X (1945), p. 429.

[49] On this very important aspect of Eastern-Western relations see Norman Daniel: *Islam and the West. The Making of an Image*. Edinburgh, 1950.

"seems to have been an accomplishment mainly of Spanish Moors living in a Christian and Mozarabic environment, therefore longer and more directly influenced by Christian and Biblical trends and motifs than the coreligionists of Asia."[50] This influence was undoubtedly present, but seeing Mohammedan eschatology as "an accomplishment of Spanish Moors" needs further qualification. His final assertion also needs qualification: "A sober and critical comparison of the two texts shows that Mohammedan eschatology as displayed in the *Book of the Ladder* contributes nothing in any appreciable way to the structural and episodic scaffold of the *Divina Commedia* or to our historical and interpretive understanding of the poem."[51] If we agree that Dante's masterpiece is not an isolated monument which can be studied independently from his world and the circumstances which formed it, Asin Palacios' theories and the *Libro della Scala* are undoubtedly contributions to our understanding of the poem.

Silverstein's (74) article on "Dante and the Legend of the Mi'raj" (1952) drew attention especially to a problem to which we have previously referred: that of the relationship of the eschatological legends in the 12th century to their classical and early Christian sources. He, in short, rejects Asin Palacios' opinions of a Muslim influence on them and stresses the continuous tradition and growth of the legends throughout the early Middle Ages. This he does in the scholarly and brilliant fashion he has accustomed us to expect. But at the same time, one cannot help noticing Silverstein's efforts to present Asin Palacios' ideas in the most extreme way: "These traditions, Night Journey and Ascension, according to him [Asin Palacios] provided a major source of matters and ideas for the Divina Commedia and to a large extent directly; but where not directly, then through their previous use (Asin's word for some instances is 'plagiarism') by other Christian visions in the Middle Ages."[52]

The arguments with which Silverstein demonstrates the continuous evolution of the Christian legends are undoubtedly convincing. On the other hand, the polemical tone of his expositions

---

[50] Ibid., p. 15.
[51] Ibid., p. 17.
[52] Ibid., p. 89.

is also unmistakable. Returning to Dante's case, he seems less convincing as he canvasses the whole Christian field in search of examples which might increase the validity of his arguments. "In the ninth-century vision of Charles the Fat the incident also appears in a form particularly suitable to Dante, who might readily have borrowed it thence, transformed by a memory of the Classical centaurs for Inferno XII." [53] In his second Part, dealing mainly with the *Libro della Scala,* Silverstein uses the more reserved approach of Cerulli's exposition as an argument against both Cerulli and Asin Palacios; this also is inappropriate, at least insofar as Cerulli's arguments are of a different nature from those of Asin, as we have shown.

It is therefore a surprise to the reader to find in the summarizing paragraph the following remark: "No one will wish to claim that it [Silverstein's survey of traditional Christian visions precursory to Dante] has proved the absence of Muslim influence among them. On the contrary, some evidence suggests that such influence may indeed have operated at certain points, and to deny this possibility, even probability, would be as intemperate as it was on Asin's part to believe that nearly everything in the tradition came from Islam." [54] And further on: "Certainly the presence in Western texts of certain motifs which the Italian poet used need not mean that he got them from a Christian work rather than a Muslim text which, by means of a translation, he could read."[55]

After Silverstein's article, Bruno Nardi's (59) discussion on the "Pretese fonti della Divina Commedia" which appeared in 1955, makes no new contribution to the controversy. It shows rather to what extent the controversy has ceased to be a problem which can be restricted solely to the study of Dante's sources. The controversy has become a problem to be solved only with a re-interpretation of our understanding of the European Middle Ages as a time in which Arabic and Jewish cultural elements as well are given the place they deserve as components of the so-called 'Western' tradition. In this light the 'influence' of a specific work on any particular author is only an episode.

---

[53] Ibid., p. 98.
[54] Ibid., p. 109.
[55] Ibid., p. 196.

With this in mind, and considering the results of the controversy so far, the conclusion at which R. Lemay arrived in an article on Dante in 1963 (42), comes as a surprise: "Si donc Dante connaissait l'arab, le problème de ses emprunts à des sources littéraires arabes deviendrait fort simplifié, n'est-il pas vrai? Dante avait les moyens de lire ce qu'il voulait ou qui l'intéressait: qu'il s'agisse de la *Risalat al-Ghoufran* d'abou 'l-'ala al-Ma'arri [not Ma'āri!] ou des divers ouvrages du grand mystique de Murcia Ibn el-'Arabi, ouvrages célèbres parmi les Arabes et très répandues tout au long de l'aire culturelle de l'Islam, les inspirations connues et surtout les nombreux passages parallèles relevés par Asin Palacios entre ces ouvrages et la *Divine Comédie* n'auraient rien pour nous surprendre!"[56] Obviously the author is not aware of the preceding controversy. "If Dante had known Arabic all this could be explained very easily." This, unfortunately, has not been proved in any way, and to explain things easily is beside the point.

---

[56] *Le Nemrod,* p. 109.

BIBLIOGRAPHY

1. ANDRÉS, JUÁN: *Del origen, progreso y estado actual de la Literatura.* Italian edition, 1782-98; Spanish edition, 1784-1806.
2. ASÍN PALACIOS, MIGUEL: *La escatología musulmana en la Divina Comedia.* Madrid, 1919.
3. ASÍN PALACIOS, MIGUEL: *La escatología musulmana en la Divina Comedia: Historia y crítica de una polémica.* In: *Il Giornale Dantesco,* XXVI (1923), XXVII (1924). Also in: *Litteris, Boletín de la Real Academia.*
4. ASÍN PALACIOS, MIGUEL: *L'Influence musulmane dans la Divine Comédie. Histoire et critique d'une polémique.* In: Revue de la littérature comparée (1924), p. 392.
5. ASÍN PALACIOS, MIGUEL: *Islam and the Divine Comedy.* (tr. and abr. Harold Sunderland) London, 1926. Translations were also announced in French, German, Italian and Arabic, but these were never published.
6. ASÍN PALACIOS, MIGUEL: *Dante y el Islam.* (Résumé with introduction by Emilio García Gómez). Madrid, 1927.
7. ASÍN PALACIOS, MIGUEL: *La escatología musulmana en la Divina Comedia. Seguida de la Historia y crítica de una Polémica.* 2nd edition. Madrid, 1943. Briefly brings up to date the controversy since the first edition.
8. BECKER, ERNEST J.: *A Contribution to the Comparative Study of the Medieval Visions of Heaven and Hell.* Baltimore, 1899. On the possible relationship between the Bridge and as-Sirat in Iranian visions and in the medieval Western visions.
9. BELLESSORT, A.: *Pour le sixième centenaire de Dante. Dante et Mahomet.* In: *Revue de Deux mondes,* Paris, 1 April, 1920. 23 pp.
10. BENCHENEB, M.: *Sources musulmanes dans "La Divine Comédie".* In: *Revue Africaine,* Alger (1919), 11 pp.
11. BLOCHET, E.: *L'Ascension au ciel du Prophète Mohamed.* In: *Revue de l'histoire des Religions* (1899). Blochet tried to prove that the Iranian legend of the Ascension had entered Greece at an early period, and that it is found in two writers who were read throughout the centuries: Plato and Plutarch.
12. BLOCHET, E.: *Les Sources orientales de la Divina Commedia.* Paris, 1901. 215 pp. He found the sources of the *Commedia* in pre-Islamic Iranian literature, from which also derives the legend of Mohammed.

13. Bosco, Umberto: *Contati della cultura occidentale di Dante con la letteratura non dotta Arabo-spagnuola.* In: Studi Danteschi, v. 29 (1950), pp. 85-102.
14. Boswell, C. S.: *An Irish Precursor of Dante.* London, 1908. "Perhaps a reference should be made to the Vision of the Other-world composed by Dante's friend, the learned Jew Immanuel ben Salamone, as the question might occur whether Dante may not, by his means, have arrived at such part of his subject as relates to Old Testament lore and Jewish tradition by a shorter cut than the usual channels... It is possible for stray pieces of information but hardly more than that." p. 241.
15. Bouvat, L.: *Le Prophète Mohammed en Europe. Légende et littérature.* In: Revue du monde musulman IX (1909), pp. 264-72. Provides some additions to the work of d'Ancona. (25).
16. Cabaton, A.: *La Divine Comédie et l'Islam.* In: Revue de l'histoire des religions LXXXI (1920), pp. 333-60. A development of the origin of the legend of Mohammed studied by Asín.
17. Cancellieri, Francesco: *Osservazioni sopra l'originalità della Divina Commedia* (1814). Ridiculed by Ugo Foscolo in: Dante in Edinburgh Review XXX, Sept. 1818.
18. Cantele, Domenico: *L'Islam e Dante. La controversa influenza delle fonti musulmane su la Divina Commedia.* Cairo, 1961. Favorable though inconclusive review of this by G. Bonfante in: La Rassegna della Letteratura Italiana LXVII (1963), v. 1, pp. 71-2.
19. Caruso, G.: *Polemiche sulla Divina Commedia.* Palermo, 1914.
20. Cattaui, Georges: *Les Sources orientales de la "Divine Comédie".* In: Annales du Centre Universitaire Méditerranéen X (1956-57), pp. 159-171; XI (1957-58), pp. 159-67. Summary of the problem; sparse bibliography, and a rather uncritical description of the themes.
21. Cattaui, Georges: *Les Sources orientales de la "Divine Comédie".* In: Bulletin de la Société d'études dantesques du Centre Universitaire Méditerranéen. VII (1958), pp. 7-15.
22. Cerulli, Enrico: *Dante e l'Islam.* In: Al-Andalus, XXI (1956), pp. 229-255. A history of the problem of the Libro della Scala in the West and in Dante.
23. Cerulli, Enrico: *Dante e l'Islam e Oriente ed Occidente nel Medio Evo.* In: Oriente ed Occidente nel Medio Evo. Rome, Acc. Naz. dei Linc., 1957, pp. 275-294, 445-458.
24. D'Ancona, Alessandro: *I Precursori di Dante.* Firenze, 1874.
25. D'Ancona, Alessandro: *La Leggenda di Maometto in Occidente.* In: Giornale Storico della Letteratura Italiana, XIII, pp. 199-281. See Bouvat (15) and Mancini (48).
26. De Fabrizio, A.: *Il "Mirag" di Maometto esposto da un frate salentino del XV secolo.* In: Gior. Stor. d. lett. ital. XLIX (1907), pp. 299-313.
27. De Gubernatis, Angelo: *Le Type indien de Lucifer chez le Dante.* In: Giornale Dantesco, III, p. 49ff. He maintains that prior to Dante, Christian art had never represented Purgatory as a mountain, the summit of which was the Earthly Paradise, and further, that this representation is only a copy of the Muslim system. According to De Gubernatis, Dante's Inferno is only a copy of the Buddhist Hell.
28. Dods, Marcus: *Forerunners of Dante.* Edinburgh, 1903.

29. EVOLA, N. D.: *Bibliografia Dantesca*. Firenze, 1932. On p. 215ff. a bibliography of works referring to the theses of Asín Palacios.
30. GABRIELI, FRANCESCO: *New Light on Dante and Islam*. In: *Diogenes. An International Review of Philosophy and Humanistic Studies*. London, n.° 6 (Spring, 1954), pp. 61-73.
31. GABRIELI, FRANCESCO: *Dante und der Islam*. In: *Diogenes. Internationale Zeitschrift fur Wissenschaft von Menschen*. Deutsche Ausgabe, Koln (1956) H 9-10, Bd. III.
32. GABRIELI, G.: *Intorno alle fonti orientali della "Divina Commedia"*. Rome, 1919. Reprinted from *Arcadia* III.
33. GABRIELI, G.: *Dante e l'Islam*. In: *Scritti vari pubblicati in occasione del VI centenario della morte di Dante Alighieri*. Varallo Sessia, 1921.
34. GABRIELI, G.: *Intorno alle fonti orientali della Divina Commedia*. In: *Arcadia* III (1949), pp. 53-59.
35. GALBIATI, GIOVANNI: *Dante e gli arabi*. In: *Studi su Dante*, ed. by Sezione Milanese della Società Dantesca Italiana, v. I (1938).
36. GILLET, LOUIS: *Dante*. Paris, 1941. In his third chapter, "Dante et l'Islam" he presents an unconditional and uncritical defense of the theses of Asin Palacios.
37. GRABHER, CARLO: *Possibili conclusioni su Dante e l'escatologia musulmana*. In: *Siculorum Gymnasium* VII, 1955. Grabher denies that Dante knew the *Libro della Scala*. A favorable review of this in *Rassegna della Letteratura Italiana* 61 (1957), p. 277.
38. GRAF, ARTURO: *Miti, leggende e superstizioni del Medio Evo*. Torino, 1892-93.
39. GRANDGENT, C. H.: *Islam and Dante*. In: *Studi Medievali*, Turin, 1930. Repeats the arguments of W. Mullert; Asin Palacios answered in *Al-Andalus* I (1933), pp. 451-53.
40. GROULT, PIERRE: *La Divine Comédie et l'Eschiele Maho-Mahomet*. Louvain, Les Lettres Romanes, IV (1950), pp. 137-49. Claims that the *Libro della Scala* proves the essentials of Asin's theory; severely criticizes Cerulli's edition of the French text: "Ce manuscrit vraiment méritait mieux qu'une édition négligée." p. 149.
41. LA BITTE, CHARLES: *La Divine Comédie avant Dante*. Paris, 1842. Used as preface to: *Oeuvres de Dante Alighieri: La Divine Comédie* (tr. A. Brizeux), Paris, 1853.
42. LEMAY, RICHARD: *Le Nemrod de l'"Enfer" de Dante et le "Liber Nemroth"*. In: *Studi Danteschi*, XL (1963), pp. 57-128.
43. LESZYNSKY, R.: *Mohammedanische Traditionen über das jüngste Gericht: eine vergleichende Studie zur jüdisch-christlichen und mohammedanische Eschatologie*, Kirchhain N. L., 1909. The first scientific study of Muslim eschatology; restricts itself to the study, edition and commentary of the Kitab al-Zuhd by Asad b. Musa b. Ibr. b. al-Walid al-Umawi (132-212 e.g.).
44. LEVI DELLA VIDA, GIORGIO: *Nuova luce sulle fonti islamiche della Divina Commedia*. In: *Al-Andalus*, XIV (1949), pp. 377-407. A review of the editions of the *Libro della Scala*, by Muñoz and Cerulli.
45. LEVI DELLA VIDA, GIORGIO: *Dante e l'Islam secondo nuovi documenti*. In: *Aneddoti e svaghi*, Milán, 1959. Published in French as *Dante et l'Islam d'après de nouveaux documents*. In: *Revue de la Méditerranée*, XIV (1954), pp. 131-46. These reproduce in the essentials the article in *Al-Andalus* (44).

46. Licitra, A.: *De la originalidad de 'La Divina Comedia' y de la leyenda islámica del isra y del mirach*. La Plata (1921), p. 118.
47. Macaluso, G.: *Dante e Maometto*. Roma, 1953.
48. Mancini, Augusto: *Per lo studio della leggenda di Maometto in Occidente*. In: *Rendiconti d. R. Acad. dei Lincei*, Ser. 6, vol. X. Roma, 1934.
49. Mandonnet, P.: *Dante et le voyage de Mahomet au Paradis*. In: *Comité français catholique pour la célébration du sixième centenaire de la mort de Dante Alighieri; Bulletin du jubilé*, n.º 5 (1921-22), pp. 544-55. The hypothesis according to which the Otherworldly journey of Mohammed could have come to Dante's knowledge through Ricoldo da Montefeltro.
50. Massignon, L.: *Les Etudes islamiques à l'étranger. En Espagne: Les recherches d'Asín Palacios sur Dante*. From: *Revue du Monde Musulman*, XXXVI (1919).
51. Merkel, R. F.: *Per lo studio della leggenda di Maometto in Occidente*. In: *Rendiconti d. R. Acad. dei Lincei*. Ser. 6, vol. X (1934). Could be developed further.
52. Modi, Jivanji Jamshedji: *The Divine Comedy of Dante and the Virafnameh of Ardai Viraf*. Lecture at the Royal Asiatic Society of Bombay, 26 Feb. 1892. With other essays, published as *Dante Papers. Viraf, Adamnan, Dante and other Papers*. Bombay, 1914.
53. Monfrin, J.: *Les Sources arabes de la 'Divine Comédie' et la traduction française du livre de l'ascension de Mahomet*. In: *Bibliothèque de l'Ecole des chartes*. Paris, t. 109 (1951), n.º 2, pp. 277-90.
54. Monneret de Villard, Ugo: *Lo studio dell'Islam in Europa nel XII e nel XIII secolo*. Città del Vaticano, 1944. (Studi e testi 110).
55. Morpurgo, Enrico: *Dante tra l'Islam e il medioevo: A proposito di una nuova pubblicazione*. In: *Neo-Philologus* (1953). Groningen 37.
56. Mullert, Werner: *Östliche Züge in der 'Navigatio Brendani'*. In: *Zeitschrift für Romanische Philologie*. Bd. 45 (1926). Against the Islamic origin of the *Divine Comedy* and of Western Christian legends. Places their origin in remote prototypes from other eschatologies which could easily have come to the West without resorting to Islamic imitations.
57. Muñoz Sendino, José: *La Escala de Mahoma. Traducción del árabe al castellano, latín y francés ordenada por Alfonso X el Sabio*. Edited, with introduction and notes by Muñoz Sendino. Madrid, 1949.
58. Nallino, Carlo Alfonso: Review of *Escatologia* (2). In: *Rivista degli Studi Orientali*, VIII (1919-21), pp. 800-19. Also in: *Raccolta di Scritti editi ed inediti*, II, pp. 436-53.
59. Nardi, Bruno: *Pretese fonti della Divina Commedia*. In: *Nuova Antologia*, XC (luglio 1955), pp. 383-89. Reprinted in *Dal Convivio alla Commedia*, Roma, 1960: See Schneider's review article on this (72).
60. Nicholson, Reynold, A.: *A Persian Forerunner of Dante*. In: *Transactions of the Royal Asiatic Society*, Bombay, 1943. Privately reprinted, North Wales, 1944.
61. Olschki, Leonardo: *Dante e l'Oriente*. In: *Giornale Dantesco*, XXXIX (1938).
62. Olschki, Leonardo: *Mohammedan Eschatology and Dante's Other World*. In: *Comparative Literature*, III (1951), pp. 1-17.

63. OSMAN, HASSAN: *Dante in Arabic*. In: *73rd Annual Report of the Dante Society* (1955). Cambridge, Mass., pp. 47-52. Discusses the state of Dante studies in the Arabic world; their interest is chiefly in Dante's eschatology, as presented by Asin Palacios, whose theories they do not extend further.
64. OTTOLENGHI, RAFFAELE: *Un Lontano Precursore di Dante*, Lugano, 1910. Originally appeared in: *Coenobium*, fasc. II-V (1909). Reviewed in *Giornale Dantesco*, XIX (1911), p. 121, and in *Giornale Storico della Letteratura Italiana*, LVI (1910), p. 250.
65. PARODI, E. G.: Review of *Escatologia* (2). In: *Bulletino della Società dantesca italiana*. Firenze (1920), XXVI, 18 pp.
66. PATCH, HOWARD R.: *The Other World*. In: *Smith College Studies in Modern Languages* (1950), Cambridge, Mass. Something like a comprehensive survey of the whole field, with a valuable bibliography.
67. PELOSI, SILVIO: *Il Paradiso e il Libro della Scala*. In: *Veltro*, III (1959), pp. 5-18.
68. PORENA, MANFREDO: *La Divina Commedia. Il viaggio di Maometto nell'oltretomba narrato nel Libro della Scala*. In: *Atti della Accad. naz. dei Lincei* Ser. 6, vol. 5 (1950), pp. 40-59.
69. RODISON, MAXIME: *Dante et l'Islam d'après des travaux récents*. In: *Revue de l'Histoire des Religions* (oct.-dec. 1951).
70. RÜEGGE, AUGUST: *Die Jenseitsvorstellungen vor Dante und die übrigen literarischen Voraussetzungen der 'Divina Commedia'*. Einsiedeln-Köln, 1945, 2 v.
71. RUSSO, G.: *Polemiche sulla Divina Commedia*. Palermo, 1914.
72. SCHNEIDER, FRIEDRICH: *Bruno Nardis angebliche Quellen der Göttlichen Komödie*. In: *Deutsches Dante Jahrbuch*, NF (1957), Bd 25-26, s. 177-82.
73. SINISCALCO LA SALA, FRANCISCO: *Dante y Abenarabi*. Montevideo, 1940. An uncritical approval of Asin Palacios' theory, especially as it refers to the allegorical interpretation of Muslim eschatology by Ibn 'Arabi.
74. SILVERSTEIN, THEODORE: *Dante and the Legend of the Mi'raj: The Problem of Islamic Influence on the Christian Literature of the Otherworld*. In: *Journal of Near Eastern Studies*, XI (1952), pp. 89-110, 187-97.
75. SÖDERHJELM, W.: *Dante et l'Islam*. In: *Neuphilologische Mitteilungen* (1921), n.º 5, 11 pp.
76. TORRACA, FRANCESCO: *I precursori della Divina Commedia*. Firenze, 1905.
77. TRONI, ARMANDO: *Dante et Mahomet. Quaderni di Cultura. Centro Studi e Scambi Internazionali*. Palermo, 1948.
78. VILLARI, PASQUALE: *Antiche Leggende e Tradizioni che illustrano la Divina Commedia*. Pisa, 1865.
79. VITTI, TOMASSO: *Le Origini della Divina Commedia*. In: *Alighieri* (1889). He admits, though vaguely, that The *Divine Comedy* is connected with previous oriental literatures, but he is wrong in quoting the *Mahabharata* which certainly has nothing to do with the work of Dante.

80. ZABUGHIN, VLADIMIRO: *Dante e l'Oriente*. In: *Roma e l'Oriente*, XXI (1921), p. 7ff.
81. ZIOLECKI, B.: *Alexandre du Pont's Roman de Mahomet, ein altfranzoesische Gedicht des XIII. Jahrhunderts, neu herausgegeben* (tr. Charles Pellat). Reprinted in *Terre d'Islam* (1943) as *La Légende de Mahomet au Moyen Age*.

DANTE AND ITALIAN NATIONALISM

CHARLES T. DAVIS
Tulane University

Among poets, Virgil and Dante have cast the longest shadows, for it is not only as artists that they have commanded men's imaginations. They have also become great historical and legendary figures, venerated both as teachers and prophets: as interpreters of the best thought of their own time and as seers who foretold the coming of a new era.

For the Middle Ages, Virgil represented the cultural and political grandeur of Rome. Legends depicted him as a sage with superhuman knowledge, a magician with supernatural powers. Christians believed that in his Fourth Eclogue he had prophesied the birth of their Saviour.

Comparetti's lengthy analysis of Virgil's medieval influence [1] could find a companion volume in a study of Dante's real and legendary fame in the modern world. To it, and particularly to Italy, he has rendered the same service that Virgil performed for medieval Christendom. Like Virgil, Dante has been the wise teacher and magical artist resurrecting a lost age and serving as guide through a universe of past thought and emotion. To some he has also been a prophet. He has been hailed as the harbinger of the Renaissance, the Reformation, nineteenth century liberalism, and the modern state. The Veltro or Greyhound that he said would come to save "lowly Italy" and chase the Wolf of cupidity and

---

[1] D. Comparetti, *Virgilio nel medio evo*, new ed. by G. Pasquali, 2 vols. (Florence, 1937).

corruption back into Hell has been identified with such figures as Luther, Kaiser Wilhelm, Garibaldi, Victor Emanuel II, and Benito Mussolini.[2] These modern extravagances are even more bizarre than the medieval belief in Virgil's prophecy of Christ, but they are perhaps no less important.

Undoubtedly some of the labels attached to the great name of Dante have been merely the catch-words of propaganda, believed no more by those who heard them than by those who used them. A great deal of what was said, however, especially in the nineteenth century, was based on a sincere faith. This faith might falsify the past, but it also helped to create the present. What was Dante's rôle in the Risorgimento, in the struggle to acquire the Trentino, in the Fascist dream of a new empire centered around Rome? This paper can only indicate briefly his own views and the travesties of later generations, the widely varying parts he was made to play in forming the political consciousness of a youthful nation with an ancient past.

One may say at the outset that it was eminently natural that the figure of Dante should have had a strong attraction for modern Italian patriots. The poet's achievement furnished a linguistic standard which could serve as a basis for developing cultural unity. He celebrated the glories of the vernacular of Italy both

---

[2] A very brief sketch of "La fama e lo studio di Dante" is given by M. Barbi, *Dante, Vita opere e fortuna* (Florence, 1952), pp. 121-129. For a short survey see V. Rossi, "Dante nel trecento e nel quattrocento"; F. Flamini, "Dante nel cinquecento e nel l'età della decadenza"; and G. Mazzoni, "Dante nell'inizio e nel vigore del risorgimento"; in *Dante e l'Italia* (Rome, 1921), pp. 285-380. See now also P. Renucci, "Dantismo esoterico nel secolo presente," and C. Dionisotti, "Dante nel Quattrocento," *Atti del congresso internazionale di studi danteschi* (Florence, 1965), pp. 305-378. For longer studies of Dante's reputation in the period between his death and 1800 see E. Cavallari, *La fortuna di Dante nel Trecento* (Florence, 1921); M. Barbi, *Della fortuna di Dante nel secolo XVI* (Pisa, 1890); U. Cosmo, *Con Dante attraverso il Seicento* (Bari, 1946); and A. Vallone, *La critica dantesca nel Settecento ed altri saggi danteschi* (Florence, 1961). For the nineteenth century see U. Micocci, *La fortuna di Dante nel secolo XIX*, 2nd ed. (Florence, 1891); P. Bellezza, *Curiosità dantesche* (Milan, 1913), pp. 95-184; G. Toffanin, *Glui ultimi nostri* (Forli, 1919, pp. 97-136); *Dante nel Risorgimento (Studi su Dante, VI)*, ed G. Galbiati (Milan, 1941); A. Vallone, *La critica dantesca nell'Ottocento* (Florence, 1958); and *Atti del I congresso nazionale di studi danteschi (Caserta-Napoli, 21-25 May 1961): Dante nel secolo dell'unità d'Italia* (Florence, 1962).

in theory and practice,³ and recognized the distinctiveness of her civilization.⁴ His Italian loyalties were moreover not merely literary and cultural but also political and historical. He mourned the civil disorders of his country⁵ and longed for her salvation through the rule of a righteous Emperor and a purified Church;⁶ he exalted her historical greatness as the garden of Empire⁷ and the seat of the Papacy.⁸ He declared that she was the noblest region of Europe, and he quoted Virgil's lines eulogizing her as the homeland of the Trojan race.⁹ Aeneas was an important figure for Dante as well as for Virgil; both poets admired the piety of the hero's return to the legendary cradle of his people to beget an empire which would dominate the world. Dante carried the theory a step further, affirming that God Himself chose Aeneas to be father of Rome and her Empire, "which were established for the holy place, where the successor of the greatest Peter sits." ¹⁰ By his birth Christ, according to Dante, sanctified the Augustan peace and the Roman power; the Eternal City was also designated as the head of his Church. It was therefore a crime to transfer the see of Peter to any other land. Dante wrote to the Italian cardinals at the conclave of 1314 urging them in the name of "our Italy" to return the Curia from Avignon to Rome, lest the Gascons be allowed to usurp the glory of the Latins.¹¹ The poet was jealous of his nation's cultural, political, and religious prestige. Was he therefore already an Italian nationalist?

If we interpret nationalism not merely as patriotic pride in a region or language or ethnic group but also as devotion to a national state, to a political entity which embodies and intensifies these loyalties, our answer must be negative.¹² For Dante Italy

---

³ *Conv.*, I, v-xiii; *De Vulg. Eloq.*, I, xvi-xix, ed. Soc. dant. (Florence. 1921).
⁴ *De Vulg. Eloq.*, I, xvi, xviii; see also *Epist.*, XI.
⁵ See especially the famous canto of Sordello, *Purg.*, VI.
⁶ Besides the passages scattered through the *Commedia* and the *Monarchia*, one can find a concentrated exposition of Dante's views on this subject in *Epistles*, V, VII, and XI.
⁷ *Purg.*, VI, 76-105.
⁸ *Epist.*, XI; *Inf.*, II; *Par.*, XXVII.
⁹ *Mon.*, II, iii, 12, quoting *Aeneid*, III, 163-166.
¹⁰ *Inf.*, II, 13-27.
¹¹ *Epist.*, XI.
¹² For definitions of modern nationalism, see H. Kohn, *The Idea of Nationalism* (New York, 1951); C. J. H. Hayes, *Essays on Nationalism* (New

was not a state. She was rather the heart and origin of the greatest state, the universal Empire. Separateness and autonomy would have destroyed her unique position, far loftier than that of independent kingdoms like England or France, though in the absence of a strong emperor more wretched. Italy was the jurisdictional head of the world; her king was the emperor and she needed no other, if he could be persuaded to rule from Rome as his rightful capital, and if she could be persuaded to submit to his residence. In his political letters Dante urged her inhabitants to receive Henry VII as their rightful lord and to bow to his *regimen*. [13] His title was not King of Italy but King of the Romans, of those willing to submit to his authority both inside and outside of Italy. But the Italians were closer to Rome, more intimately a part of Roman history and civilization, than any other people. Italy was the cradle of the Empire, and that Empire, at least in Dante's theory, was worldwide. The poet's firm belief in the universality of Roman power made any exclusive theory of nationalism impossible. Dante condemned France for her usurpations and Florence for her intransigence; he reacted violently against the growing strength of particularist sentiment in his own time. In his great invective against Italy [14] he attributed her anarchy not only to the desertion of Rome by the Emperor but also to the refusal of the Italians to

---

York, 1926); L. L. Snyder, *The Meaning of Nationalism* (New Brunswick, N. J., 1954); and B. C. Shafer, *Nationalism: Interpreters and Interpretations* (Washington, American Historical Association, 1959). For the vast literature on this subject see K. Pinson, *A Bibliographical Introduction to Nationalism* (New York, 1934) and K. W. Deutsch, *An Interdisciplinary Bibliography on Nationalism, 1935-1953* (Cambridge, Mass., 1956). The elusive beginnings of national sentiment in the Middle Ages have naturally attracted much less scholarly interest. The following articles are among those which deal with this problem: G. G. Coulton, "Nationalism in the Middle Ages," *Cambridge Historical Journal*, V (1935), 15-40; V. H. Galbraith, "Nationality and Language in Medieval England," *Transactions of the Royal Historical Society*, Fourth Series, XXIII (1941), 113-128; H. Koht, "The Dawn of Nationalism in Europe," *American Historical Review*, LII (1947), 265-280; B. C. Keeney, "Military Service and the Development of Nationalism in England, 1272-1327," *Speculum*, XXII (1947), 534-549; E. H. Kantorowicz, "Pro Patria Mori in Medieval Political Thought," *American Historical Review*, LVI (1951), 472-492 (included in revised form in *The King's Two Bodies* (Princeton, 1957), pp. 232-272); G. Post, "Two Notes on Nationalism in the Middle Ages, *Traditio*, IX (1953), 281-320.

[13] *Epist.*, V, VI.
[14] *Purg.*, VI.

recognize their rightful master. As long as she continued to follow her selfish desires, Italy, he said, would be a ship without a helmsman, devoid of justice and peace.

This was a severe judgment. Yet Dante pitied his distracted country and prophesied her eventual redemption through restoration of the imperial power and reform of the Church. Again and again the poet denounced evil prelates, ecclesiastical interference in secular affairs, and Constantine's supposed gift of the western half of his empire to the Church. Dante regarded this alleged cession as a blunder which enabled greedy clerics and wicked popes to poison the life of Christendom and mar the "good world" which Rome had made.[15] From this decline Italy, since she was the seat of the Empire and the Papacy, had naturally suffered most of all. But Dante never proposed curing her ills by the establishment of an independent "regno d'Italia." Her recovery, he believed, could only come through a general *renovatio*, spiritual as well as political, of all Christendom. It was to help persuade men of this necessity that he wrote the *Commedia*.

In subsequent centuries, Italy was neither reformed nor unified. She remained turbulent and anarchic and soon became the prey of France, Spain, and Austria; Dante's ideal seemed increasingly remote.[16] Some Italians of the early modern era admired his poetry and some did not; his works were usually read, when they were read at all, as literature and not as political philosophy. "In the years of slavery," Italians were later fond of saying, "Dante was silent." But with the rising murmurs of revolt against Bourbons, Habsburgs, and the temporal power of the papacy, Dante was transformed once more into a contemporary.

In the growth of his nineteenth and twentieth century cult, various phases may be discerned, though they cannot be sharply separated; it is often more a matter of emphasis than of clearcut divisions. First, the anti-clerical Dante holds the stage; second,

---

[15] *Inf.*, XIX, 115-117; *Purg.*, VI, 88-96; XVI, 106-114, 127-129; XXXII, 124-129; *Par.*, XVIII, 124-136; XX, 55-57; XXVII, 40-60, 139-141; XXX, 133-148.

[16] See, however, Hans Baron, *The Crisis of the Early Italian Renaissance*, 2 vols. (Princeton, 1955), for an account of the lively discussions in humanist circles, particularly in that of Coluccio Salutati, recorded by Leonardo Bruni, of Dante's political ideas. They naturally aroused adverse criticism among republicans.

the Catholic and patriotic Guelf; third, the prophet of Italian unity; fourth, the herald of a greater Italy and of a totalitarian state.

The first phase, that of rebellion against the Church, begins at the turn of the nineteenth century, though it endures much longer, finding adherents among such later neo-Ghibellines as Settembrini and Carducci. Its prologue may be found in the strange ceremony organized by Vincenzo Monti at Ravenna in 1797 to celebrate the freeing of the Romagna from papal rule. The *Divine Comedy* was carried in triumph through the streets and Monti harangued the throng which gathered at the poet's tomb, proclaiming Dante "the ancient victor over priestly imposture." [17] Two decades later, while on his way to exile in England for agitating on behalf of the Neapolitan constitution of 1820, Gabriele Rossetti saw a vision. Dante appeared to him in a dream and said, "Italy will drive the Wolf into Hell." For Rossetti, the stronghold of the Wolf was papal Rome, and the letters of the word VELTRO or UELTRO might be transposed to read LUTERO. [18] Rossetti's fellow exile in England, Ugo Foscolo, did not indulge in the esoteric interpretations of the *Commedia* of which Rossetti was so fond, but he too continued the same attacks against the papacy, affirming that anyone who saw in Dante only the poet and not the religious reformer proved himself ignorant both of the writer and of his century. Dante had expressed his Italian patriotism, Foscolo asserted, from the viewpoint of a Ghibelline; he had been a lover of his country but a violent lover, ready to see parts of it devastated in order to purify the rest. He did not share the mawkish sentimentality of his modern compatriots; if they should read his political letters commanding Italy to submit to Henry VII, they would be gravely shocked. They were still incapable of understanding "the indomitable force which characterized the old Ghibelline." [19] Dante's works, therefore, if properly studied, should

---

[17] See G. Mazzoni, "Dante nell'inizio e nel vigore del Risorgimento," *Dante e l'Italia* (Rome, 1921), p. 345, and G. Zippel, "Monumenti a Dante," *Il Trentino a Dante Alighieri* (Trento, 1896), p. 63.

[18] Mazzoni, *op. cit.*, p. 364, and Maria Sticco, "Dante e Gabriele Rossetti," *Dante nel Risorgimento*, pp. 51-116.

[19] Ugo Foscolo, *La Commedia di Dante Allighieri* (London, 1842), I, 78, 225-227; *Lezioni e orazioni* (Lugano, 1836), p. 202.

help to rouse Italy from her torpor and make her aware of her decadence. They were a whip and not a sedative, a rebuke to inertia and not a eulogy of complacency under the foreign and priestly yoke.

Mazzini, in his introduction to Foscolo's commentary on the *Divine Comedy*, remarked that the latter "sought in Dante not merely the poet, not merely the father of our language, but the citizen, the reformer, the religious apostle, the prophet of the nation." [20] Mazzini declared, however, that Foscolo did not go far enough: he did not make Dante the prophet of a unified Italian state. Later the neo-Ghibellines would extend and develop Foscolo's ideas in this direction.

First, however, the neo-Guelfs attempted to claim Dante for their party. Cesare Balbo, who published his *Vita di Dante* in 1839, stood at the head of a school which included Gioberti, Giuliani, and Tommaseo. Balbo's biography laid the groundwork for the second phase in the development of the cult of Dante; it presented the poet as an Italian patriot who in his better moments defended the independence of his city and the authority of his church. Balbo sought to sketch the life of "the most Italian among the Italians" for the inspiration of his countrymen." [21] "If Dante had been only a poet or a literary figure," Balbo said, "I should have left the task of writing about him to the many others far better prepared than I... But Dante is a great part of the history of Italy... Therefore, since I have not been able to depict the life of the whole Italian nation, I shall at least attempt to depict that of the Italian who more than any other combined in himself the genius, the virtue, the vices, and the fortunes of our country." [22] Balbo confessed himself to be enough of a Guelf to believe that in the past the papacy had served as "a counterweight ... to impede ... the renewal of the tyranny of the old Roman Empire." [23] Writing as an aristocratic liberal, a lover of the com-

---

[20] *La Commedia, ed. cit.,* p. xviii.

[21] Cesare Balbo, *Vita di Dante,* annotated by E. Rocco (Naples, 1840), p. 155.

[22] *Ibid.,* p. 7. Balbo acknowledges his debt to the work he regards as the first serious attempt at the historical reconstruction of Dante's life and time, Carlo Troya's *Del Veltro allegorico di Dante.*

[23] Balbo, *op. cit.,* p. 81.

munal idea, and a devoted Catholic, he could not accept the Dante of the *Monarchia* as the voice of true Italian patriotism. He regarded that book as the poet's great error, composed under the spur of wrath at the injustice done him by his countrymen. Here, Balbo believed, Dante had abandoned "the party of the people and of the independence of Italy" and embraced the party of foreign domination.[24] A sin so grievous, however understandable, was redeemed only by the magnitude of Dante's other achievements, by his reverence for the Church, and by the intensity of his patriotic sentiment.

Balbo's *Vita di Dante* revealed the dilemma which confronted all those who wished to see in the poet the prophet of Italian independence. How could a nationalist invoke the aid of a foreign prince to discipline his country? How could the supporter of the German Emperor be called the father of Italy? It was a question to try the wits even of the most skillful controversialist; that controversialist, however, soon appeared in the person of the subtle Jesuit Hegelian Vincenzo Gioberti.

Gioberti's synthesis, linking the pagan and Christian eras of Roman-Italian history, attempted to dispose of these obstacles to a Guelf interpretation of Dante's thought.[25] Each era, Gioberti said, had a first, clerical phase: in early pagan times kings were also priests, in early medieval times popes were also kings. Then each society was transformed by the lay spirit with "civil independence" replacing "sacerdotal tutelage" both in ancient Rome and modern Italy. Just as the sway of Roman arms gave place to that of Latin civilization, so the "civil primacy" which Italian popes like Gregory VII held was succeeded by the moral and cultural primacy achieved through the genius of such "spontaneous monarchs" as Dante, Machiavelli, Vico and Alfieri. Slowly but surely, according to Gioberti, "the priestly age drew to a close and the Pope laid aside the symbols of his dictatorial authority and exchanged them for those of a judge and conciliator."[26]

Gioberti believed that the Pope still possessed his absolute jurisdiction, but that circumstances determined whether it should

---

[24] *Ibid.*, pp. 75-76.
[25] Vincenzo Gioberti, *Opere,* ed. Ugo Redanò, of which vols. II and III contain the *Del Primato Morale e Civile degli Italiani.*
[26] *Ibid.*, II, 22, 177-181.

be invoked. The clergy, he said, should rule not with force or fraud but with ideas. The Italy he envisaged was a union of states under papal presidency. Papal presidency, however, should confine itself within desirable limits and welcome the opportunity to share its power with laymen.[27]

Dante was the prophet of the new secularized order. Gioberti said that thirteenth century Italy produced in him "the founder of the lay and Catholic civilization of the modern world". He was therefore an enemy of the exercise of that authority which Pope Boniface VIII possessed rightfully but used unskillfully. Yet the poet recognized its legitimacy when he denounced the attack on Boniface at Anagni. Dante's defence of the rights of the old empire was an anachronistic evocation of the lay phase of Roman imperial civilization. At the same time, he foresaw and in large part created the second phase of Christian civilization,[28] in which Italian culture stimulated and refined that of other nations.[29]

In Gioberti's theory, Dante became simply the pivot of an historical scheme which denied him all individual reality. Gioberti accounted for the troublesome side of his thought by applying it to the earlier pagan dispensation whose lay period ran parallel to the new lay age of Christianity which the poet supposedly inaugurated. Dante, according to Gioberti, founded the modern cultural supremacy of Italy. He drew inspiration from Christianity and remained loyal to the Church; at the same time he created political philosophy and secularized the science of history. From the *Divine Comedy*, moreover, all modern literatures had sprung. Dante's genius was universal, and it was a sign of the reawakening of Italy to her role as redemptress of Europe that his works were again studied in all their manifold aspects, linguistic, philosophical, poetic, moral, and political. This was the most hopeful indication, according to Gioberti, that the high cultural and religious destiny of Italy would be at last fulfilled.[30]

Gioberti's dream was as grandiloquent as his rhetoric; a modern critic has compared it to "a gigantic ephemeral medieval

---

[27] *Ibid.*, II, 189 ff.
[28] *Ibid.*, II, 181.
[29] *Ibid.*, II, 32.
[30] *Ibid.*, III, 109, 139, 156.

castle" which looms for a moment above the horizon of history and then is swept away.[31] The rival vision of Mazzini, in spite of all its exaggerations, proved a better prophecy of the future of Italy, and a truer mirror of the patriotic aspirations of her people. Mazzini regarded Dante as the seer of Italian unity and world brotherhood; the disciple of Foscolo went far beyond his master. In the newspaper which he edited for Italians in England Mazzini set forth his credo in defiant tones: "Those foreigners most eager to vilify us and to declare us eternally impotent draw back almost with terror before that name which neither centuries, nor vileness of servitude, nor the tyranny of strangers, of our own princes, and of Jesuits [a thrust at Gioberti], have ever or shall ever be able to blot out." Mazzini asserted that Dante fought always for the People and for the future Nation; he wished to absorb the German Empire in Rome. "Italian workers," asked Mazzini in conclusion, "do you wish to honor the memory of your great men and to give peace to the soul of Dante Alighieri? Give substance, then, to the dream which burdened him in his terrestrial life... And when you become worthy of Dante in love and in hate, when your land is *yours* and not another's, when the soul of Dante can behold you without grief, joyful in the holiness of Italitan pride, we will raise the statue of the poet on the loftiest eminence of Rome and inscribe on its base: TO THE PROPHET OF THE ITALIAN NATION [FROM] THE ITALIANS WORTHY OF HIM."[32] Nearly twenty years later, in his second London journal *Pensiero ed Azione*, he hailed Dante as the apostle of progress, who chose as the symbol of human unity the holy city of Rome.[33] This symbol was at once Italian and universal; it was, as Chabod has phrased it, "the Rome of Mazzini, the third Rome, the Rome of the People, after that of the Caesars and the Popes."[34]

---

[31] Toffanin, *op. cit.*, pp. 101 ff.

[32] *Apostolato italiano*, ed. Giuseppe Mazzini, N.º 3 (15 Sept. 1841), pp. 21-24.

[33] The articles expressing these views were published first in 1858-59 and then gathered into the well-known work *Dei doveri dell'uomo* (Lugano, 1860).

[34] F. Chabod, *Storia della politica estera italiana dal 1870 al 1896*, Vol. I: *Le Premesse* (Bari, 1951), p. 195.

Certainly Dante was the poet of the people during the struggle for independence. They, like their leaders, regarded him as the great prophet of Italian nationalism. The *Divine Comedy* was carried to war in the knapsacks of volunteers. It was read by condemned men in prisons. It furnished slogans for battle, and supplied inscriptions for medals, buildings, and ships of war. In 1865, after the capital of Italy had been transferred from Turin to Florence, the dedication of the statue of Dante in Piazza Santa Croce was a solemn national festival. [35] Bernardino Zendrini summed up the general feeling when he said, "The *Comedy* was to us, like the Bible to the Jewish wanderers, the symbol of fatherland and nationality during the years of foreign domination." [36]

In the early period of the life of the new nation, interest in Dante became a kind of mania; the poet "was cooked in every sauce, served hot and cold, broiled and in jelly, whole and in croquettes, ... prepared for strong stomachs and weak, for female taste and male, for children in kindergarten and for those in second childhood in the academies." [37] But critics of integrity attempted to raise the study of Dante to a more serious level and to correct patriotic excesses. Carducci, for example, reprinting in 1874 a poem written twenty years earlier which represented Dante as desiring an Italy "united in arms, in laws, in language," said now that it was time to leave such things to those who "sweated to flatter the Veltro." [38] As early as 1858 the great De Sanctis also criticized the current political interpretations; he was far more concerned with questions of psychology and aesthetics than with Dante's "Ghibellinism," which he cautiously defined as "a dream which in part becomes history." Because Dante looked as much to the past as to the future, De Sanctis said, it was inaccurate to find a clear-cut political message in his work: it might be claimed by all parties, but it was really understood by none. [39]

In spite of this critic's wide influence, the rising tide of Italian imperialism in the late nineteenth and early twentieth centuries

---

[35] Mazzoni, *op. cit.*
[36] Bellezza, *op. cit.*, p. 103.
[37] *Ibid.*, p. 510; the quotation is from E. Thovez.
[38] *Ibid.*, pp. 101-102.
[39] F. De Sanctis, "Carattere di Dante e sua utopia" (1858), *Saggi danteschi*, ed. L. Taroni (Milan, 1954), pp. 1-24.

found a further rôle for Dante the nationalist, that of helping to extend the boundaries of Italy. Many Italians believed that his delineation of the boundaries of their country gave a kind of imprimatur to their territorial claims. Had he not spoken of Lake Garda, still in Austrian hands, as lying "in beautiful Italy at the foot of the Alps which shut in Germany"? Had he not mentioned Carnaro, the gulf on which Fiume was located, as "closing Italy and bathing her boundaries"? Had he not recognized the dialect of Trento as Italian, however impure, and thereby claimed the district as a part of the nation? [40] Thus the bond of language was tightened by Dante's voice, and patriots discussed the poet's alleged visit to the Trentino as if his bodily presence could hallow still more the Italian quality of that ground.

Listen to Bonghi's words in 1890 at the first congress of the Società Dante Alighieri, designed to keep alive the language and culture of Italy wherever Italians lived: "We must form an association as large and powerful as the poetry of Dante Alighieri, as large and powerful as his influence on the whole intellectual life of Italy, of all Italy, not within the narrow circle of her legal limits, but within the more ample circle of her ideal boundaries." [41] The appeal was directed especially to *Italia irredenta*. Mazzoni, who signed the manifesto which created the Society, wrote of the embarrassment of government officials who wished to sign it but could not, because it would have been inadvisable so publicly to commit themselves to *irredentismo*. "They found it convenient," he declared, "to place between themselves and the outbursts of patriotism, between themselves and European diplomacy, such a Society, which at one moment could be aided surreptitiously and at another disavowed publicly." [42]

The response from the Trentino also took the form of a tribute to Dante. Groups were organized to collect money for a statue of the poet, begun at Trento in 1893 and dedicated in October, 1896, at a gathering which rivalled the famous celebration of 1865 at Santa Croce. Carducci wrote a poem for the occasion

---

[40] *Inf.*, XX, 61-63; IX, 112-114; *De Vulg. Eloq.*, I, xv, 8.

[41] G. Mazzoni, "Il nome di Dante e le due società intitolate da lui," *Almae luces malae cruces* (Bologna, 1941), p. 92.

[42] *Ibid.*, p. 90.

ending with the well-known line: "And now he stands still, and seems to wait, at Trento." [43] There he waited another twenty-three years until the end of the First World War and the festival of 3 November 1919 celebrating Italy's possession of the region.

The African and European wars whipped up more patriotic fervor, and Dante's name was again invoked. In 1915 Gabriele d'Annunzio addressed the youth of his country with an Italian version of the Beatitudes. "Blessed are the young men who hunger and thirst after glory," he cried, "for they shall be filled... Blessed are the pure in heart, blessed are those who return with victories, for they will see the fresh countenance of Rome, her brow crowned again by Dante, and the triumphant beauty of Italy." [44] After the unsatisfactory peace this ardent proto-Fascist declared Fiume to be "the ultimate bearer of the Dantesque banner." [45]

In 1918 the Hegelian and later Fascist philosopher Giovanni Gentile claimed for the author of the *Monarchia* foreknowledge of the nature of the modern state: an entity created by a concord of wills, possessing its own religion and its own ethical life. [46] Twenty years later, in a lecture on the canto of Sordello, Gentile eulogized Dante in emotional terms: "Dante, our father, the first of the Italians, the first to summon Italy into the world and make her live in his song as an eternal reality, a holy fatherland." [47]

It was natural that later Fascist propaganda should fasten on Dante's reverence for Rome. In the periodical *L'Idea di Roma*, published from 1938 to 1941, an article was devoted to the subject of Dante's conception of the Roman mission of Italy. All the old clichés were there: Dante as father of his country, as reformer of the Church, and as prophet of a restored Empire. His Veltro had come, the author said, in the person of Benito Mussolini,

---

[43] See the volume *Il Trentino a Dante Alighieri, con versi di Giosuè Carducci* (Trento, 1896), and G. Zippel, *Dante e il Trentino: Lectura Dantis* (Florence, 1920)..

[44] Gabriele D'Annunzio, "Orazione per la sagra dei Mille. V. Maggio MDCCCLX" (1915), *per la più grande Italia* (Il Vittoriale degli Italiani, 1940), VIII, 30.

[45] D'Annunzio, *La fiamma intelligente*, 1920-24, p. 179.

[46] G. Gentile, "La profezia di Dante," first delivered at the Casa di Dante in Rome, 17 February 1918, and printed in *Dante e Manzoni* (Florence, 1923), pp. 9-61.

[47] Gentile, "Il Canto di Sordello," *Nuova Antologia*, 16 May 1939, p. 130.

who had recalled Italy to an awareness of her primacy among the nations, had continued the civilizing work of Rome, and had established concord between Church and State. At last the ideas propounded by Dante in the *Monarchia* were a reality and Italy stood again at the center of the world.[48]

The same identification of the Veltro with Mussolini was made by the Russian novelist Demetrio Merejkowsky,[49] an exile from his own country who was anxious to find in Italy that "divine communism" which would counteract the "diabolical communism" of the Bolsheviks. Merejkowsky reported an interview with the Duce in which he asked three questions of Mussolini: did Fascism envisage a national or an international paradise? Was eternal war or eternal peace the most desirable state for man? How could the antinomy between Church and State be resolved? Mussolini said only, "I cannot answer your questions." Then Merejkowski was certain of the great truth which he had already discerned: Mussolini, the Spirit of the Earth, could not answer in words but only in action, for he was the complement of Dante. "Between You and Dante," said Merejkowski, "there exists a harmony which is preordained... Dante in contemplation, in speculating, makes us understand Mussolini; Mussolini in action, *in operating*, makes us understand Dante."[50] So Mussolini and Dante divided the world between them and there was no third. But what was one to say of Hitler's Germany?

The obvious response was provided in an article written in the early forties and published in 1944 by the distinguished historian Arrigo Solmi, then Undersecretary to the Ministry of National Education. He declared that the Wolf of Greed whom Dante's Veltro was to overcome was represented by the plutocracies of

---

[48] G. Forte, "L'ideale di Dante nella sua realtà storica," *L'idea di Roma*, III (1940), 370-398.

[49] D. Merejkowsky, *Dante*, trans. by R. Küfferle (Bologna, 1940), pp. 3-22. This is also the burden of D. Venturini's book, *Dante Alighieri e Benito Mussolini (Pubblicazioni d'opere per l'incremento della letteratura fascista*, Rome, n.d.).

[50] It should be said, however, that a look at the numerous but brief references to Dante in Benito Mussolini, *Opera omnia*, ed. by E. and D. Susmel (Florence, 1953), reveals a rather traditional view of the poet. For Mussolini, "Dante aspettava a Trento," (XI, 458-9) and helped to create an Italian cultural unity, but he did little more.

the West. They were opposed, however, by the two nations which had once been joined in Dante's Holy Roman Empire and which were again united in an effort to redeem the world. Thus Solmi in the middle of the twentieth century offered a solution to the problem posed by Balbo a century before of how Dante could be a good Italian and also welcome a foreign emperor. [51]

In general, however, it must be noted that Dante did not speak to Fascist Italy with the same clarity that he spoke to the Risorgimento. A look at the leading Italian journal devoted to the poet, the *Studi danteschi,* will show that serious scholars remained on the whole unmoved by propaganda. It is true that Francesco Ercole's theory of Dante's belief in the existence of a medieval Italian kingdom [52] commanded a natural popularity and was eventually accepted by Michele Barbi. [53] But Ercole's view was first put forward in 1917 and had no specifically Fascist content. Dante was a political prophet for the whole nation in the Risorgimento; in the Fascist era he provided inspiration only for a limited amount of propaganda. No doubt it would be an exaggeration to say again that "in the years of slavery, Dante was silent." Under Fascism, however, his voice reflected mainly the shrillness of official diatribes.

After the ardors of Fascistic Italy, one may hope that Dante will now be left to the perhaps less biased and at least more cautious, attentions of aesthetes and academicians. But in view of the well-proven exegetical energy of patriots and politicians, it would be rash to venture such a prediction.

---

[51] A. Solmi: "L'idea imperiale di Dante," *Studi su Dante,* VII, ed. G. Galbiati (Milan, 1944), pp. 1-31. G. A. Borgese's counter-propaganda also indicates the importance of Dante as a political symbol at this time. In his tract *Golia: Marcia del Fascismo,* a work first published in English and later translated into Italian by Doletta Caprin-Oxilia (Verona, 1946), pp. 35, 37, 84, 391, Borgese said that Roman aspirations had poisoned the history of Italy and likened Dante's poem to the Cretan labyrinth: it contained two Minotaurs, the twin superstitions of imperial and ecclesiastical mythology, united by the accord betwen Fascism and the Church.

[52] F. Ercole, "L'unità politica della nazione italiana e l'impero nel pensiero di Dante," *Archivio storico italiano,* LXXV (1917), 79-144.

[53] M. Barbi, "L'Italia nell'ideale politico di Dante," *Studi danteschi,* XXIV (1939), 5-37.

The Department of Romance Studies Digital Arts and Collaboration Lab at the University of North Carolina at Chapel Hill is proud to support the digitization of the North Carolina Studies in the Romance Languages and Literatures series.

www.ingramcontent.com/pod-product-compliance
Lightning Source LLC
Chambersburg PA
CBHW022019220426
43663CB00007B/1143